SCHOOL SUBJECTS AND CURRICULUM CHANGE

CROOM HELM CURRICULUM POLICY AND RESEARCH SERIES
Edited by William Reid and Ian Westbury

EVALUATING CURRICULUM PROPOSALS
A Critical Guide
Digby C. Anderson

THE CLASSROOM SOCIETY
The Construction of Educational Experience
Herbert A. Thelen

INNOVATION IN THE SCIENCE CURRICULUM
Classroom Knowledge and Curriculum Change
Edited by John Olson

School Subjects
and Curriculum Change

IVOR GOODSON

CROOM HELM
London & Canberra

©1983 Ivor Goodson
Croom Helm Ltd, Provident House, Burrell Row,
Beckenham, Kent BR3 1AT

British Library Cataloguing in Publication Data

Goodson, Ivor
 School subjects and curriculum change.—
 (Croom Helm curriculum policy and research
 series)
 1. Curriculum planning
 I. Title
 375'001   LB1570

 ISBN 0-7099-1104-1

Printed and bound in Great Britain by
Biddles Ltd, Guildford and King's Lynn

CONTENTS

To my Dad and Mum
FRED AND LILY GOODSON
for all their sacrifice
and support

FOREWORD

This is a rare and important book. It is rare in that few attempts
have been made to bring together first-hand historical work on
curriculum change with the perspectives on change held by
people whose interest is in the processes and products of teaching; it is important because it raises in a very concrete and
practical way questions about the failures and successes of the
comprehensive school, about how its curriculum should be related
to the political and economic conditions of society at large, and
about what kind of an image of an educated person it should be
promoting.

In spite of efforts to formulate new bases for the curriculum,
the story of change in the secondary school over the last 80
years has been largely the story of the growth, decline and
evolution of the traditional subjects of the curriculum (science,
mathematics, languages), or of the newer subjects (geography,
economics) which have modelled themselves on established ones.
Historical accounts of school subjects have been written, but
they are usually constructed either from the standpoint of
interested participants, or from that of historians viewing events
as historical rather than educational phenomena. On the other
hand, writers and theorists who have taken curriculum change
as their central theme have tended to relegate the question or
how subjects change to a subsidiary status in favour of macro-
level explanations which have led to over-optimistic prescriptions
for innovation. Moves towards integrated curricula and mixed
ability teaching which began in the 1960s have proved transitory.
Recent official documents on the secondary school curriculum
have re-emphasised the role of subjects (even to the extent of
resurrecting proposals very close to the spirit of the 1904
Regulations), and comprehensive schools which had set up
schemes of teaching based upon long established traditions of
mixed ability grouping have been progressively dismantling them.

In this book, Dr Goodson looks in detail at one very well
documented instance of an attempt to establish a new integrated
'subject' - the case of environmental studies, and especially of
the move on the part of Hertfordshire teachers and advisors to
introduce an 'A' level syllabus and examination. His interest,
however, is not simply in the *story* of environmental studies,
but in what the story means for the understanding of curriculum
change generally and, consequently, for the possibilities that
exist for reform and innovation in the comprehensive school. The
activities of the environmentalists are, therefore, set against

the necessary background of developments in the school curriculum as a whole, and especially in the established subjects most affected by the growth of the new area of study - Biology and Geography. And beyond this, the whole complex of political, disciplinary and educational activity is comprehended within a framework through which 'meaning' can be attached to it. The book accomplishes its task clearly and cogently; never neglecting the complexities, but always keeping close to the central and important themes and issues.

But the purpose of the book is not simply to offer explanations for social phenomena. It is to help educators and supporters of education at all levels to see what are the limits and possibilities of the comprehensive school as a social institution in the 1980s. It should be read by all who are looking for realistic ways in which the curriculum of the school can be brought into a closer relationship with the educational needs of children and society.

William A. Reid
University of Birmingham

Ian Westbury
University of Illinois

Editors

ACKNOWLEDGEMENTS

In particular to Sean Carson for his generosity and patience in providing a series of interviews and access to his personal papers; to Dr W.A. Reid for help and support beyond the call of editorial duty; to Dr M. Eraut for his considerable help in commenting on the many drafts of the book; to Dr M. Waring for her unselfish academic support, particularly with respect to the sections on Biology; to Paul Topham, Martyn Hammersley, Carl Parsons, Rodger Gomm, Simon Duncan.

To my wife Mary, and latterly son Andrew, whose warmth and love have helped enormously and who have generously covered the many gaps left in the 'domestic economy' during the writing of this book.

PART ONE

Becoming an Academic Subject: Case Studies in the
Social History of the School Curriculum

1 INTRODUCTION

This book provides a number of historical case studies of school
subjects and examines underlying patterns of change and conflict both within and between these subjects. The focus of the
case studies is on the 'process of becoming a school subject'
and therefore concentrates on the promotion of subjects as they
seek establishment in the school curriculum. The concern is not
to provide a general explanation of school subjects and curriculum change but rather to raise issues and generate insights
about past and current work which does seek to provide such
explanatory theories. Central to the book is a belief in a socio-
historical approach to curriculum studies.

In particular and in summary the book seeks to present
evidence for three hypotheses: firstly, that subjects are not
monolithic entities but shifting amalgamations of sub-groups and
traditions. These groups within the subject influence and change
boundaries and priorities. Secondly, that in the process of
establishing a school subject (and associated university discipline) base subject groups tend to move from promoting
pedagogic and utilitarian traditions towards the academic tradition.
The need for the subject to be viewed as a scholarly discipline
will impinge on both the promotional rhetoric and the process of
subject definition, most crucially during the passage to subject
and discipline establishment. Thirdly, that, in the cases studied,
much of the curriculum debate can be interpreted in terms of
conflict between subjects over status, resources and territory.

Above all historical case studies of school subjects provide
the 'local detail' of curriculum change and conflict. The identification of individuals and sub-groups actively at work within
curriculum interest groups allows some examination and assessment of intention and motivation. Thereby sociological theories
which attribute power over the curriculum to dominant interest
groups can be scrutinised for their empirical potential.[1]

To concentrate attention at the micro level of individual school
subject groups is not to deny the crucial importance of macro
level economic changes or changes in intellectual ideas, dominant
values or educational systems. But it is asserted that such macro
level changes may be actively reinterpreted at the micro level.
Changes at macro level are viewed as presenting a range of new
choices to subject factions, associations and communities. To
understand how subjects change over time, as well as histories
of intellectual ideas, we need to understand how subject groups
take up and promote new ideas and opportunities. It is not con-

tended that subject groups are all-powerful in engineering curriculum change but that their responses are a very important, and as yet somewhat neglected, part of the overall picture.

Besides seeking to examine sociological explanation of the school curriculum the emphasis on the social history of school subjects generates insights and questions of importance for the future of the comprehensive school. The differential status (and available resources) of the various school subjects derive from their origins in the separate educational sectors which preceded comprehensivation. For instance, craft and practical subjects still carry with them the low status which originated through their elementary school background. School subjects, therefore, represent the deep structures of curriculum differentiation at work within contemporary schools. Recent studies of comprehensives have shown how a divisive system arises as these differentiated curricula are allocated to different pupil clienteles. Changing the internal processes of schooling in line with the comprehensive ideal will require detailed understanding of the origins and continuing strengths of the subject-based curriculum. The present pattern of subject definition and syllabus construction, of associated status and resources, ensures that school subjects play their part in preserving entrenched social divisions in the face of organisational change.

EXPLANATIONS OF SCHOOL SUBJECTS

The juxtaposition of intellectual 'disciplines' and school subjects has for some time been a starting point in the work of certain philosophers of education. Hirst, for instance, talks of school subjects 'which are indisputably logically cohesive disciplines'.[2] But such a philosophical perspective is rooted in particular educational convictions, notably in the assertion that 'no matter what the ability of the child may be, the heart of all his development as a rational being is, I am saying, intellectual'.[3] In accordance with these convictions Hirst (and Peters) argue that 'the central objectives of education are developments of mind'. Such objectives are best pursued by 'the definition of forms of knowledge'[4] (later broadened to include 'fields of knowledge'). These forms and fields of knowledge can provide the 'logically cohesive disciplines' on which school subjects are based.

The philosophy of Hirst and Peters, therefore, provides a explanatory basis for the school curriculum aspiring to promote the intellectual development of its pupils. In this model of school subject definition it is often implied that the intellectual discipline is created by a community of scholars, normally working in a university, and is then 'translated' for use as a school subject. Phenix defines the intellectual discipline base in this way: 'The general test for a discipline is that it should be the characteristic activity of an identifiable organised tradition of men of knowledge, that is of persons who are skilled in certain specified functions that they are able to justify by a set of intelligible standards'.[5]

Once a discipline has established a university base it is persuasively self-fulfilling to argue that here is a field of knowledge from which an 'academic' school subject can receive inputs and general direction. But this version of events simply celebrates a fait accompli in the evolution of a discipline and associated school subject. What is left unexplained are the stages of evolution towards this culminating pattern and the forces which push aspiring 'academic' subjects to follow similar routes. To understand the progression along the route to academic status it is necessary to examine the social histories of school subjects and to analyse the strategies employed in their construction and promotion.

The manner in which philosophical studies offer justification for the academic subject-based curriculum has been noted by sociologists. Thus philosophers such as Hirst present a view of education that Young states: 'appears to be based on an absolutist conception of a set of distinct forms of knowledge which correspond closely to the traditional areas of the academic curriculum and thus justify, rather than examine, what are no more than socio-historical constructs of a particular time'.[6] Whilst accepting Young's critique it is important to note that this book will contend that school subjects represent substantial interest groups. To view subjects as 'no more than socio-historical constructs of a particular time', whilst correct at one level, does severe injustice to all those groups involved in their continuance and promotion over time.

As long ago as 1968 Musgrove made what, at the time, was a fairly original suggestion to sociologists. He recommended that they:

> Examine subjects both within the school and the nation at large as social systems sustained by communication networks, material endowments and ideologies. Within a school and within a wider society subjects as communities of people, competing and collaborating with one another, defining and defending their boundaries, demanding allegiance from their members and conferring a sense of identity upon them . . . even innovation which appears to be essentially intellectual in character can usefully be examined as the outcome of social interaction . . .

Musgrove remarked that 'studies of subjects in these terms have scarcely begun at least at school level'.[7]

A number of studies have sought to follow Musgrove's exhortation, for instance recent work by Eggleston, but a very influential work in the field of the sociology of knowledge was the collection of papers in 'Knowledge and Control' edited by M.F.D. Young in 1971. The papers reflect Bernstein's contention that 'how a society selects, classifies, distributes, transmits and evaluates the educational knowledge it considers to be public, reflects both the distribution of power and the principles of social control'.[8] Young likewise suggests that 'consideration of the assumptions underlying the selection and organisation of knowledge by those in positions of power may be a fruitful perspective for raising sociological questions about curricula'.[9] The emphasis leads to general statements of the following kind:

> Academic curricula in this country involve assumptions that some kinds and areas of knowledge are much more 'worthwhile' than others: that as soon as possible all knowledge should become specialised and with minimum explicit emphasis on the relations between the subjects specialised in and between specialist teachers involved. It may be useful, therefore, to view curricular changes as involving changing definitions of knowledge along one or more of the dimensions towards a less or more stratified, specialised and open organisation of knowledge. Further, that as we assume some patterns of social relations associated with any curriculum, these changes will be resisted insofar as they are perceived to undermine the values, relative power and privileges of the dominant groups involved.[10]

The process whereby the unspecified 'dominant groups' exercise control over other presumably subordinate groups is not scrutinised, although certain hints are offered. We learn that a school's autonomy in curriculum matters 'is in practice extremely limited by the control of the VIth form (and therefore lower form) curricula by the universities, both through their entrance requirements and their domination of all but one of the school examination boards'. In a footnote Young assures that 'no direct control is implied here, but rather a process by which teachers legitimate their curricula through their shared assumptions about "what we all know the universities want"'.[11] This concentration on the teachers' socialisation as the major agency of control is picked up elsewhere. We learn that:

> The contemporary British educational system is dominated by academic curricula with a rigid stratification of knowledge. It follows that if teachers and children are socialised within an institutionalised structure which legitimates such assumptions, then for teachers high status (and rewards) will be associated with areas of the curriculum that are (1) formally assessed (2) taught to the 'ablest' children (3) taught in homogeneous ability groups of children who show themselves most successful within such curricula.[12]

Young goes on to note that it 'should be fruitful to explore the syllabus construction of knowledge practitioners in terms of their efforts to enhance or maintain their academic legitimacy'.[13]

Two papers by Bourdieu in 'Knowledge and Control' summarise

his considerable influence on English sociologists of knowledge.[14]
Unlike many of the other contributors to 'Knowledge and Control',
Bourdieu has gone on to carry out empirical work to test his
theoretical assertions. His recent work, though concentrated
at university, not school, level, looks at the theme of reproduction through education and includes an important section on The
Examination within the Structure and History of the Educational
System.[15] Young also has come to feel the need for historical
approaches to test theories of knowledge and control. He wrote
recently 'One crucial way of reformulating and transcending the
limits within which we work, is to see . . . how such limits are
not given or fixed, but produced through the conflicting actions
and interests of man in history'.[16] Likewise Bernstein has subsequently argued that 'if we are to take shifts in the content of
education seriously, then we require histories of these contents,
and their relationship to institutions and symbolic arrangements
external to the school.'[17]

TOWARDS A SOCIAL HISTORY OF SCHOOL SUBJECTS

A number of recent studies have employed historical approaches
to explore curriculum issues pertinent to the questions addressed
in this book. Wilkinson's study of the classical academic curricula
of nineteenth-century public schools is of this sort and draws
ideas from an earlier study by Weber.[18] Weber investigated
Confucian education and identified three crucial elements in the
education of Chinese administrators at this time. The main
emphasis was on propriety and 'bookishness', with a curriculum
largely restricted to the learning and memorising of classical
texts. This curriculum comprised a very narrow selection from
the available knowledge in a society where mathematicians,
astronomers, scientists and geographers were not uncommon.
However, all these fields of knowledge were classified by the
literati as 'vulgar' or perhaps in more contemporary terms 'non-
academic'. The use of examinations, based on this narrow
curriculum, for controlling entry into the administrative elite
meant that the non-bookish were for the purposes of the Chinese
society of the time 'not educated'.[19] Wilkinson draws an analogy
between Confucian education and late Victorian public school
education in which it is not bookishness but the 'gentleman ideal
that maintains the political elite'. The public school curriculum
by 'the very criteria themselves, emphasizing classical knowledge
and a certain set style, favoured the gentry individual'.[20]

The Wilkinson article appeared in an important collection of
papers in 'Sociology, History and Education' edited by P.W.
Musgrave. Two other articles rehearse similar arguments to
those of Wilkinson. Campbell's study of Latin and the Elite
Tradition in Education notes that 'there is a direct relationship
between a school's social prestige in the community and the
extent to which it is classically based'.[21] Goody and Watts present

some general considerations about 'literate culture'. They note that the main characteristics of literate culture are 'an abstraction which disregards an individual's social experience . . . and a compartmentalisation of knowledge which restricts the kind of connections which the individual can establish and ratify with the natural and social world'.

Historical studies of the elite education provided in universities have been undertaken, notably by Davie and Rothblatt. Davie's study concerned patterns of curriculum change in the nineteenth-century Scottish universities and pointed to an increasing emphasis on literature rather than oral expression.[23] Rothblatt's study of nineteenth-century Cambridge described the successful strategies which the dons pursued to maintain the dominance of classical studies over the less favoured 'useful knowledge':[24]

> So deeply rooted was the disdain for commerce and industry, for the values which they were supposed to represent, that numerous dons and non-resident M.A.s decided the worth of an academic subject by its usefulness to commerce and industry. In their view no subject which could be turned to the benefit of business deserved university recognition . . . whenever it was suspected that the impetus for curricular reform came from commercial or political sources, Cambridge dons arose to denounce the proposed changes as technical, illiberal, utilitarian and soft options.[25]

A number of studies have focused on the traditions within separate subjects and on the pursuit of status and academic acceptability within subjects. Layton's study 'Science for the People' traces a number of traditions in nineteenth-century science which sought to relate science to people's lives. The book generates a number of hypotheses as to why these versions of science were ultimately dominated by a more thoroughly academic version cushioned in laboratories, textbooks and syllabi. The role of subject associations in this pursuit of increased academic status is documented by Hanson with reference to Society of Art Masters. The Society showed great concern for the academic dress and titles which bestowed, or appeared to bestow, high status on other knowledge categories.[27]

Dodd has recently reviewed the history of Design and Technology in the School Curriculum, following earlier work on Design Education by Eggleston.[28] A major theme in the work is the desire among teachers of the subject for higher status:

> Heavy craft activities have been referred to by a number of different titles as their nature and contribution has changed. Concealed in this on-going discussion is the matter of 'status' and 'respectability', and although the most recent change from Handicraft to Design and Technology reflects a change of emphasis, there is something of the former argument. 'Practical' describes quite adequately an essential part of the

subject, but it is an 'emotionally charged word'. As the subject has developed there have been efforts made to encourage its acceptability by participation in certain kinds of external examinations (which have not always been the best instruments of assessment), the use of syllabuses (often malformed to make them acceptable by other institutions), and by euphemisms like the 'alternative road', but these have failed to hide the underlying low status which practical subjects have by tradition.[29]

Among more general studies of the history of curriculum, Raymond Williams' brief work, written in 1961, relating educational philosophies to the social groups holding them, is deeply suggestive. He writes: 'an educational curriculum, as we have seen again and again in past periods, expresses a compromise between an inherited selection of interests and the emphasis of new interests. At varying points in history, even this compromise may be long delayed, and it will often be muddled'.[30] This view of the history of curriculum focusing on interest groups has been recently considerably extended by Eggleston who contends that: 'The fundamental conflicts are over the identity and legitimacy of the rival contenders for membership of the groups who define, evaluate and distribute knowledge and the power these confer'.[31]

Bank's study 'Parity and Prestige in English Secondary Education' is a valuable complement to these studies, again the close relationship between curriculum and social class emerges. Williams had noted that the academic curriculum was related to the vocations of the upper and professional classes. The curriculum related to the vocations of the majority was slowly introduced and Banks notes that 'as the proportion of children from artisan and lower middle class homes increased, it was necessary to pay more attention to the vocational needs of the pupils, and even to amend the hitherto academic curriculum to admit subjects of a vocational nature.[32] But the subjects related to majority vocations were persistently viewed as of low status. A TUC pamphlet written in 1937 maintained that school time used for vocational training 'not only gives a bias to study but takes up valuable time and effort better employed in a wider and more useful field. Moreover it stamps at an early and impressionable age, the idea of class and inferior status on the scholar, which it is the aim of a noble education to avoid'.[33] Viewed in this way the notion of vocational training is seen not to refer to the pervasive underlying objective of all education as preparation for vocations but to the low-status concern of preparing the majority for their work. The academic curriculum is, and has historically been, vocational in purpose, but the preparation is for the high-status professions. Indeed Banks' study concludes that 'the persistence of the academic tradition is seen as something more fundamental than the influence, sinister or otherwise, of teachers and administrators. It is the vocational qualification of the academic curriculum which enables it to exert such a pressure on all forms of secondary education'.[34]

The term vocational as applied to the qualification function of the academic curriculum can of course be disputed. The fact that such a curriculum helps people to secure professional jobs, which is an aspect of the selection function of education, does not necessarily imply that it prepares them for the job through the provision of skills relevant to their work. The continuing dominance and high status of academic subjects is undoubtedly grounded in their acceptance as qualifications for desirable jobs. This, however, does not explain why so few new 'academic' subjects are born, nor whether these subjects are 'academic' at 'birth' or only develop a more academic character as they pursue status escalation.

Layton has analysed the evolution of science in England from the nineteenth century and in a brief article has developed a tentative model for the evolution of a school subject in the secondary school curriculum. Layton defined three stages in this evolution. In the first stage:

> the callow intruder stakes a place in the timetable, justifying its presence on grounds such as pertinence and utility. During this stage learners are attracted to the subject because of its bearing on matters of concern to them. The teachers are rarely trained specialists, but bring the missionary enthusiasms of pioneers to their task. The dominant criterion is relevance to the needs and interests of the learners.

In the interim second stage:

> a tradition of scholarly work in the subject is emerging along with a corps of trained specialists from which teachers may be recruited. Students are still attracted to the Study, but as much by its reputation and growing academic status as by its relevance to their own problems and concerns. The internal logic and discipline of the subject is becoming increasingly influential in the selection and organisation of subject matter.

In the final stage:

> the teachers now constitute a professional body with established rules and values. The selection of subject matter is determined in large measure by the judgements and practices of the specialist scholars who lead inquiries in the field. Students are initiated into a tradition, their attitudes approaching passivity and resignation, a prelude to disenchantment.[35]

Layton's model warns against any monolithic explanation of subjects and disciplines. It would seem that, far from being timeless statements of intrinsically worthwhile content, subjects and disciplines are in constant flux. Hence the study of patterns of knowledge in our society should move beyond philosophical or macro-sociological analysis towards a detailed historical investigation of the motives and actions underlying the presentation and promotion of subjects and disciplines.

In this respect the study by Ben-David and Collins provides useful guidelines. They tried to isolate the 'social factors in the origins of a new science'; namely psychology. They postulated firstly that the ideas necessary for the creation of a new discipline are normally available over a prolonged period of time and in several places; secondly that only a few of these potential beginnings lead to further growth, and finally that 'such growth occurs where and when persons become interested in the new idea, not only as intellectual content but also as a means of establishing a new intellectual identity and particularly a new occupational role'.[36]

From a consideration of historical and social factors an alternative set of hypotheses about the way knowledge is organised and promoted begins to emerge. The traditional explanation is that new knowledge is generated by dispassionate scholarship and taken up according to considerations relating to its intrinsic and pedagogic validity. Sociologists of knowledge counter this with explanations citing the activities of 'dominant interest groups particularly the universities'.

The alternative view would hold that it is really much more complex than that. Subjects and disciplines are made up of teachers and scholars attracted to differing factions and traditions within their subject's concern; and these factions and traditions develop or decline as the subject evolves. By and large, the more 'mature' the subject, the more 'academic' its content and the predispositions of its members. Thus when new intellectual problems or areas arise for solution or enquiry, a differential response would be expected according to the direction and stage of evolution of the various subjects and disciplines involved. New knowledge would be scrutinised for its potential contribution to the furtherance of the subject or the interests of particular factions within the subject. The take-up and promotion of the knowledge could then accord with both the status position of the subject/discipline practitioners involved and their need and perception of its potential in offering new occupational identities.

To pursue this alternative view of school subjects further it is necessary to briefly outline the historical background to curriculum issues, and the main patterns of change in curricula and examinations as the secondary school system has evolved. Describing the changing educational system provides a contextual background for analysing the conflicts over the school curriculum in particular periods of history. The hypotheses that have so far been tentatively formulated can thereby be reformulated in the light of the specific characteristics of the English educational system in the twentieth century.

NOTES

1 As in M.F.D. Young (ed.), 'Knowledge and Control', (London, Collier Macmillan, 1971).
2 P.M. Hirst, The logical and psychological aspects of teaching a subject, in R.S. Peters (ed.), 'The Concept of Education' (London, Routledge and Kegan Paul, 1967), p. 44.
3 Schools Council Working Paper No. 12, 'The Educational Implications of Social and Economic Change' (HMSO, 1967).
4 P.M. Hirst and R.S. Peters, 'The Logic of Education' (London, Routledge and Kegan Paul, 1970), pp. 63-4.
5 P.M. Phenix, 'The Realms of Meaning' (McGraw-Hill, 1964), p. 317.
6 Op. cit., M. Young, 1971, p. 23.
7 F. Musgrove, The contribution of sociology to the study of curriculum', in J.F. Kerr (ed.), 'Changing the Curriculum' (University of London Press, 1968).
8 B. Bernstein, On the Classification and Training of Educational Knowledge, op. cit. M. Young (ed.), p. 47.
9 Op. cit., M. Young, 1971, p. 31.
10 Ibid., p. 34.
11 Ibid., p. 22.
12 Ibid., p. 36.
13 Ibid., p. 40.
14 P. Bourdieu, Systems of Education and Systems of Thought, op. cit. Young (ed.), 1971.
15 P. Bourdieu and J.C. Passeron, 'Reproduction in Education, Society and Culture' (London, Sage, 1977).
16 M. Young, Curriculum Change: Limits and Possibilities, in, M. Young and G. Whitty (eds.), 'Society, State and Schooling' (Falmer Press, 1977), pp. 248-9.
17 B. Bernstein, Sociology and the Sociology of Education a brief account, in J. Rex (ed.) 'Approaches to Sociology' (Routledge and Kegan Paul, 1974), p. 156.
18 R. Wilkinson, 'The Prefects' (London, Oxford University Press, 1964).
19 M. Weber, 'Essays in Sociology', translated and edited by M. Certz and C.W. Mills (London, Routledge and Kegan Paul, 1952).
20 M. Young, 'Knowledge and Control', p. 30.
21 F. Campbell, Latin and the Elite Tradition in Education, in Musgrave, ibid.
22 J. Goody and I. Watt, Literate Culture: Some General Conclusions, in Musgrave, ibid.
23 G.E. Davie, 'The Democratic Intellect' (Edinburgh, Edinburgh University Press, 1961).
24 S. Rothblatt, 'The Revolution of the Dons' (London, Faber and Faber, 1969).
25 Ibid., Rothblatt, pp. 256-7.
26 D. Layton, 'Science for the People' (London, Allen and Unwin, 1973).

27 D. Hanson, The Development of a Professional Association of
   Art Teachers, 'Studies in Design Education' 3, 2, 1971.
28 J. Eggleston, 'Developments in Design Education' (London,
   Open Books, 1971).
29 T. Dodd, 'Design and Technology in the School Curriculum'
   (Hodder and Stoughton, London, 1978).
30 R. Williams, 'The Long Revolution' (Harmondsworth, Penguin,
   1961), p. 172.
31 J. Eggleston, 'The Sociology of the School Curriculum'
   (London, Routledge and Kegan Paul, 1977).
32 O. Banks, 'Parity and Prestige in English Secondary Education' (London, Routledge and Kegan Paul, 1955), p. 5.
33 TUC, 'Education and Democracy' (London, TUC 1937).
34 Op. cit. O. Banks, 'Parity and Prestige', p. 248.
35 D. Layton, Science as General Education, 'Trends in
   Education', January 1972.
36 T. Ben-David and R. Collins, Social Factors in the Origins
   of a New Science: the case of psychology, 'American Sociological Review' August 1966, Vol. 31, No. 4.

2 THE GROWTH OF THE ENGLISH EDUCATION SYSTEM:

CHANGING PATTERNS OF CURRICULA AND EXAMINATIONS

The emergence of a national system of education followed in
slow and haphazard fashion the rapid series of economic and
demographic changes which affected Britain between the mid-
eighteenth and mid-nineteenth centuries. In the period from
1751 to 1871 the British population quadrupled. With the
development of factories and other urban industry a growing
proportion of the population worked in industrial occupations
and moved to the rapidly developing industrial towns to be near
their work. Williams has contended that at the beginning of the
nineteenth century: 'The process of change from a system of
social orders based on localities, to a national system of social
classes . . . was virtually complete.' The result of this changing
pattern he asserted was 'a new kind of class-determined education. Higher education became a virtual monopoly, excluding
the new working class, and the idea of universal education,
except within the narrow limits of "moral rescue" was widely
opposed as a matter of principle'.[1] For the working class the
main educational institutions were the Sunday Schools, run by
the churches, and the industrial schools set up to provide
manual training and instruction, but to classes that often comprised several hundred children. In 1851 the average duration
of schooling for working-class children was approximately two
years. The Revised Code introduced in 1862, whilst severely
limiting the curriculum, attempted to raise and monitor educational standards by introducing payment by results in reading,
writing and arithmetic (the three Rs). The limited nature of
the educational institutions and experiences available to the
working class was acknowledged by the 1870 Education Act which
sought to make primary education available for all children. In
1880 attendance was made compulsory up until the age of ten.

For older children education was available in public and grammar
schools but, generally speaking, only for the middle and upper
classes. The Taunton Commission which reported in 1868 on the
state of secondary education defined three grades of education
according to the time spent at school: the first grade school
continued until 18 or 19 or beyond, the second grade until 16
and the third grade until 14. Taunton asserted:

> The difference in the time assigned makes some difference in
> the very nature of education itself; if a boy cannot remain at
> school beyond the age of 14 it is useless to begin teaching him
> such subjects as require a longer time for their proper study;

14

if he can continue till 18 or 19, it may be expedient to postpone some studies that would otherwise be commenced early. Both the substance and the arrangements of the instruction will thus greatly depend on the length of time that can be devoted to it.

In terms of its relationship to the contemporary social structures the convenience of this pattern of curriculum differentiation was duly noted because 'these instructions correspond roughly but by no means exactly, to the gradations of society. Those who can afford to pay more for their children's education will also, as a general rule, continue the education for a longer time.'[12] The curriculum of the public and grammar schools was extremely specialised and, in line with the avowed intention of educating 'christian gentlemen', stressed classics and religious instruction. The classical educational orientation echoed that in the universities described in Rothblatt's study of nineteenth-century Cambridge.[3] The close connections between secondary and university curricula were far from coincidental for as Williams reminds us: 'By the 1830's, the examination system between these schools [the public and grammar schools] and the universities was firmly established and this, while raising educational standards within the institutions, had the effect of reinforcing the now marked limitation of the universities to entrants from a narrow social class.'[14]

In fact, from this period onwards the curricula of the public schools began, in uneven and idiosyncratic fashion, to broaden. By 1868, when the Public Schools Act was passed, the curriculum covered not only classics but mathematics, one modern language, history, geography, two natural sciences, drawing and music. This broadening curriculum was again partly a reflection of changes in university curricula although some of the changes in the schools in this period did pre date university developments. Curriculum change was strongly advocated in government circles because of the increasing challenge from countries like Germany and America to Britain's economic and military supremacy. The broadening of the public and grammar school curriculum must not be overstated, however, for inside the new and wider curriculum classical studies for the moment maintained their dominant position. Ryder and Silver noted: 'Science and modern subjects had gained a foothold, but the classical-literary tradition continued to be considered the right kind of cultural and moral contribution to the preparation of an educational and social elite.'[15]

Meanwhile in the elementary school sector, growing rapidly following the 1870 Act, new patterns of curricula began to emerge. The School Boards administering schools that were innovative and responsive to local demands began to provide more vocational curricula covering commercial, technical and scientific subjects. These developments were considered by the 1895 Bryce Commission whose findings helped form the basis of the 1902 Education Act. One result of the Act was that these schools were removed from the elementary sector and absorbed into the new secondary system defined by Bryce. Vocational and technical curricula were henceforth put on a separate limb in the central schools, which were higher elementary schools for the purposes of administration, and in the junior technical schools: 'Though valuable work was done in both these types of school, and though the junior technical schools came to challenge more orthodox secondary education, the official view was that their status was, and should be, below that of the secondary school.'[6]

The 1902 Act had two main results. Firstly, the 'arenas' in which educational policy were decided were substantially altered and/education became the local responsibility of county and borough authorities. Secondly, the secondary sector was to follow the pattern of curriculum then enshrined in the public and grammar schools. The Act ensured that: 'Whatever developments in secondary education might occur, it should be within a single system, in which the dominant values would remain those of the traditional grammar school and its curriculum.'[7]

Other developments, at the national level, confirmed this trend. The Board of Education, formed in 1899, devised a four-year secondary course in 1904. Although this closely echoed public and grammar school curricula the movement within these schools to a broader curriculum was strikingly confirmed. The course covered mathematics, science, English language and literature, geography, history, a language other than English, drawing, manual work, physical training and household crafts for girls. The tendency growing quite markedly in some areas towards the inclusion of technical and commercial curricula in elementary schools was effectively checked. With classical curricula on the other hand the Boards preferences were clear where Latin is not taught the Board will specifically inquire and require satisfaction that the omission of Latin is for the good of the schools'.

The dominant influence of the Board of Education as expressed in the Secondary Regulations was much resented by the local authorities whose own power had been established by the 1902 Act. However, the influence of the Board was not to remain dominant for very long. In 1917 the School Certificate was introduced and from this date onwards the Examination Boards began to exert considerable power in the control of the secondary school curriculum. The examinations were closely tied, as we noted earlier, to the public and grammar schools and by the 1850s 'a system of University Local Examinations, first called "Middle Class Examinations", had enabled endowed and proprietary schools of the first and second grades to aim at some recognised standard of education'.[8]

Control of the curriculum by the University Examination Boards ensured that substantially the same values as those promoted by the Board of Education were enshrined in school curricula.

The Joint Matriculation Board, for instance, in 1918 offered the following main subjects for those seeking to pass the Higher Certificate:

Group I: Greek, Latin and Roman History.
Group II: English Literature, French, German, Russian, Spanish, History (either 1(a) or 1(b) and either 2(a) or 2(b)), Latin, Pure Mathematics or Higher Pure Mathematics.
Group II(B): Economics, Geography, History (1 and 2), French, German, Italian, Russian, Spanish.
Group III: Pure Mathematics or Higher Pure Mathematics, Applied Mathematics, Physics, Chemistry, Botany, Zoology.

Candidates had to satisfy the examiners in one of the four groupings (as well as passing one of a broader range of 'subsidiary' subjects).[9] The use of the University Examinations Boards by public and grammar schools facilitated the establishment of viable sixth forms 'able to act as a focal point for . . . academic goals'.[10] These academic goals, linked to specialised course requirements of university departments, developed a common sixth form pattern and 'teacher opinion seemed to accept the value of specialisation. It stimulated interest, maintained high standards of work, kept teachers close to university methods and material and added to their status'.[11]

The linking of the definition of curricula to examination boards controlled by the universities, enabled state education to be established as a 'ladder' leading to professional occupations. Building upon the three-grade classification offered by Taunton, the Bryce Commission had argued for scholarships to offer access for the most talented of all classes to the educational ladder. The ladder to the professions, with the associated curricula thereby implied, affected the social classes differentially. Less than a fifth of the generation of boys born between 1910 and 1929 reached a secondary school; a seventh of these (approximately 3 per cent of the total age group) went on to university. Two-fifths of the middle-class boys and one-tenth of the working-class boys went to secondary school, giving an opportunity ratio of 4:1. For universities the ratio for the same 1910-29 generation of boys was 6:1.[12]

Lacey has traced how the spread of university-controlled school examinations affected the functions of 'Hightown Grammar' school. Up until 1922 the school was: 'used as a jumping-off place, one of higher status than the ordinary or higher elementary school, from which it was possible to obtain the best clerical, commercial, technical and trade apprenticeships in local industry.' The implications for the school curriculum were clear: 'For this purpose a two-year course was often as good as a three-year course. Given the conditions in local industry, academic qualifications were to a large extent ignored in favour of the "secondary school boy" with a good family.[13] After this date the content and emphasis of the headmaster's reports to the governors underwent a noticeable change and from 1923 onwards there were detailed reports on examinations, school certificates (and later Higher School Certificates) and the number of boys staying on beyond matriculation (at 16 years of age).[14] This has continued to be a major feature of secondary school reporting and associated organisation to this day. Moreover, it is interesting to note that for those boys who stay on beyond compulsory leaving age the same subject-based curriculum has remained almost totally intact for the 60 years following the 1904 Regulations. The major reasons for this stabilised subject-based pattern were the considerable power over the curriculum held by the examination boards and, secondly, the founding and growth of separate subject groups and associations. The combined activities of examination boards and subject groups and associations sustained and developed the secondary school curriculum pattern.

This pattern was critically scrutinised by the Norwood Report of 1943 which argued that throughout Europe, 'the evolution of education' had, 'thrown up certain groups, each of which can and must be treated in a way appropriate to itself.' In England three clear groups could be discerned. Firstly:

> The pupil who is interested in learning for its own sake, who can grasp an argument or follow a piece of connected reasoning, who is interested in causes, whether on the level of human volition or in the material world, who cares to know how things came to be as well as how they are, who is sensitive to language as expression of thought, to a proof as a precise demonstration, to a series of experiments justifying a principle; he is interested in the relatedness of related things, in development, in structure, in a coherent body of knowledge.

These pupils form the continuing clientele of the traditional subject-based curriculum for as Norwood states, 'such pupils, educated by the curriculum commonly associated with the Grammar School, have entered the learned professions or have taken up higher administrative or business posts.'[15] The needs of the intermediate category, 'the pupil whose interests and abilities lie markedly in the field of applied science or applied art,' were to be fulfilled by the technical schools. Finally, Norwood states with a very partial view of educational history, 'There has of late years been recognition, expressed in the framing of curricula and otherwise of still another grouping of occupations.' This third group was to provide the clientele for the new secondary modern schools.

> The pupil in this group deals more easily with concrete things than with ideas. He may have much ability, but it will be in the realm of facts. He is interested in things as they are; he finds little attraction in the past or in the slow disentanglement

of causes or movements. His mind must turn its knowledge or its curiosity to immediate test; and his test is essentially practical.[16]

This curriculum, whilst ruling out certain occupational futures, certainly facilitated those destined for manual work. It 'would not be to prepare for a particular job or profession and its treatment would make a direct appeal to interests, which it would awaken by practical touch with affairs'.[17]

The Norwood Report summarises the patterns of curriculum differentiation which had emerged through 'the evolution of education' over the past century or so. The close alliance between patterns of curriculum differentiation and social structure was often conceded (e.g. in the Taunton Report in 1868): different curricula are explicitly linked to different occupational categories. The academic tradition was for the grammar school pupil destined for the learned professions and higher administrative or business posts. The more utilitarian curriculum in the technical schools was for the pupil destined to work in 'applied science or applied art'. Whilst for the future manual worker in the secondary modern the emphasis was on utilitarian and pedagogic curricula; these studies were to 'make a direct appeal to interests which it would awaken by practical touch with affairs'. The close identity between different curriculum traditions, occupational destinations (and social classes) and different educational sectors was confirmed in the 1944 Education Act.

THE TRIPARTITE SYSTEM AND THE RAISING OF THE SCHOOL LEAVING AGE

The 1944 Education Act foreshadowed the tripartite system of grammar, technical and secondary modern schools. The compulsory school leaving age was raised to 15 in 1947. The Act marks the beginning of the modern era of curriculum conflict, not so much because of its details but because from this date onwards curriculum conflict becomes more visible, public and national. Glass has noted that in this respect there was no 'prewar parallel' for there was now 'a recognition that Secondary education is a proper subject for discussion and study . . . in striking contrast to the pre-war position when attempts to investigate access to the various stages of education tended to be looked at by the Government as attacks on the class structure.'[18]

In the emerging secondary modern schools the curriculum was initially free from the consideration of external examinations. This freedom allowed many of the schools to experiment with their curricula and to pursue vocational and child-centred objectives. Social studies and civic courses, for instance, were rapidly established in a number of the schools. Kathleen Gibberd

has argued that the secondary modern school as conceived in
1944 was never intended to work to any universal syllabus or
take any external examination: 'It was to be a field for experiment.' She considered that: 'Behind the official words and
regulations there was a call to the teacher who believed in education for its own sake and longed for a free hand with children
who were not natural learners. Many of those who responded
gave an individual character to their schools.'[19] However, the
period during which secondary moderns were 'a field for experiment' with vocational, child-centred and integrated curricula
was to prove very limited. More parents began to realise that
certification led to better jobs, teachers found examinations a
useful source of motivation and heads began to use examinations
as a means of raising their schools' reputation and status. For
some heads support for GCE may have stemmed from an initial
rebellious non-acceptance of the whole tripartite philosophy. But
soon 'success in this examination started a national avalanche'.[20]
By 1961-3, when Partridge studied a secondary modern school,
the competitive nature of the 'examination race' was clearly
apparent: 'with the public demand for academic attainments,
reflecting the fact that education has become the main avenue
of social mobility in our society, GCE successes would immeasurably enhance the repute of such a school, and hence the standing and status of the headmaster.'[21] The rapid take-up of the
GCE and other examinations in secondary moderns led to an
exhaustive inquiry by the Ministry of Education, culminating
in the Beloe Report which recommended that secondary modern
schools should have their own examinations. In 1965, therefore,
the CSE was inaugurated.

The rapidity with which external examinations came to dominate
secondary modern school curricula meant that many of the
characteristics of grammar school curricula were reproduced.
Paradoxically it was the growth of public debate about education
which produced this pressure for the convergence of educational
patterns whatever sector of the tripartite system was under
consideration. But the public debate also identified considerable
objections to the whole tripartite philosophy. Evidence accumu-
lated that the 11-plus was often arbitrary and unfair. As a
result support grew for a more 'comprehensive system'. The new
comprehensive schools, however, also had to justify themselves
in terms of examination success. They had to perform as well as
the examination-oriented grammar and secondary modern schools;
and for many years their examination results were to constitute
a major piece of evidence in the 'comprehensive debate'.

THE CHANGEOVER TO A COMPREHENSIVE SYSTEM AND THE
FURTHER RAISING OF THE SCHOOL LEAVING AGE

When the Labour Government took office in 1964, an early
declaration was made of the intention to end divisions within

secondary education along tripartite lines and to move towards a
phased introduction of comprehensive schooling. The intention
was publicised both in a House of Commons resolution passed in
January 1965 and in the two circulars issued by the DES.
Circular 10/65, 'The Organisation of Secondary Education', was
issued in July 1965 to be followed by Circular 10/66 issued in
March 1965 on the subject of 'school building programmes'.

The government's pronouncements met with a patchy response,
even though in the year the government took office 71 per cent
of all authorities either had established, or intended to establish,
some form of comprehensive education.[22] In the years between
1965 and 1970 the number of comprehensive schools grew from
262 to 1,415, a growth in percentage terms from 8.5 to 31 per
cent.[23] More important than the actual progress was the fact
that more and more local authorities were planning comprehensive
schemes: this added a sense of momentum and a growing feeling
that all sectors would have to prepare for the inevitable change.

As these figures show, the belief that the Labour Government
of the late sixties effected rapid changeover to comprehensives
is misleading when examined in detail. The growth of the comprehensive sector in this period took place very largely at the
expense of the secondary modern schools. Between 1961 and
1970 the proportion of secondary school pupils attending comprehensive schools increased from 4 per cent to 29 per cent.
These pupils came mainly from secondary modern schools whose
share of the secondary schools population declined by 17 per
cent. In comparison the grammar school population declined by
only 3 per cent and the proportion of pupils in independent,
direct grant and assisted schools by only 2 per cent.[24] For the
grammar and independent schools, bastions of traditional
academic education in this period, comprehensivisation often
remained a threat rather than a reality, albeit a threat often
perceived in a highly emotional manner (a common phrase in
currency at the time referred to the 'vandals of comprehensivisation'). From 1970, however, comprehensive schooling spread
rapidly and in 1979 approximately 80 per cent of secondary
school children attended such schools.

Besides the organisational reform considerable curriculum
reform was envisaged at this time. A range of influences was
at work which partly arose from comprehensivisation and partly
from the moves to raise the school leaving age (ROSLA). Walker
and MacDonald have judged the latter as 'a far more threatening
shadow on the teachers' horizon' than America's fear of the 'red
menace'.[25] Though this may overstate the case, it was plain that
many teachers feared the plan and took every opportunity to
criticise it. Nonetheless, in 1972 the change, originally planned
for 1970, was implemented. Comprehensivisation and ROSLA drew
attention to the large group of students who did not even take
CSE - the 'non-examination' classes. Alongside this practical
problem the ideology of mixed ability teaching also argued for the
provision of more 'relevant' and 'child-centred curricula'.

The curriculum reform movement gained insight and support from the preceding movement in the USA. The decision of the Nuffield Foundation to fund school curriculum development projects was partially influenced by these American developments. The Foundation began a number of projects beginning with Nuffield 'O' level projects in physics, chemistry and biology in 1962 but covering many other subjects besides science, for instance, classics and languages. When the Schools Council for Curriculum and Examinations was established in 1964, development projects began in co-operation with Nuffield. Robert Morris, one of the first Joint Secretaries of the Council, states that its work 'was initially carried on the shoulders of Nuffield finance into a curriculum development role'.[26] Several of the early Schools Council projects grew out of Nuffield initiatives, for instance two of the science projects: Science 5-13 and Integrated Science. Other projects, like the Humanities Curriculum Project, were jointly funded by Schools Council and the Nuffield Foundation.

Rubinstein and Simon have left a summary of the climate of educational reform in 1972 following ROSLA, and the rapid growth of the comprehensive system:

> The content of the curriculum is now under much discussion, and comprehensive schools are participating actively in the many curriculum reform schemes launched by the Schools Council and Nuffield. The tendency is towards the development of the interdisciplinary curricula, together with the use of the resources approach to learning, involving the substitution of much group and individual work for the more traditional forms of class teaching. For these new forms of organising and stimulating learning mixed ability grouping often provides the most appropriate method; and partly for this reason the tendency is towards the reduction of streaming and class teaching. This movement in itself promotes new relations between teachers and pupils, particularly insofar as the teacher's role is changing from that of ultimate authority to that of motivating, facilitating and structuring the pupils' own discovery and search for knowledge.[27]

The belief that rapid curriculum reform, with a range of associated political and pedagogical implications, was well underway was commonly held at this time. Professor Kerr asserted in 1968 that 'At the practical and organisational levels, the new curricula promise to revolutionise English education.'[28]

At the very time when some teachers were seeing integrated or interdisciplinary courses as the strategy for establishing new curricula, other voices were warning of the dangers inherent in curriculum reforms then being pursued. Marten Shipman read a paper before the British Sociological Association in 1969 which argued that the curriculum reforms were in danger of perpetuating the two nations approach inside the educational system what he called a 'Curriculum for Inequality'. He spoke of the 'unintended consequences of curriculum development':

> Coming less from actual content than from the introduction of new courses into a school system that is still clearly divided into two sections, one geared to a system of external examinations, the other less constrained. The former is closely tied to the universities and is within established academic traditions. The latter has a short history and is still in its formative stages. It is the consequences of innovation into these two separate sections rather than the curricula themselves which may be producing a new means of sustaining old divisions.[29]

The connecting traditions are elucidated later in the paper:

> One is firmly planted in revered academic traditions, is adapted to teaching from a pool of factual knowledge and has clearly defined, if often irrelevant subject boundaries. The other is experimental, looking to America rather than our own past for inspiration, focusses on contemporary problems, groups subjects together and rejects formal teaching methods. One emphasises a schooling within a framework of external examinations, the other attempts to align school work to the environment of the children.[30]

The divisive effects of curriculum reform were not, however, the major features to gain attention. In October 1976 the Prime Minister, James Callaghan, drew together the major themes of public anxiety about curriculum in a speech he made at Ruskin College which launched the so-called 'Great Debate' on education. He was worried about what kind of curriculum pupils were being offered, about modern teaching methods, about educational standards and about the relationship between school and industry. In effect he was calling into question the whole pattern and efficiency of curriculum reform. 'No new policies were proposed but the government had now established that educational standards, and the relationship of education to the economy, were to be as much of a priority as comprehensive reform in isolation.' The concern with school-industry links touches on a recurrent and illustrative theme in curriculum history. Callaghan stated that he was concerned to find that many of 'our best trained students who have completed the higher levels of education at university or polytechnic have no desire to join industry.' He concluded that there seemed to be a need for 'a more technological bias in science teaching that will lead towards practical applications in industry rather than towards academic studies.'[31] Thus it would seem that despite radical changes in the organisational structure of the educational system, the underlying fabric of curriculum has remained surprisingly constant.

A footnote is provided in a recent book by Hopkins on the
'School Debate'. He notes that 'part of the theory behind comprehensive reform was to extend the opportunities for practical
study so as to favour technological advance'. But concludes
'the resulting technological advance appears to have been
small (why, otherwise, a great Debate) and the status of
practical subjects remains low'.[32] It would appear that, despite
the unification behind comprehensivisation, despite an explicit
desire to broaden the appeal of practical (and also the more
pedagogic) subjects, patterns of status differentiation have been
substantially sustained. It seems that it will be impossible to
realise the ambitions of comprehensive educational reform unless
we have a better understanding of the part played by the
subjects of the curriculum in preserving a divided system in
the face of organisational change. We may understand the
apparent paradox more fully if we analyse the role of subject
associations, sub-groups and traditions in modifying and sus-
taining patterns of curriculum differentiation in the era of
comprehensive schooling. This will be the subject of the next
chapter.

NOTES

1   R. Williams, 'The Long Revolution' (Harmondsworth, Penguin,
    1961), pp. 156-7.
2   Report of the Royal Commission known as the Schools Inquiry
    Commission (the Taunton Report), 1868, Ch. 7, p. 587.
3   S. Rothblatt, 'The Revolution of the Dons' (London, Faber
    and Faber, 1968).
4   R. Williams, 'Long Revolution', p. 158.
5   J. Ryder and H. Silver 'Modern English Society, History
    and Structure 1850-1970' (London, Methuen, 1970), p. 97.
6   D.V. Glass, Education and Social Change in Modern
    England, in R. Hooper, (ed.), 'The Curriculum Context,
    Design and Development' (Edinburgh, Oliver and Boyd,
    1971), p. 25.
7   Ryder and Silver, 'Modern English Society', p. 98.
8   R. Williams, 'Long Revolution', pp. 159-60.
9   'Joint Matriculation Board Calendar' (Manchester, 1918),
    pp. 41-2.
10 W.A. Reid, 'The University and the Sixth Form Curriculum'
    (London, Macmillan, 1972), p. 88.
11 A.D. Edwards, 'The Changing Sixth Form' (London, Rout-
    ledge and Kegan Paul), p. 34.
12 Glass, in R. Hooper (ed.), pp. 28-9.
13 C. Lacey, 'Hightown Grammar', (Manchester University
    Press, 1970), p. 15.
14 Ibid., p. 21.
15 The Norwood Report, 'Curriculum and Examinations in
    Secondary Schools', Report of the Committee of the

Secondary School Examinations Council appointed by the President of the Board of Education in 1941 (London, HMSO, 1943), p. 2.

16 Ibid., p. 3.

17 Ibid., p. 4.

18 Glass, in R. Hooper (ed.), p. 35.

19 K. Gibberd, 'No Place Like School' (London, Michael Joseph, 1962), p. 103.

20 Ibid., p. 102.

21 J. Partridge 'Life in a Secondary Modern School' (Harmondsworth, Penguin, 1968), p. 68.

22 National Foundation for Educational Research, 'Local Authorities Practices in the allocation of Pupils to Secondary Schools' (Slough, NFER, 1964).

23 D. Rubinstein and B. Simon, 'The Evolution of the Comprehensive School 1926-1972' (London, Routledge and Kegan Paul, 1973), p. 108.

24 Ibid., pp. 110-12. The figures are completed by a 2 per cent reduction in separate 'technical schools'.

25 B. Macdonald and R. Walker, 'Changing the Curriculum', (London, Open Books, 1976), p. 32.

26 Interview with Robert Morris, 26.7.78.

27 Rubinstein and Simon, 'Comprehensive School 1926-1972,' P. 123.

28 J. Kerr, The Problem of Curriculum Reform, op. cit., R. Hooper (ed.), p. 180.

29 M. Shipman, Curriculum for Inequality, op. cit., R. Hooper (ed.) 1976, pp. 101-2.

30 Ibid., p. 104.

31 Speech by James Callaghan, Prime Minister 18 October 1976, Ruskin College.

32 A. Hopkins, 'The School Debate' (Harmondsworth, Penguin, 1978), p. 139.

3 ACADEMIC 'SUBJECTS' AND CURRICULUM CHANGE

INTRODUCTION

The historical background presented in Chapter 2 points to the emergence of a hierarchy of high-status 'examination subjects' associated with 'revered academic traditions'. The direct connection between 'O' and 'A' level examinations and the academic tradition is one of the most enduring features of our educational system and it is normally assumed that 'able pupils' are those who can pass 'O' and 'A' level examinations. These assumptions have been faithfully reproduced in the changeover from a tripartite to a comprehensive system.

The taken for granted assumption that 'O' and 'A' level examinations cover 'academic' content and are aimed at 'able' pupils, represents the culmination of a conflict that is briefly recorded in Chapter 2. In this conflict a number of alternative traditions to the academic tradition could be discerned: for instance the technical and vocational curricula promoted within the elementary schools in the late nineteenth century. These alternative traditions represent fundamental and recurrent elements in curriculum conflict. To understand their continuing subservience to the academic tradition, it is necessary to first define the major 'alternative' traditions and then to analyse the conflict over the curriculum, particularly with reference to the nature of 'examinable knowledge'. In this conflict the varying 'traditions' gain the allegiance of different sub-groups of factions among subject teachers. The academic tradition's dominance needs above all to be understood through an analysis of the nature of its appeal to these groups.

The process model developed by Bucher and Strauss for the study of professions provides valuable guidelines for those studying school subjects. Within a profession, they argue, are varied identities, values and interests, hence professions are to be seen as 'loose amalgamations of segments pursuing different objectives in different manners and more or less delicately held together under a common name at particular periods in history.'[1] The most frequent conflicts arise over the gaining of institutional footholds, over recruitment and over external relations with clients and other institutions. At times when conflicts such as these become intense professional associations may be created, or if already in existence, become more strongly institutionalised.

The Bucher and Strauss model of professions suggests that perhaps the 'subject community' should not be viewed as a

homogeneous group whose members share similar values and
definitions of role, common interests and identity. Rather the
subject community could be seen as comprising a range of conflicting groups, segments or factions. The importance of these
groups might vary considerably over time. As with professions,
school subject associations often develop at particular points
in time when there is an intensification of conflict over school
curricula and resources and over recruitment and training.

In this book the subject community is therefore seen as comprising a shifting network of sub-groups, segments or factions.
These sub-groups might, for instance, be organised around
different schools of thought with different views about which
knowledge should be emphasised within the subject: field work
or laboratory work in biology, or regional geography as against
new geography.

One of the main sources of argument between these sub-
groups (and indeed between subject communities) is the nature
and purpose of the school curriculum. There is a long history
of these arguments and it is useful to discern three major
traditions: the academic, the utilitarian and the pedagogic.

Since the nineteenth century 'academic subjects' and written
examinations have become closely interconnected. This alliance,
whether viewed as divine or malign, was formally enshrined in
the School Certificate examination defined in 1917. Since that
date certain material implications have followed for those sub-
groups and school subjects promoting or representing the
academic tradition. Questions of theoretical base or methodological
perspective have often been subsumed by or channelled into
the construction of acceptable written examinations. For the
groups and associations promoting themselves as school subjects,
and irresistibly drawn to claiming 'academic status', a central
criterion has been whether the subjects' content could be tested
by written examinations for an 'able' clientele. Acceptance of
the criterion of examinability affects both the content and form
of the knowledge presented but carries with it the guarantee of
high status. The academic tradition is content-focused and
typically stresses abstract and theoretical knowledge for examination.

The utilitarian tradition is conversely of low status, dealing
with practical knowledge sometimes not amenable to the current
'A' level mode of written examination. Utilitarian knowledge is
related to those non-professional vocations in which the majority
of people work for most of their adult life. The low status of
utilitarian knowledge also applies to the personal, social and
commonsense knowledge stressed by those purusing the
pedagogic tradition. Whilst all school knowledge has at least an
implicit pedagogy this tradition places the 'way the child learns'
as the central concern in devising subject content.

These traditions are viewed as three 'centres of gravity' in
the arguments about styles of curriculum. They do not represent
a complete list of the 'traditions' in English curricula nor are

they timeless entities; they simply represent three clear con-
stellations of curriculum styles which recur in the history of the
school subjects under study. In this sense they are perhaps
best viewed as strategic clusters employed to help in the
scrutiny of curriculum changes and conflicts.

At certain stages in their history, subjects may come to be
represented by subject associations. These associations present
a formal arena wherein sub-groups can promote their varied
interests and where the arguments about curriculum traditions
can be pursued. The range of groups involved in school subjects
- sub-groups, factions, associations and communities - will be
broadly referred to as subject groups.

SCHOOL SUBJECT 'TRADITIONS' AND CURRICULUM CHANGE

The historical background of the English curriculum and the
studies of historical elements in curriculum (notably by Layton,
Williams and Banks) point to the existence of several leading
traditions. Often these traditions can be related to the social
class origins and occupational destinations of their pupil
clienteles. Hence the curricula of public and grammar schools
aimed at middle- and upper-class children preparing for
professional life were primarily academic, whilst the elementary
schools educating the majority stressed utilitarian training.

Writing of the 'traditions' in English primary education, Blyth
discerned three different kinds: the preparatory, the elementary
and the developmental. The preparatory tradition was 'almost
exclusively related to what we now call grammar-school education,
which developed in its turn mainly as an upper middle-class
phenomenon.' Conversely the elementary tradition 'with its
characteristic emphasis on the basic skills' was aimed at the
lower classes. 'For those who were unfortunate, indolent or
culpable enough to be poor, the minimum of education was proper
and sufficient.'[2] The third tradition, the developmental, based
its principles on concern with developing each child's interest
in learning along the lines recommended by Rousseau and
Pestalozzi. Broadly speaking Blyth's three primary traditions
can be equated with three leading traditions discerned within
secondary education: the preparatory with the academic, the
elementary with the utilitarian and the developmental with the
pedagogic traditions.

Academic, Utilitarian and Pedagogic Traditions

The definition of public and grammar school subjects in the
nineteenth century which was established in the 1904 regulations
and confirmed in the School Certificate examinations clearly
followed the aims of education as a preparation for professional
and academic life. Eggleston, commenting on the early nineteenth
century, found that 'A new and important feature of the time

that was to prevail, was the redefinition of high-status knowledge as that which was not immediately useful in vocation or occupation.' Hence the study of Classics 'now came to be seen as essentially a training of the mind and the fact that a boy could be spared from work long enough to experience this in full measure was in itself seen as a demonstration not only of the high status of the knowledge itself but also of the recipient - the mark of a 'gentleman' rather than a worker.'[3] Eggleston's last sentence points up the contradiction: it was not so much that classical liberal education was non-vocational but that the vocations were only those fit for upper-class gentlemen. 'As educational history shows', Williams reminds us, 'the classical linguistic disciplines were primarily vocational but these particular vocations had acquired a separate traditional dignity, which was refused to vocations now of equal human relevance.[4]

For this reason we have avoided the use of the terms vocational education or vocational knowledge. Instead we refer to the subject-based curriculum confirmed by the examination system as the 'academic' tradition, and to low-status practical knowledge as the 'utilitarian' tradition. Utilitarian knowledge thus becomes that which is related to those non-professional vocations in which the majority of people work for most of their adult life.

Despite being advocated by a number of influential government committees and commissions, neither commercial nor technical education was ever seriously considered as a new dimension of comparable status to be added to the existing classical curriculum. It was specialised training for a particular class of man, and its confinement to low-status areas of the curriculum has remained a constant feature of English curriculum conflict. For example, Layton's research on the development of science education in the nineteenth century has shown how the emphasis was increasingly placed on abstract knowledge with a consequent separation from the practical world of work.[5] Nevertheless, the alternative view of a narrowly utilitarian curriculum is still powerful, as is shown by the constant pressure for utilitarian subjects in spite of their recurrent failure to earn high status. The manpower needs of a changing industrial economy provoke continuing advocacy of utilitarian training, by industrialists although these demands are at their most shrill at times of pervasive crisis in the economic and social system. When widespread industrial failure is endemic the continuing ambivalence of educational status systems causes serious concern and pressure for change. The Great Debate was one symptom of this concern and it was recently argued in 'The Times' that:

> strategies for furthering the inter-relationship between industry and the educational system need to address the complex question of status systems. The established patterns of status represent an enormously powerful historical legacy, a kind of indirect pressure group. Only if high status areas in the educational system such as the public schools and Oxbridge

are willing to remodel their value systems do current strategies stand any chance of success.[6]

The low status of utilitarian knowledge is shared by the personal, social and commonsense knowledge stressed by those pursuing a child-centred approach to education. This approach with its emphasis on the individual pupil's learning process can be characterised as the pedagogic tradition within the English curriculum. Child-centred or progressive education does not view the task of education as preparation for the 'ladder' to the professions and academia or as an apprenticeship to vocational work; rather education is seen as a way of aiding the child's own 'inquiries' or 'discoveries', a process facilitated by 'activity' methods which move the pupil away from the role of passive recipient to one of active agent in the learning process. The approach was found in the Social Studies movement of the 1930s and 1940s: 'The outlook is essentially broad and exploratory and the course is broken up into a series of cor-related units of study rather than conducted as a rigid sequence of lessons. It thus offers endless opportunities for active learning; for relating the lesson to contemporary events for co-operative study by the form as a group.'[7] The pedagogic tradition often challenges the existing professional identity of teachers at two levels: (1) as a 'specialist' in a school subject, for which the teacher had normally been specifically trained; and (2) as an all-pervading authority figure within the classroom. The Interdisciplinary Enquiry (IDE) workshops run by Goldsmiths College in the sixties clarify the dual nature of the challenge. The workshops were specifically instituted as pilot courses for experienced teachers involved with those school leavers that would be staying on as a result of ROSLA.

The IDE booklets contained a series of stark messages for teachers of traditional subjects and suggested that 'the subject based curriculum has fundamental educational disadvantages'. For instance, 'the school day is fragmented into subject periods and time allocated to each subject is always regarded as insufficient by the subject specialist, as indeed it is.' Apart from the disadvantages in terms of time:

> The arbitrary division of knowledge into subject-syllabuses, encourages a didactic form of teaching with the pupils' role reduced to passive assimilation. Any enquiry resulting from a keen interest shown by children in a section of work they are doing in a subject inevitably takes them over the bound-aries of the subject into another, perhaps several others. Good teachers would like to encourage this evidence of interest, but they simply cannot afford the time, especially if their syllabus is geared to external examinations.[8]

As a solution to the problems engendered by the didactic teaching of traditional subjects the Goldsmiths team advocated organising schemes of work around interdisciplinary enquiries.[9]

Another curriculum project aimed at young school leavers underlined both the need to reappraise 'subjects' and to clearly define new pedagogic relationships. The Humanities Curriculum Project (HCP) began in 1967 with Lawrence Stenhouse as its director. HCP pursued the pedagogic implications of curriculum reform through the notion of 'neutral chairmanship'. This meant: 'That the teacher accepts the need to submit his teaching in controversial areas to the criterion of neutrality . . . i.e. that he regards it as part of his responsibility not to promote his own view,' and further that 'the mode of enquiry in controversial areas should have discussion, rather than instruction as its core'.[10] The pedagogic tradition has been closely allied to the so-called 'progressive' movement in education. As Shipman noted in 1969, the more progressive curricula have come to be concentrated on those sections of the pupil clientele not considered suitable for 'O' and 'A' level examinations.[11] In this way the pedagogic tradition has often suffered from the comparatively low status also accorded to the utilitarian tradition.

Examinations and Academic Subjects

The connection between the subjects taught in school and external examinations was established on the present footing with the birth of the School Certificate in 1917. From this point on, the conflict over the curriculum began to resemble the contemporary situation in focusing on the definition and evaluation of examinable knowledge. The School Certificate rapidly became the major concern of grammar schools and the academic subjects it examined soon came to dominate the school timetable. Thus when, the Norwood Report assessed the importance of examinations it found that

> A certain sameness in the curricula of schools seems to have resulted from the double necessity of finding a place for the many subjects competing for time in the curriculum and the need to teach these subjects in such a way and to such a standard as will ensure success in the School Certificate examination.

As a result of 'these necessities' the curriculum had 'settled down into an uneasy equilibrium, the demands of specialists and subjects and examinations being nicely adjusted and compensated'.[12] Despite these warnings, the academic subject-centred curriculum was strengthened in the period following the 1944 Education Act. The introduction of the GCE in 1951 allowed subjects to be taken separately at 'O' level (whereas the School Certificate was a 'block' exam in which a group of main subjects all had to be passed), and the introduction of 'A' level increased subject specialisation in a manner guaranteed to preserve if not enhance the largely 'academic' nature of the 'O' level examination.

There was little chance that a lower-status examination such as the CSE which was introduced in 1965, would endanger the academic subject-centredness of the higher status 'O' and 'A' levels.

Indeed the CSE has proved remarkably adaptive to maintaining the status differentiation noted by Shipman and has even extended it. A recent study by Ball shows four bands within a comprehensive school allocating pupils as follows: band 1 to subject-based 'O' levels; band 2 to subject-based CSE mode 2; band 3 to 'integrated' subjects (e.g. Maths. for Living) for CSE mode 3; and band 4 to non-examined 'remedial' classes.[13]

The hegemony of the academic subject-based curriculum for 'O' level and 'A' level candidates was confirmed by the organisational structure of the Schools Council. An early role for the Council in the examinations field was advising the Beloe Committee set up to consider the proliferation of examinations in secondary modern schools. Beloe employed the subject-based framework of the Secondary Schools Examination Council, set up in the interwar years to ensure uniformity of examinations, mainly at 'O' and 'A' levels. As Robert Morris, one of the two founding joint secretaries, explained: 'You can now see why the Schools Council developed a committee structure based on subjects. It was simply logical . . . we just inherited the structure of the Secondary Schools Examinations Council who had already developed a pattern for examination in academic subjects.'[14]

Accepting this structure of academic subject examinations, interest groups promoting new subjects have focused since 1917 on the pursuit of high-status examinations and qualifications. Subjects like art, woodwork and metalwork, technical studies, book-keeping, typewriting and needlework, domestic science and physical education, have consistently pursued status improvement by arguing for enhanced academic examinations and qualifications. But as we have seen, few subjects have been able to challenge the hegemony of the academic subjects incorporated in the 1904 Regulations and 1917 School Certificate. This academic tradition has successfully withstood the recent waves of comprehensive reorganisation and associated curriculum reform. The upheaval of the 'Great Debate' is a reminder that this survival appears to have been at the expense of certain 'dominant interests' in the economy.

Academic Subjects, Status and Resources

The strong historical connection between academic subjects and external examinations is only partly explained by 'the need to teach these subjects in such a way and to such a standard as will ensure success in the School Certificate examination'.[15] The years after 1917 saw a range of significant development in the professionalisation of teachers. Increasingly with the establishment of specialised subject training courses, secondary school teachers came to see themselves as part of a 'subject community'. The associated growth of subject associations both derived from and confirmed this trend. This increasing identification of secondary teachers with subject communities tended to separate them from each other, and as schools became larger, departmental forms of organisation arose which reinforced the separation. Thus the subject-centred curriculum developed to the point where the Norwood Report in 1943 expressed considerable concern and, in doing so, hinted at the political as well as academic side of curriculum conflict:

> Subjects have tended to become preserves belonging to specialist teachers; barriers have been erected between them, and teachers have felt unqualified or not free to trespass upon the dominions of other teachers. The specific values of each subject have been pressed to the neglect of the values common to several or all. The school course has come to resemble the 'hundred yards' course, each subject following a track marked off from the others by a tape. In the meantime we feel, the child is apt to be forgotten.

Norwood summarises the position by saying that 'subjects seem to have built themselves vested interests and rights of their own'.[16] In explaining the continuing connection between external examinations and academic subjects, the part played by the vested interests of the subject groups needs to be analysed. The dominance of academic subjects with high-status examination credentials would need to be in close harmony with the vested interests of subject groups to explain the strength of this structure over so long a period.

The 'subject' label is important at a number of levels. Obviously as school 'examination' category, but also as a title for a 'degree' or 'training course'. Perhaps most important of all the subject defines the territory of a 'department' within each school. With the important exception of administrative and pastoral work, the subject is the major reference point in the work of the contemporary secondary school: the information and knowledge transmitted in schools is formally selected and organised through subjects. The teacher is identified by the pupils and relates to them mainly through his subject specialism. Given the size of most comprehensive schools a number of teachers are required for each subject; and these teachers are normally organised in subject 'departments'. The departments have a range of 'graded posts' for special responsibilities and for the 'head of Department'. In this way the teacher's subject provides the means whereby his salary is decided and his career structure defined, and his influence on school policy channelled.

Within school subjects there is a clear hierarchy of status which is based partly upon assumptions that certain subjects, the so-called 'academic' subjects, are suitable for the 'able' students whilst other subjects are not. In her study of resource

allocation in schools Eileen Byrne has shown how more resources
are given to these able students and hence to the academic
subjects. She drew attention to two assumptions 'which might be
questioned' that have been seen 'consistently to underly educational planning and the consequent resource-allocation for the
more able children: First, that these necessarily need longer in
school than non-grammar pupils, and secondly, that they
necessarily need more staff, <u>more highly paid staff and more
money for equipment and books</u>.'[17] Byrne's research ended in
1965 before widespread comprehensivisation, and therefore
refers to the tripartite system. However, referring to the new
comprehensive system she wrote in 1974 that there was 'little
indication that a majority of councils or chief officers accept in
principle the need for review and reassessment of the entire
process of the allocation of resources in relation to the planned
application, over a period of years, of an approved and progressive policy, or coherent educational development.'[18]

That comprehensive schools do place overwhelming emphasis
on academic examinations, in spite of the growth of 'pastoral
systems', has been recently confirmed by Ball's study of
Beachside Comprehensive. He notes that 'once reorganised as a
comprehensive, academic excellence was quickly established as
a central tenet of the value system of the school.'[19] He provides
a range of qualitative and statistical indicators to confirm this
contention and concludes that 'while the division is less clear-
cut and stark than in the grammar school' nonetheless it is
evident that 'the teacher-resources within the comprehensive
school are allocated differently according to the pupil's ability.
Thus the most experienced teachers spend most of their time
teaching the most able pupils. This is a reflection of the fact
that the social and psychological rewards offered by the school
to its pupils accrue to those who are academically successful
and that academic achievement tended to be the single criterion
of success in the school.'[20]

Through the study of Beachside Comprehensive considerable
evidence is assembled to prove Marsden's prediction that 'if
we give the new comprehensive the task of competing with
selective schools for academic qualifications, the result will be
remarkably little change in the selective nature of education.
Selection will take place within the school and the working-
class child's education will still suffer.'[21] The importance of
different curriculum traditions for each ability band of pupils
is central in confirming these selective patterns. After the
first term we learn 'the increasing differences of syllabus and
curriculum which develop between the bands mean that band 2
or band 3 pupils would have to perform exceptionally well if
not brilliantly to overcome the limitations placed upon them
by the organisation of the syllabus.'[22] Ball notes that the
pattern of curriculum differentiation is 'not unlike that made in
The Norwood Report for fourth and fifth year pupils.[23] At the
top of the hierarchy of subjects are the traditional 'O' level

subjects like maths, English, the languages, sciences, history and geography. These high-status subjects have 'an academic orientation in common; they are concerned with theoretical knowledge. They are subjects for the brighter, the academic, the band 1 pupil. Below these in status come "O" levels in practical subjects like technical studies and metalwork. For band 2 and 3 pupils there are traditional C.S.E.s and lowest of all in status new Mode III C.S.E.s.[24]

In a detailed and illuminating study of how the option system works it is possible to discern how curriculum categories and pupil clienteles (and futures) are 'matched' by the teachers. Ball shows how this works for two classes – the band 1 class 3CU and the band 2 class 3TA. After the option system has worked the '3TA pupils have been directed away from the "academic" to the practical, while the reverse has happened for the 3CU pupils'.[25] The study shows clearly that working-class pupils concentrate in bands 2 and 3 and further that the 'differentiation of access to high status knowledge with high negotiable value is crucially related to socio-economic status'. He concludes:

> Option-allocation is a point at which school careers become firmly differentiated and at which the informal differences between pupils in terms of social reputation and their experiences of the curriculum lower down the school are formalised into separate curricular routes and examination destinations. It is here that the stratified nature of the occupation structure is directly reflected in the ability stratification within the school.
>
> Both the differential status of the knowledge areas in the curriculum and the access to the sixth form that certain courses provide are aspects of the selection of pupils for further and higher education and the occupation market. The selection process and negotiation of meanings that go to make up the option-allocation procedure are part of the structural relationships within the school which label pupils with different statures and educational identities.[26]

A number of studies confirm that a status hierarchy exists for school subjects. Warwick reports that a 1968 survey showed that over 7 per cent of the male teachers who had studied within the languages and literature group (forming just over 19 per cent of the total sample), had become head teachers, compared with less than 1 per cent of those who had studied in the field of technology and handicraft (who formed just over 11 per cent of the total sample). Similarly, among male teachers 'former students of languages and literature had apparently four times as many chances as former students of music and drama, and $1\frac{1}{2}$ times the chances of former students of science and mathematics of becoming headmasters.'[27] The hierarchy of subjects is clearly derived from traditional grammar school preferences. Stevens reports that here

'English, science, languages and mathematics are in general the subjects in which success or lack of it is significant for the children. The fact that practical subjects come low on the scale does not in itself support an assumption that more intelligent children are weak, even comparatively, at practical subjects . . . The figures are interesting rather as indicating the degree of importance with which several people, but chiefly the staff, invest subjects for the children.[28]

Also important in confirming the hierarchy of status in favour of academic subjects is the part played by university admissions policies. Reid found that the universities 'exercise almost complete control over their own admissions policies; they are seldom compelled by pressures of supply and demand, or by public policy, to revise their selection criteria; and they occupy positions of high prestige in the social structure of the disciplines.[29] In the hierarchy of subjects no subject found complete support in its acceptability to university departments but mathematics came very close. Most of the subjects which are well established as university studies are strongly supported but 'practical and aesthetic subjects are accorded sharply lower recognition'.[30] Other subjects less well accepted were those, such as General Studies, 'which are not clearly associated with a specific discipline'. The full version of Reid's findings are presented in Table 3.1.[31]

Table 3.1: Acceptability of 'A' Level Subject Passes to a Sample of University Departments (n = 84)

Pure mathematics	0.92	German	0.63
Pure mathematics w.stat.	0.83	Economics	0.62
Pure mathematics w.mech.	0.82	Greek	0.62
Physics	0.81	Geology	0.61
SMP mathematics	0.78	Nuffield biology	0.60
Further mathematics	0.78	Latin	0.60
Physical science	0.71	British government	0.49
Chemistry	0.70	General studies	0.49
SMP further mathematics	0.69	Engineering science	0.46
History	0.67	Scripture knowledge	0.46
Biology	0.66	Music	0.44
Geography	0.66	Art	0.37
French	0.65	Elements of eng. design	0.27
English literature	0.64	Geom. and eng. drawing	0.24
Nuffield chemistry	0.64	Housecraft	0.15
Spanish	0.64		

The evidence presented confirms that in secondary schools the self-interest of subject teachers is closely connected with

the status of the subject in terms of its examinable knowledge.
Academic subjects provide the teacher with a career structure
characterised by better promotion prospects and pay than less
academic subjects. Seen from this viewpoint the conflict over
the status of examinable knowledge is therefore partly a
battle over the material resources and career prospects available to each subject community. Of course many other arguments
are mobilised in the decisions over how knowledge is defined –
the utilitarian and pedagogic traditions owe their existence to
radically different visions of the assumptions and intentions
which underpin school subjects. Despite the recurrence of
these traditions we would hypothesise that subject sub-groups
or associations whose paramount concern is the material interests
of their members, would over time pursue academic status.[32] In
this pursuit the aspiration to gain 'O' and 'A' level examinations
in the subject is of central importance. By examining the case
of a new subject contender for 'O' and 'A' level status the
process of curriculum conflict and change can be analysed in
detail.

SUBJECTS IN EVOLUTION AND THE CASE OF ENVIRONMENTAL EDUCATION

The studies in this book have been devised to test a number of
hypotheses generated from previous curriculum studies and from
a historical review of the changing contexts within which the
curriculum is negotiated. The starting point is the belief that
subjects should not be viewed as monolithic entities but as social
communities containing groups with conflicting loyalties and
intentions and with variable and changing boundaries. The major
sub-groups or factions of subject communities often ally themselves to particular traditions and three main traditions have
been tentatively discerned: the academic, the utilitarian and the
pedagogic.
  The material interests of teachers – their pay, promotion and
conditions – are broadly interlinked with the fate of their
specialist subject communities. The 'academic' subject is placed
at the top of the hierarchy of subjects because resource allocation
takes place on the basis of assumptions that such subjects are
best suited for the able students who, it is further assumed,
should receive favourable treatment. For this reason, a second
hypothesis is that subject groups pursuing the material interests
of their members will move progressively away from the utilitarian and pedagogic traditions and promote themselves as 'academic'
subjects. The associated model of internal subject change would
postulate a number of stages culminating at the point where 'the
selection of subject matter is determined in large measure by the
judgements and practices of the specialist scholars who lead enquiries in the field'. In the final stage the subject has its own
intellectual leadership to confirm its academic character and to

aid in establishing academic examinations in the subject's area
of knowledge.

In order to develop a model of subject change in Part Two,
three subjects have been studied in evolution: geography, biology
and rural studies. Where possible, documentary evidence and the
personal accounts of subject members are presented, so as to
build on the existing studies in the field. The fates of the three
main traditions are then traced as the subjects evolve.

Patterns of status and change do not, however, determine the
curriculum solely through internal subject change. The major
part of the book tries to analyse the role that the pursuit of
academic status plays in the relationship between subjects. In
particular the book focuses on a new contender for academic
status in the form of environmental education. The main subjects
involved in the aspirations of this new contender for a place in
the curriculum were again geography, biology and rural studies.
Curriculum conflict between subjects takes place over the issue
of external examination, for if the new contender can gain high
status 'O' and 'A' level examinations which are broadly accepted,
then it claims academic, and therefore material and financial
parity.

To analyse the nature of subject group responses it is necessary
to focus on the main strategies such groups utilise to promote
their members' interests. Curriculum conflict takes place against
a changing background both in terms of the organisation of the
educational system and the broader fabric of the national economy.
Within this changing 'arena' it is possible to discern both changes
in the rules of conflict and changes in the 'weaponry' employed.
Certain features of the 'battlefield' have remained remarkably
unchanged since 1917. The year which saw the introduction of
the tank and the aeroplane heralding the modern era of warfare,
also saw the birth of the School Certificate examinations which,
together with their successor the GCEs, have dominated the
modern era of curriculum conflict. As we shall see, it is these
examinations which have shaped the rules and weapons with
which rival subject groups have contested the 'territory' of the
school timetable.

Among the subject groups and communities considered in this
book the power which is conferred by academic examinations
means that they are drawn inexorably into playing the 'status
game' concerning the nature of examinable knowledge in their
subject. Such status promotion most often follows the rules of
professional debate among 'associations', but the central concern
is to move away from pedagogically pupil-centred or utilitarian
knowledge to abstract, theoretical knowledge embodied in 'A'
level examinations.

By laying claim to high-status 'academic' formulations of the
subject these subject associations ensure that the special
interests of their members are best served. 'Child-centred'
or 'utilitarian' formulations of the subject would be at the expense
of the subject communities' self-interest. This is because it is the

status rather than the usefulness or relevance of each subject's examinable knowledge which ultimately takes priority. 'A' level examinations characteristically stress theoretical and 'academic' knowledge - not child-centred or basic utilitarian content; and for the subject community the establishment of an 'A' level base is crucial. It usually guarantees a subject's territory in terms of a separate 'department' or even 'faculty'; and it also ensures priority inside the school in terms of finance, rooms, furnishings, equipment, resources and graded posts. Further, 'academic' status ensures that members can claim priority in the allocation of pupil clienteles inside the school.

To develop a detailed understanding of how the conflict over examinable knowledge actually takes place, Part Three of the book concentrates on a study of an attempt to develop an 'A' level in environmental studies. Fortunately, this instance is extremely well documented, partly because the main protagonists believed publicity would further their cause. The 'A' level was promoted to establish 'a discipline of sufficient rigour as to be recognised by universities generally', and followed a Schools Council working paper which in 1969 perceived 'the need for a scholarly discipline' which would 'take the form of an integrated course of study based upon environmental experience'.[33]

The main promoters of the 'A' level in environmental studies were the rural studies teachers: for this reason the book will focus more on the rural studies group as the instigators and pioneers in the definition of this new area of knowledge. In the early stages of the enterprise the biologists and geographers were merely unconcerned, or latently hostile, observers. The next two chapters deal with the histories of these two school subjects as a precursor to examining their reactions to the development of 'environmental studies' by rural studies teachers.

NOTES

1   R. Bucher and A. Strauss Professions in Process, in M. Hammersley and P. Woods (eds.), 'The Process of Schooling' (London, Routledge and Kegan Paul, 1976), p. 19.
2   W.A.L. Blyth, 'English Primary Education, A Sociological Description', Vol. 2 (London, Routledge and Kegan Paul, 1965), p. 30 and pp. 124-5.
3   J. Eggleston 'The Sociology of the School Curriculum' (London, Routledge and Kegan Paul, 1978), p. 25.
4   R. Williams, 'Long Revolution', 1961, p. 163.
5   D. Layton 'Science for the People' (London, George Allen and Unwin, 1973).
6   I. Goodson, Why Britain Needs to Change its Image of the Educated Man, 'The Times' 14 February 1978.
7   J. Hemming, 'The Teaching of Social Studies in Secondary Schools' (London, Longmans, 1949). Quoted in D. Gleeson and G. Whitty, 'Developments in Social Studies Teaching'

(London, Open Books, 1976), p. 5.

8   University of London, Goldsmiths College, The Raising of the School Leaving Age, Second Pilot Course for Experienced Teachers (Autumn Term, 1965), p. 4.

9   Ibid., p. 5.

10   The Schools Council/Nuffield Foundation 'The Humanities Project: an Introduction' (London, Heinemann, 1972), p. 1.

11   Shipman, in R. Hooper (ed.), 1970.

12   The Norwood Report, 'Curriculum and Examinations in Secondary Schools', Report of the Committee of the Secondary School Examinations Council Appointed by the President of the Board of Education in 1941 (London, HMSO, 1943), p. 61.

13   S. Ball, 'Processes of Comprehensive Schooling: A Case Study' (D. Phil., Sussex University, 1978); subsequently published (see note 19).

14   Interview with Robert Morris, 26.7.78.

15   Norwood Report, p. 61.

16   Ibid.

17   E.M. Byrne, 'Planning and Educational Inequality' (Slough, NFER, 1974), p. 29.

18   Ibid., p. 311.

19   S.J. Ball, 'Beachside Comprehensive' (Cambridge University Press, 1981), p. 16.

20   Ibid., p. 18.

21   Ibid., p. 21.

22   Ibid., pp. 35-6.

23   Ibid., p. 138.

24   Ibid., p. 140.

25   Ibid., p. 143.

26   Ibid., pp. 152-3.

27   D. Warwick, Ideologies, Integration and Conflicts of Meaning, in M. Flude and J. Ahier (eds.), 'Educability, Schools and Ideology' (London, Croom Helm, 1976), p. 101.

28   F. Stevens, 'The Living Tradition: The Social and Educational Assumptions of the Grammar School' (London, Hutchinson, 3rd Ed. 1972), pp. 117-18.

29   W.A. Reid, 'Universities and Sixth Form', p. 61.

30   W.A. Reid, 'Universities and Sixth Form', ibid., p. 49.

31   Ibid., p. 50.

32   See B. Turner, 'For Weber' (London, RKP, 1981), p. 9. Using Weber's distinction between 'material' and 'ideal' interests, subject groups will be seen continuously pursuing 'material' interests. Debates about 'ideal' considerations were mainly left to university scholars once a 'discipline' base had been successfully established.

33   Schools, Council Working Paper No. 24, 'Rural Studies in Secondary Schools (London, Evans/Methuen Education, 1969).

PART TWO

School Subjects: Patterns of Internal Evolution

THE HISTORICAL BACKGROUND

This chapter outlines the historical background of biology with particular reference to the ensuing curriculum conflict over environmental education. As will be seen later the biologists played a far less central role than the geographers in this conflict. Hence the chapter deals only with the broad progress of biology and avoids a number of the complexities explored in the case of geography. In particular, the relationship between school biology and university biology (both teachers and courses) is not fully explored, neither are the details of 'O' and 'A' level courses, nor the full diversity of groups within the biology subject community. It will become clear, however, that biology has been subject to many of the same fears about fragmentation as those experienced by the geographers at much the same point in time. Moreover, many of the features to be discerned in the evolution of geography can also be traced in reviewing the history of biology.

In the early nineteenth century, a number of initiatives sought the inclusion of scientific subjects in secondary school curricula. Physics and chemistry were the leading science subjects, botany and zoology followed some way behind in popularity, and biology hardly existed as an identifiable discipline. Public opinion was mobilised by the advances in scientific knowledge promoted by such men as T.H. Huxley and Faraday. Advocates of science stressed not only the intrinsic value of their subject as a disciplinary training, but also the utilitarian potential.

To progress, the branches of science had therefore to exhibit these dual characteristics, and as a result we learn botany and zoology could find support 'only in so far as they contributed to useful ends, such as the extermination of insects destructive to timber in the dockyards'.[1] The teaching of these areas of science was limited throughout the nineteenth century but, significantly, whilst botany declined as a school subject, biology began to emerge in the curricula of some schools.[2]

In fact, the growth of biology in schools was extremely slow in the late nineteenth century and early decades of the twentieth century. This can be attributed to two main factors. Firstly, the more utilitarian and applied aspects of biology remained substantially undeveloped at this stage. Further, the value of the subject for 'disciplinary training' remained limited, not least because 'biological science in the nineteenth century was immature.

43

Usually the material studied was not of any potential economic
value and the subject was often considered to be more hobby or
pastime of county gentlemen [sic] rather than a serious scientific
study.[13] Jenkins argues that

> a satisfactory scheme of work in biology, capable of involving
> pupils in both observation and experiment and self-evidently
> something more than an amalgam of topics drawn from the
> contributing sciences can be constructed only after the appro-
> priate biological – as distinct from botanical or zoological –
> principles have been firmly established. Despite the advances
> made in the nineteenth century, it is doubtful whether such
> biological principles existed in sufficient number or were
> sufficiently clearly formulated in 1900.[4]

The changing 'image' of biology was mainly facilitated by the
work of scientists in a number of emerging specialist fields.
Their work both developed the utilitarian potential of the subject
and its claim to 'disciplinary rigour'. For instance, following the
work of Louis Pasteur, the branch of medicine and biology
called bacteriology was developed; marine biology developed
through studies of the nutrient bases of marine life and the
biological characteristics of marine animals, particularly fishes,
that are used as human food; agricultural biology developed,
focusing on soil studies, crop cultivation research and studies
of the animal and plant breeding; physiological research
broadened into the study of human function and genetics. That
the establishment of the subject's utilitarian potential was an
important factor determining its early progress, can be deduced
by analogy with the physical sciences. Their acceptance followed
closely the associated developments which may be grouped as
the 'Industrial Revolution':

> The spectacular achievements of the mechanical and physical
> sciences during the Industrial Revolution and its aftermath
> appealed to the imagination of a generation immensely interested
> in the development of industry. The steam engine, the tele-
> graph, the internal combustion engine and, latterly the aero-
> plane, all pointed to the utilitarian value of a knowledge of
> physics and chemistry for boys, if not for girls.[5]

The consequent chronological priority of the physical sciences
was probably of considerable import for the history of biology
in schools and it has been claimed that because physics and
chemistry were 'first in the field' the task of establishing biology
in school curricula was rendered immeasurably more difficult.
   The slow growth of biology is eloquently attested to by the
activities of examination boards. The Oxford and Cambridge
examining board introduced biology into its examinations in 1885.
Initially it attracted few candidates, but as Waring has noted, by
1904 'a new biology paper was attracting more candidates than

chemistry'. She notes that 'as pressures mounted for recognition of the schools as institutions for the pre-clinical scientific training (in chemistry, physics and biology) of intending medical students going on to study for the Diploma of the Conjoint Board of the Royal College of Physicians and of Surgeons, the numbers rose.' At first only a limited number of schools were allowed to train candidates but in 1911 all public schools were granted such recognition.[6]

Following the introduction of the new School Certificate between 1918 and 1927, several boards ignored the claims of biology as a 'School Certificate subject' - notably the University of Bristol Board and the Cambridge Local Examinations Syndicate. Even the University of London, historically somewhat more flexible, ignored the subject at matriculation level. Total entries for School Certificate and matriculation in the subject in 1924 were 18 students (Universities of London and Durham) and in 1927, 175 students (London, Durham and Oxford Local). The Northern Universities Joint Matriculation Board ran an exam in 'Natural History' which covered a broadly biological field and attracted 535 School Certificate and 15 matriculation candidates in 1927. Entries for Higher Certificate exams also reflected the stunted development of the subject during these years.[7]

The figures for the Northern Board in 'Natural History' imply that this subject provided an important arena for the development of biology. As Tracey notes:

On its initiation biology had little option but to accept the legacy of Junior School natural history, develop it further, and try to lay the foundations of the two sciences, botany and zoology. In doing so it was bound to have growing pains, for natural history is concerned with the ways of life of living creatures, and the botany and zoology which accrue to it have, until comparatively recently been more concerned with their anatomy. This inheritance has influenced its significance and acceptance in schools all along, and still influences the content of the teaching where it is governed by external examinations.[8]

The implications of the social history of biology for the teaching of the subject in school suggest further analogies with the histories of geography and rural studies. Hence:

The teachers who taught biology in its early days were not well equipped academically to teach the subject efficiently. They did not have the experience of their own school days to fall back upon since, if they had learned any biological science then the stress had been on the botanical side. Moreover botany and zoology have been kept in water-tight compartments in the universities, and very few students have gone on with both subjects in their final examinations.[9]

Besides exam board statistics, considerable evidence is available that biology was neglected in the decade or so following the First World War. In 1918, Jenkins states, 'biology in boys' secondary schools was represented almost exclusively by nature study, taught to the lower forms, and by botany and zoology taught to the few senior pupils intending to study medicine'.[10] Contemporary evidence judged that biology was 'disgracefully neglected' throughout the 1920s and a report of the Imperial Agricultural Research Conference in 1927 noted 'inadequate provision for biological teaching' in every level and type of school.[11] But rapid change was on the way and Jenkins has argued that 'it was the decade after 1930 which, more than any other, saw biology gain an established place in the secondary school curriculum'.[12] By 1931 all eight examination boards had adopted biology as a school certificate examination.

The growth in the utilitarian aspects of biology helps to explain a sudden expansion in the subject in the late 1920s and 1930s. The utilitarian function which had so facilitated the growth of physical sciences was enormously influential and Tracey argues that for biology it cleared the way for its introduction into the school as gradually there was a growing recognition in government and elsewhere that 'biology was capable of economic application and exploitation in industries such as fishing, agriculture and forestry, and also in medicine'.[13] Associated with the development of biology's applied uses was a new promotion of the subject. From the late 1920s onwards government agencies, the British Association for the Advancement of Science, the British Social Hygiene Council and the Science Masters Association promoted the cause of biology in schools.

The Prime Minister's 'Committee to enquire into the position of Natural Science in the Education System of Great Britain' began the process of inter-war reappraisal of official policy in 1918. The 1926 'Education of the Adolescent' report advocated biology teaching. So too did the British Association in a report on the teaching of animal biology published in 1928 and even more importantly the Chelmsford Report in 1932 on 'Education and Supply of Biologists', the 1938 Consultative Committee on Secondary Education and finally, in 1943, the report of the Committee of the Secondary Schools Examinations Council. Significantly the last report suggested that physics, chemistry and biology should be taught in schools 'without any attempt at vocational training but on orthodox academic lines'.[14] Throughout the 1930s the issue of biological education was debated and advocated in educational journals and even in the correspondence columns of 'The Times'.[15]

These landmarks in official acceptance can be partly attributed to the work of a number of agencies promoting biology. The British Social Hygiene Council developed from the National Council for the Control of Venereal Disease and adopted the slogan 'the only sure foundation for social hygiene is a biological one'. Waring has summarised their work, often conducted through specially created sub-committees:

They established and sustained contact with virtually every educational institution and administrative organisation. They enlisted massive and extended support from leading biologists, psychologists, sociologists and educationists . . . At a time of desperate shortage of biology teachers they organised a quite staggering programme of two and three-day conferences, of lecture series and workshops (extending over three, six or twenty sessions, and run many times over), courses and summer schools. At all of them, eminent speakers dealt with the method and content of biology teaching, in an attempt to give practical help to teachers struggling with unfamiliar materials and subject matter. Attendance figures for these meetings are very impressive indeed. Starting in the thirties, they continued throughout the war years and for some time afterwards.[16]

In 1938 the Council launched a journal for 'schools and teachers' initially called 'Biology' but after 1942 changed to 'Biology and Human Affairs'. The journal was to 'foster the development of biological teaching'.[17]

Although active in framing syllabuses, the Council allowed the Science Masters Association to handle the submission of syllabuses to the school examination boards whilst offering support and materials. In 1936 the Science Masters Association convened a conference with representatives of five of the eight examining boards to discuss biology syllabuses. A biology sub-committee was formed by the SMA to plan a biology syllabus and in 1937 this was published in a further initiative to promote the subject. One immediate reason for the increase in numbers taking biology in the 1930s was that 'many schools, particularly boys', which had taught little biology before 1930 introduced it as an examination subject, and many girls' schools replaced the study of botany by that of biology'.[18] Significantly, at the same time general science was introduced into the timetable of many schools. Since the subject was studied by less able pupils who had previously studied physics and chemistry this meant that biology's growth relative to the physical sciences was even more dramatic. The Northern Universities Joint Matriculation Board statistics, shown in Table 4.1 reflect this pattern.

Table 4.1: Percentage of Total Number of Candidates each Year Offering Biology, Chemistry and Physics, 1925-1949

	1925	1928	1934	1937	1949
Biology	2.7	4.0	13.1	23.5	31.4
Chemistry	47.1	50.4	51.1	45.8	31.9
Physics	33.4	39.7	43.0	40.1	30.3

During this period the total entries for all three subjects virtually tripled from 13,474 to 34,790.[19]

The growth up until 1949 was consolidated in the subsequent decades, although there were certain continuing problems in establishing complete parity of esteem with physics and chemistry. The figures for 'O' level show biology emerging as the major scientific subject in the 1950s; 73,001 candidates in 1959 as opposed to 60,029 in physics and 53,803 in chemistry. However, at 'A' level the subject remained a poor relation: 5,086 candidates compared with 27,450 for physics and 22,188 for chemistry.[20] These figures imply that the moves to invest biology with high status still had some way to progress.

THE STRUGGLE FOR RECOGNITION AFTER 1945

The continuous struggle to establish biology after the Second World War was reflected in a number of articles in the 'School Science Review'. As early as 1942 M.P. Ramage argued the case for an expansion of biology in schools,[21] and in the same year M.L. Johnson stressed the virtues of the subject as a 'training in observation'.[22] Johnson later extended the argument to stress that if taught successfully the subject could serve as a 'training in scientific method',[23] and F.S. Russell reiterated the case for teaching the subject in a consideration of its aims and objectives.[24] In 1949 the British Social Hygiene Council held the first of a series of conferences on 'new trends in biology teaching'. A number of bodies such as the Science Masters Association, British Association and the main teacher unions were involved in the organisation which later grew into the Joint Biology Committee.[25]

Despite the growth in examination entries in the late 1940s and throughout the 1950s the overall influence of biology in the curriculum continued to be more limited than that of the physical sciences. The subject was of apparently equal importance only in the fourth and fifth year examination groups. The report on science in secondary schools compiled in the late 1950s found that biology 'makes very little impact upon the broader education with which the schools are concerned' and significantly that 'the place which is occupied by advanced biological studies in schools, especially boys schools, at present, is unfortunately that of vocational training rather than of an instrument of education'.[26] Thus the limited number of 'A' level students noted earlier is explained because the subject was taken only by those who required it for professional qualification.

Biology appears at this stage to have been confined, not only at the upper end of the secondary school but also in the early years. This point was made by the Study Group on Education and Field Biology set up in 1960. They felt that there was a need for 'a new approach to the teaching of biology in schools. Biology is particularly well suited as an introduction to science, but it is often taught as an incompletely fused amalgam of classical botany and zoology.[27] The solution they favoured was that biology 'should instead be treated as a comprehensive discipline in its own right, with a bearing on the teaching of geology and geography. It should involve much more field work than is customary at present. In this revised form biology should be an integral part of the junior and middle school curriculum.[128]

The Study Group's analysis of the problem confronting biology in schools and their re-emphasis of the need for 'a comprehensive discipline' underlines the newness of biology as an intellectual synthesis. The teachers who taught the new subject in the 1940s and 1950s were by and large trained as specialists in botany and zoology. A university teacher who taught school biology at this time recalls that among the specialists 'there was an antagonism to union', and that 'specialist teachers were simply reflecting the attitudes in universities which were to stick to bot. and zoo.[29] The stress on needing a comprehensive discipline echoes the arguments presented by Bernal in 1939. He argued that biology was waiting for 'the arrangements for greater coordination' of the various biological disciplines which might come from advances in the field of research. Until that happened biology could not move from being the cinderella of the sciences as an essentially descriptive and taxonomic study to being a 'unitary, experimental, quantitative science'.[30]

The establishment of a unitary science besides awaiting advances in research was enormously hampered by both the continuing strength of botany and zoology and the existence of separate traditions within biology. In school biology a major division arose between the medical tradition which focused on the pre-medical training role noted earlier, and the natural history or ecology tradition. 'The medical tradition in biology with its emphasis on the destructive investigation of killed specimens, contrasted sharply with the approach of the naturalists who were concerned to foster a love of nature and an interest in the activities and interests of living organisms.[31] Although 'field work and ecological studies' tended to 'suffer the most' from the medical bias of biology 'efforts to increase their part in biology syllabuses remained very tentative.[32] Jenkins has judged that 'the "medical problem" of sixth form biology was not to be resolved until the 1960s when grammar school biology courses were redesigned as part of a wider programme of curriculum development and there were significant changes in the structure and content of medical education.[33] The 'redesigning' of school biology; notably through the Nuffield schemes, was related to the changes in university biology towards a more unitary science, but with a place for ecological studies within this rigorous scientific conception.

THE FIELDWORK AND ECOLOGY TRADITION IN BIOLOGY

The natural history element had been present in biology from
the very beginning; the naturalist approach depended on field
observation and outdoor studies. Such work within biology might
clearly have led into the broadly-conceived field of environmental
education. In fact field studies and ecology remained firmly
defined within a conception of biology as a rigorous science. In
explaining this 'containment' of the field studies tradition the
role of the Study Group on Education and Field Biology and the
Nuffield Project were centrally important: both groups saw
biology as a rigorous experimental science to which field studies
might provide a gateway. 'I think ecology came in to biology
through the notion of conservation . . . not in the sense we
know it now. This was conservation in the strictly limited sense
of the Nature Conservancy . . . we were conserving areas of
natural beauty and scientific interest, that sort of thing . . .'
(Dowdeswell).

In 1960 the Nature Conservancy set up the highly influential
Study Group on Education and Field Biology. The aim of the
group was to 'examine the role of field studies and their relation
to school education and to science teaching in particular: the
requirements in terms of curricula and examinations, teachers
and teacher training; the facilities needed . . .'[34] The study
group made it clear that it firmly rejected 'the view that biology
in general, and field studies in particular, are less scientific
or less essential in an education programme than the physical
sciences. It aims to show that if their full educational potential
can be realised field studies are one of the best gateways to the
teaching of the sciences and one of the best bridges between
biology and other sciences.'[35] In expressing this view the group
made it clear which other competing views of education it was
opposed to:

> there is little educational value in taking groups of children
> to stare uncomprehendingly and unguided at nature or to
> listen to sentimental, superficial, discourses by people without
> scientific understanding. The poverty of such teaching is
> only matched by that of the indoor 'parrot' learning of the
> correct examination answer or the so-called 'experiments'
> often masquerading as science teaching, not only in biology
> but also in physics and chemistry.[36]

The challenge to more traditional patterns of teaching was
consistently pursued to the point where the divisions into
scientific subjects were called into question in line with the
fashion for 'interdisciplinary enquiry'. 'Field studies have been
held in check by the fact that science and science teaching
have become confined in arbitrary compartments. One of the
main objects of a new approach must be to reduce such artificial
barriers to a minimum.' To achieve this 'flexible arrangements'

were needed to 'enable scientific topics to be pursued wherever they lead, thus making servants instead of masters of the disciplines involved, and never seeking to deny the altogetherness of science'.[37]

At the beginning of the 1960s field studies were being promoted by a number of prominent biologists. This development at tertiary level was of crucial importance because, when few graduates or teacher trainees were taught ecological or field studies, they in turn could teach little of the subject when they took up positions in schools. This seems to have been the case in the 1950s. According to a report issued in 1953 by a research committee of the British Association for the Advancement of Science: 'A vicious circle is in operation. Neglect of field work at universities in the past has led to neglect in training colleges (who employ biology graduates on their staff) and in schools (who have graduates or training college diploma holders on their staff).' The results of this were clear for 'if members of staff neglect the subject the great majority of pupils will naturally do so, with the result that training colleges and universities then receive students whose interest in field work has not been aroused in earlier formative years.'[38] The neglect of field studies at the tertiary level was confirmed by the study group. They found that the average amount of time spent out of doors was 'a mere 130 hours in zoology departments and 225 hours in botany departments in "single subject/special honours" courses of three or four years duration'.[39]

Of course interdisciplinary constraints were only one factor limiting the growth of field studies. Other factors inhibited the growth of the approach at all educational levels. The study groups listed some of the constraints inside schools in the form of a series of questions:

. . . is the advance of field studies inhibited by lack of teachers trained to conduct them, Are the procedures of educational administration and rigidities in the school curriculum obstructing local opportunities for teaching children outside the classroom, Are teachers deterred by lack or remoteness of facilities, and generally by the sheer difficulty of coping with field studies of a higher standard on a more widespread basis, Is the examination system penalising schools which show initiative in this field as against those which stick to the indoor routine[40]

The latter point was extended elsewhere in arguing that it was possible for a candidate who has 'never strayed outside a laboratory door and who knows no ecology whatever, nonetheless to obtain a "creditable pass" (possibly a distinction!). Schools are fully aware of this fact and many of them make the best of it.'[41] The Report of the Study Group on Education and Field Biology, whilst detailing the problems faced by ecology and field studies, remains a strongly propagandist document. Field studies were to be 'the gateway to scientific education as a whole'[42] for 'It is plain that future citizens will need a much better induction into the principles and ways of science, a deeper and more satisfying sense of values and a firmer and stronger emotional feeling of being anchored and really belonging to contemporary civilisation.'[43]

The importance of the Report was stressed by Dowdeswell who in 1962 began directing the Nuffield biology project. From the beginning he stressed the educational value of ecological studies: 'I looked upon ecology as applied natural history and I meant that that was one of the ways that one introduced children to biology . . . I would reckon "science out of doors" reflected my philosophy very well.' Therefore ecology became a very important section of Nuffield biology: 'I think we were very lucky to have a go . . . I was a fanatic so we decided we would go to town on ecology.' The results were less impressive than the intentions: 'In point of fact, as you probably know, that was in many ways the least successful part of the Nuffield 'O' level project . . . partly because there were many teachers who still didn't accept ecology at all and it failed because it was well in advance of the thinking of teachers . . . ' This statement gives the impression that it was mainly a conceptual problem on the part of the teachers, an impression Dowdeswell was quick to correct.

I think there are problems of teaching methodology . . . I think there is a problem of time: There's a problem of basic attitude and thinking . . . It involves more of a different way of thinking than any other aspect of Nuffield and the organisational problems are great . . . It meant you had to organise things and take children out of doors.[44]

The organisational prerequisites became a rallying cry for opponents of ecology and field studies: 'it was used as an excuse . . . of that there was no doubt. Whether the excuse was valid or not I'm not sure but it was used as the great excuse - ecology whether we liked it or not was impractical because of the demands it made on organisation . . .'[45]

In spite of the opposition and constraints evident in Dowdeswell's statements other initiatives promoted field studies in the middle of the 1960s. Ecology grew as a new intellectual synthesis within the universities. A number of the new universities established departments of ecology or 'environmental science' and there were equally significant developments in the older universities. Sir Arthur Tansley, who had been the first president of the Council for the Promotion of Field Studies, developed the subject at Oxford in line with a strongly-felt tradition at that university (Dowdeswell had studied there).

The definition of ecology as a university-based discipline within the more traditional science paradigm and the other developments in biology 'contained' the purer environmental and naturalist traditions. By and large therefore biologists stood aside from environmental education. We learn that 'the good ship "environment" was launched but not fitted out with engines or steering gear some time ago. It then proceeded to sail into uncharted sea with a very motley crew aboard. Many might feel that the Institute of Biology has been left on the shore . . .'[146] In a paper on biology, Waring has written that in consequence 'as the environmental lobby gained momentum, the field studies movement grew rapidly, but the field studies biologists and the geographers ensured that the "environmentalists" remained in a subordinate position.'[147]

BIOLOGY AS 'HARD SCIENCE'

Despite the broad initiatives from the study group, from the Nuffield Project, from certain university personnel and from the Keele Conference, evidence of any broad-based change in biology teaching was not forthcoming. In 1967, writing of the 'crisis' in biology, Dyer argued that the growth of 'such essentially unifying disciplines' as ecology was being ignored because of 'the unhappy separation of botany and zoology which persists in our sixth forms and so many of our universities'.[48] Even in 1971, 33 out of 44 university-taught undergraduates were in separate botany and zoology departments.[49]

Dyer's comment on the continuing separation of botany and zoology and his implicit plea for a 'unifying discipline' presents interesting similarities to the attempt in America in the early 1960s to produce a definition of school biology. The diversity of biology led the Biological Sciences Curriculum Study to produce three 'versions' of school biology, covering the 'biochemical', 'ecological' and 'cellular' aspects of the subject, but their reluctance to expose this apparent lack of unity led to the versions being designated 'blue', 'green' and 'yellow'. As the director later explained:

> to identify these versions as 'biochemical', 'ecological' or 'cellular' might have unintended and unfortunate implications, since some persons might then consider the versions to be courses on ecology, biochemistry or cell biology rather than as general biology programs written by groups of biologists with different backgrounds. Thus it was necessary that the versions be indicated by neutral terms . . .[50]

The study also noted the difference between biology and the 'established' sciences of physics and chemistry. They argued that the absence of a clear unifying structure for biology was a result not of its immaturity but of its sophistication:

> The nature of biology itself, as a science built upon the physical sciences, is automatically of a more inclusive level of complexity and so characterisation of its structure appro-

priate for secondary school students may involve increased
complications.

Aware of the dangerous implications of this claim it is noted that
this should not be taken to imply that

> Biology represents the ultimate complexity of discipline struc-
> ture remaining to be analysed by educators for presentation
> in curricula . . . One simply needs to add to these consider-
> ations the human implications of the social sciences and the
> humanities to enter into still further complexities well beyond
> those contemplated by the biologist in confronting his science.[51]

A solution to the unstructuredness and disunity of biology
came with the development of molecular biology. Here at last
was the rationale for claiming parity of esteem with the physical
sciences. Molecular biology provided both high prestige and an
overarching theory which unified many aspects of the subject.
Moreover, since plants and animals look very similar at the
cellular level, the division between botany and zoology appeared
far less justifiable. Jenkins summarised the development in this
way: 'The enormous success of crystallographic and cytochemical
studies in the field of molecular biology of which the elucidation
of the structures of DNA is the best-known example led to
pressure to reform the teaching of the life sciences so as to
incorporate both the relevant biochemistry and the reductionist /
experimental approach which had brought such triumphs.' At
last the 'arrangements for greater coordination' which Bernal
in 1939 had argued could come from advances in research were
at hand and for a period biology could be presented as a unitary
science.[52]
The breakthrough was rapidly achieved and teachers at the
time noted the change: 'I remember the rise of molecular biology
. . . Crick and Watson and the rest . . . that paved the way for
the breakthrough in biology's fight to become a science. From
then on there was a strong possibility that biology could become
a "hard science" alongside physics and chemistry.'[53] Speaking
of the late 1960s Professor Dowdeswell confirmed: 'Status
followed the rise of molecular biology. The great discoveries of
Crick and Watson changed everything.' Alongside these developments, however, Dowdeswell noted another theme when commenting that, 'there was a feeling that if it wasn't quantitative it
wasn't science'.[54] Another university biologist explained the
trend in this way: 'Biology had been . . . often still is more
descriptive than physical science . . . in consequence weaker
candidates were pushed into it . . . when quantitative things
were pushed it was for more respect for the subject, increased
status.'[55] The twin themes of molecular biology and quantification
were incorporated into school biology. The first theme on 'A'
level syllabuses is now often 'the Cell' and focuses on structure,
molecular organisation and functions. Similarly quantification is

now a prominent feature of many 'A' level syllabuses. For example, the JMB syllabus specifically states that 'an understanding of the principles of the application of mathematics and statistics is required'.
However, school biology 'A' level courses retained elements of earlier stages in the history of biology. As was to be the case with geography there was both resistance to and a time lag in the incorporation of new versions of biology, even the hard science version. Jenkins comments that 'both the "principles" and "type" approach to constructing biology syllabuses were to survive throughout the 1960s and beyond, producing greater differences in advanced level syllabuses in biological science than at any time the past.'[56] But both the versions Jenkins mentioned fell within the 'scientific' paradigm of biology. For the fieldwork tradition the consequences were clearer: a final result of the rise of molecular biology and quantification to dominance in biology was to finally confirm the relegation of the human and environmental aspects of ecology and field biology within the subject.

The great problem was that the environmentalist pressures came at more or less the same time as biology was making its big push to become a hard science subject with all the status that involved . . . the environmental thing came right in the middle of biology's final fight to be accepted as a hard science and was therefore pushed to the margins of the subject.[57]

By the mid-1960s biology, as a laboratory-based hard science, was being rapidly institutionalised in the expanding universities and in the schools (especially through the Nuffield project). Molecular biology, by providing high prestige and an over arching theory, finally sealed biology's establishment as a fully-fledged, scientifically rigorous, academic discipline.

CONCLUSION

In the evolution of biology the subject first developed as an integrated area of knowledge which bridged certain segments of traditional botany and zoology. In the early stages, with a few exceptions, only the latter specialisms were taught in the universities. Biology developed initially in two arenas. Firstly, in the early years of the secondary school, biology built upon the already developed junior school courses in 'natural history'. Then, with the growing appreciation of the economic uses of biology in medicine and agriculture, fishing and forestry, new careers began to open up in which specialised biological training was valuable. Hence the second arena in which biology developed was in the sixth form. This development gained momentum throughout the twentieth century but increasingly from the 1930s onwards. In the 1950s it was noted that: 'The place which is occupied by advanced biological studies in schools, especially boys schools at present, is unfortunately that of vocational training rather than of an instrument of education.' This quote confirms the low status of utilitarian elements within the status hierarchy of subjects, as does an earlier contention that biology like the other sciences should be taught 'without any attempt at vocational trend but on orthodox academic lines'.

The traditional pursuit of 'academic' status through university establishment of the subject was rendered difficult because of the hegemony of botany and zoology. In the 1950s the sixth form specialist teachers in botany and zoology reflected their training at, and the contemporary attitudes within, universities which favoured the teaching of these two subjects in watertight compartments – 'there was antagonism to union'. Without establishment at the tertiary level biology was, therefore, confined to the early years of the secondary school and to vocational training at 'O' and 'A' level. In 1967 Dyer noted the consequently low popularity of the subject at sixth form level and spoke of 'the unhappy separation of botany and zoology which persists in our sixth forms and so many of our universities'.

The utilitarian and pedagogic elements in biology which so retarded its progress to high academic status were found within human biology and in certain fieldwork aspects of the subject. Hence the development of field biology sometimes ran counter to the pressures for status escalation. Status through a vision of biology as 'hard science' was increasingly pursued in the 1960s through an emphasis on laboratory investigations and mathematical techniques. In 1962, the Nuffield project confirmed the crucial importance of laboratories as status symbols and directed much of the Nuffield Foundation's money and resources towards their development. The rise of molecular biology, with the work of Crick and Watson, finally confirmed biology as a laboratory-based hard science. As a result the subject was rapidly expanded in the universities (themselves expanding apace), and, with the training of a new generation of biology graduates, the subject's incorporation as a high-status 'O' and 'A' level school subject was finally assured.

In fact, biology's establishment as a scientific discipline has been recently commented on by Waring. She writes that:

> The word 'biology' tends to conjure up an image of a clearly-defined body of knowledge, built up through recognisable sorts of activity and validated on the basis of agreed criteria and, indeed, this view would seem to be confirmed by the existence of the Biological Council, the Institute of Biology and a range of biology departments, courses and examinations in all types of educational institution.[58]

Yet Waring's article is concerned with whether biological science is faced by 'integration or fragmentation'. There is considerable evidence of a continuing fear of the latter: confirming the view that school subjects and academic disciplines are normally temporary coalitions. Hence we find the 'Journal of Biological Education' warning in 1975 that biology could be 'dispersed to the four winds'.[59] A year later the Biological Education Committee of the Royal Society and the Institute of Biology expressed concern over the burgeoning popularity of human biology. A working party set up to consider the problem revealed a proliferation of broadly biological courses all considerably overlapping but each with idiosyncratic features. In 1977 a discussion paper at the conference of university biology education tutors dealt with the question of teacher training.

All these committees and associated papers expressed a consensus among professional biologists that biological education must reflect, 'a rigorous, experimental science' alongside considerable 'ambivalence about the place, in biology, of the study of man, and about the implications for education of the blurring of the boundaries between biology and the social sciences.'[60] This view reflects that held by the promoters of the subject that to progress the subject needs to outgrow its pedagogic and utilitarian origins and the randomness occasioned by its concern with social and human issues. Status and resources have been achieved through promotion as a hard, experimental and rigorous science. The recurrence of pressures for more social and human biology therefore threaten the uneasy establishment of the subject as a scientific discipline which alone assure the status and resources so valued by the members of the biology subject community.

NOTES

1   D. Layton, 'Science for the People' (London, George Allen and Unwin, 1973), p. 21.
2   C.W. Tracey, Biology: Its struggle for recognition in English Schools during the period 1900-60, 'School Science Review', Vol. XCIII, No. 150, March 1962, p. 429.
3   Ibid., p. 430.
4   E.W. Jenkins, 'From Armstrong to Nuffield: Studies in Twentieth Century Science Education' (London, John Murray, 1979), p. 116.
5   Tracey, 'Biology: Its struggle', p. 429.
6   M. Waring, unpublished paper on 'History of Biology', 1980, p. 7.
7   Tracey, op. cit., p. 429. The low status of biology is testified to in J. Huxley, Biology in Schools, 'School Science Review' Vol. 4, No. 13, 1972, pp. 5-11.
8   Tracey, 'Biology: Its struggle', p. 424.
9   Ibid.
10 Jenkins 'Armstrong to Nuffield', p. 119.
11 Ibid. Jenkins, p. 121.
12 Ibid. Jenkins, p. 123.

13   Tracey, 'Biology: Its struggle', p. 423.
14   'The Norwood Report', Report of the Committee of the
      Secondary School Examinations Council appointed by the
      President of the Board of Education in 1941, 'Curriculum
      and Examinations in Secondary Schools' (London, HMSO,
      1943), p. 112.
15   Waring, 'History of Biology'.
16   Ibid., pp. 11-12.
17   Jenkins, 'Armstrong to Nuffield', p. 134.
18   Tracey, 'Biology: Its struggle', p. 426.
19   J.A. Petch, 'Fifty Years of Examining, the Joint Matriculation
      Board, 1903-53' (London, Harrap, 1953), p. 84.
20   Tracey, 'Biology: Its struggle, p. 425.
21   M.P. Ramage, Educational Biology, 'School Science Review',
      Vol. 23, No. 91, (1943), pp. 312-19.
22   M.L. Johnson, Biology and Training in Observation 'School
      Science Review' Vol. 24, No. 92, 1942, pp. 56-8.
23   M.L. Johnson, Biology and Training in Scientific Method,
      'School Science Review', Vol. 29, No. 108, (1948), pp.
      139-47.
24   F.S. Russell, What is Biology?, 'School Science Review',
      Vol. 28, No. 104, 1946, pp. 69-79.
25   Waring, 'History of Biology', p. 12.
26   Ministry of Education, 'Science in Secondary Schools',
      Ministry of Education Pamphlet No. 38 (London, HMSO, 1960).
27   Study Group on Education and Field Biology, 'Science Out
      of Doors' (London, Longmans, 1963), p. 196.
28   Ibid., p. 197.
29   Interview, 24.10.77.
30   Jenkins Armstrong to Nuffield, pp. 139-40.
31   Ibid., pp. 146-7.
32   Ibid., p. 148.
33   Ibid., p. 147.
34   Study Group, 'Science Out of Doors', p. vi.
35   Ibid., p. 5.
36   Ibid.
37   Ibid., p. 7.
38   'British Association for Advancement of Science Report',
      1953.
39   Study Group, 'Science Out of Doors', p. 55.
40   Ibid., p. 185.
41   Ibid., p. 27.
42   Ibid., p. 10.
43   Ibid., p. viii.
44   Interview, 24.10.77.
45   Ibid.
46   See M. Waring Biological Science: Integration or Fragmen-
      tation, 'History of Education Society Conference Papers'
      December 1978, p. 57.
47   M. Waring, 'History of Biology', p. 20.
48   K.F. Dyer, Crisis in Biology: An Examination of the

Deficiencies in the Current Expansion of Biological Education, Journal of Biological Education', 1967, Vol. 1, no. 2, p. 112.

49 M. Waring, 'Biological Science', p. 51.

50 A.B. Grobman, The Changing Classroom, 'The Role of the Biological Sciences Curriculum Study' (New York, Doubleday, 1969), p. 64.

51 Ibid., p. 65.

52 Jenkins Armstrong to Nuffield, p. 153.

53 Interview with biology teacher, 15.3.77.

54 Interview 24.10.77.

55 Interview 26.10.76.

56 Jenkins Armstrong to Nuffield, p. 155. The number of 'A' level entrants is noted in Jenkins, p. 156, for 1961 and 1971.

	1961	1971	% change
Botany	4,729	1,981	-58.1
Zoology	7,409	4,428	-40.2
Biology	7,099	21,575	+204

57 Interview, 15.3.77.

58 M. Waring, 'Biological Science', p. 49.

59 J.A. Baker, Comment 'Journal of Biological Education', 9 (1975), p. 59. Quoted ibid. Waring.

60 M. Waring, 'Biological Science', p. 149.

INTRODUCTION

This chapter seeks to provide a historical background to the
geographers' part in the curriculum conflicts surrounding the
emergence of environmental studies. Hence the focus is directed
to those aspects of geography's history concerned with its
promotion and maintenance as a subject with its own territory,
status and resources. The concern is with those elements of the
geographical enterprise which stress the 'survival of the discipline' rather than its intellectual advance. Whilst these cannot
always be distinguished, Gregory has noted that geography has
had a problem 'in so far as an exclusive concern with the survival of the discipline required a degree of pragmatism which
many regarded as an abandonment of principle. The difficulty
was that pragmatism was uncomfortably close to opportunism.'[1]
Such opportunism has left geography with perhaps the most
chameleon nature of any of the so-called 'fields of knowledge'.
As a subject with a recurring crisis of identity the 'survival of
the discipline' has the kind of priority among subject practitioners
which sometimes seems to border on obsession.

The promotion of geography has taken place against a background of social change which has provided a range of arenas
for subject advocates to react to and utilise. In the late Victorian
period, a period of rapid imperial expansion, geography was
promoted by strategies such as Sir George Robertson's description of it as 'the Science of Distances - the science of the
merchant, the statesman and the strategist'; as Gregory notes,
'a characterisation which appeared to make a command of
geography vital both for the maintenance of the Empire itself
and the ascent of men to the most acclaimed positions of profit
and power within it.'[2] In more recent times, geography has
responded to society's needs 'for spatial efficiency and regional
planning,'[3] and geographical studies have been used 'to provide
an essential technical foundation for the elaboration of private
and public policy'.[4] Our concern though is not with social change
per se but with the milieu and associated opportunities such
changes present to those people involved in geography's maintenance and promotion as a discipline - those concerned with its
material and pragmatic, rather than intellectual, advance.

We begin with a brief historical introduction which summarises
the recent background of geography in England. Certain themes
are identified here, notably geographers' concern with achieving

'scientific' discipline status. The moulding of geography in
pursuit of status has been commented on by Gregory in explaining that 'the early reluctance to consider man in society' was
'prompted at least in part by an important search for intellectual
respectability, and a belief that by structuring human geography
in terms of physical geography such a goal could be attained'.[15]
Another theme picks up the evolving relationship between school
geography and university geography. A third theme focuses on
the promotional role of the subject association.

The 'fieldwork tradition' is then analysed for, as we shall see
later, this was the tradition within the subject which was closest
to 'environmental studies'.

Finally, the launching of new geography is considered and
related to the aspirations and promotional strategies of geographers as they have been evidenced at work during the last
century.

THE ESTABLISHMENT OF GEOGRAPHY IN SCHOOLS AND UNIVERSITIES

The writings of two German scholars, von Humboldt[6] and Ritter,[7]
in mid-nineteenth century mark the stage at which 'modern
geography is often said to begin'.[8] Because their conception of
geography dominated the formative years in the evolution of the
subject it has been titled 'classical geography'.[9] Classical
geography sought to organise knowledge in two stages; in the
first stage facts and details of geographical phenomena were
collected and presented and in the second stage these were
'given coherence and made intelligible by being subsumed under
a number of laws'.[10]

Towards the end of the nineteenth century in Germany,
classical geography came under question from scholars like
Heffner, who studied alongside Max Weber at Heidelberg, and in
the early part of the twentieth century in France, notably in
the work of Brunthes,[11] classical geography was attacked for its
rigidity, because it encouraged notions of geographical determinism and because 'the new ideas about methodology in the
social sciences made its whole approach to the understanding of
social action and social change seem unrewarding'.[12] In England,
in the absence of any alternative native models, classical
geography remained for a time the subject 'model' to which to
aspire. In 1901 in the first issue of the 'The Geography Teacher',
T.C. Rooper, and HMI, noted that Britain 'awaits the birth of
an epoch-making writer on geography'. The country had 'no
such series of geographers as Humboldt, Ritter and Pescher,
whose names add so much lustre to the fame of German learning'.[13]

In late nineteenth-century England, geography was in the
process of establishing itself as a subject in schools, but had
obtained only a tentative place in a few universities. The widespread comments about the teaching of the subject imply that

much of the knowledge that was taught remained at the first
stage of classical geography's twinstage objective. Thus in 1887
when MacKinder posed the question 'Can geography be rendered
a discipline instead of a mere body of information?' he noted that
when 'the method of description has been adopted and still more
that of enumeration, each additional fact adds an ever-increasing
amount to the burden to be borne by the memory.'[14]

Since at the stage MacKinder was writing geography was predominantly a school subject, his criticisms had considerable
significance for its progress. In the schools, particularly the
public and grammar schools, geography teachers were seeking
to establish the intellectual as well as pedagogical credibility of
the subject. By 1870 many public and grammar schools gave one
or two periods to geography. Likewise in 1875 'elementary
geography' was added to the 'class subjects' examined in
elementary schools.[15] But the teaching of the subject left a good
deal to be desired. In 1901 Rooper asserted that in British
schools geography: 'has ever been a dull and uninteresting
subject:' It has been, he said, 'a dreary recitation of names
and statistics, of no interest to the learner, and of little use
except perhaps in the sorting departments of the Post Office.'[16]
Writing a decade later Holmes confirmed this view of geography
teaching when he stated that the children were 'the victims of
an unintelligent oral cram, which they were compelled, under
pains and penalties to take in and retain till the examination was
over.'[17]

The problems of geography partly stemmed from the difficulty
of promoting a new intellectual synthesis in the school arena,
where examinations and timetable constraints predominated.
Writing in 1901 a Rochester headmaster identified two major
problems. Firstly that 'the overcrowding in the school timetable
makes it impossible to give more than one at most two lessons
per week in geography', and secondly that as a school subject,
geography 'suffers from the fact it generally falls into the hands
of a master who takes no special interest in it and has no special
knowledge of it or of the methods of teaching it.'[18]

Given the problems at university level and the limited base in
the elementary and secondary school sector, the promoters of
geography began to draw up plans for a subject association.
In 1893 the Geographical Association was founded: 'to further
the knowledge of geography and the teaching of geography in
all categories of education institutions from preparatory school
to university in the United Kingdom and abroad.'[19] The formation
of the Association in 1893 was extremely well-timed. Two years
later the Bryce Commission reported, and some of its recommendations were built into the 1902 Education Act. Furthermore,
when the 1904 secondary regulations effectively defined the
subjects to be offered in secondary schools, geography's
inclusion in the regulations was a major staging-post in its
acceptance and recognition, and in the broad-based take-up of
external examinations in geography in secondary schools. As

can be seen on the membership chart in Fig. 5.1, this change
was clearly reflected in the sharp increase in the Association's
membership from this date.[20]

Figure 5.1: Geographical Association
Membership 1893-1968

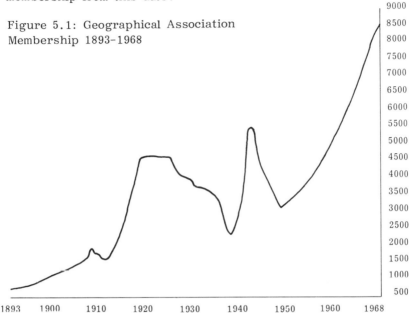

At this stage geography was included in many exam board
regulations, both at School Certificate and Higher School
Certificate, as a main subject. Certain boards, however,
included geography only as a 'subsidiary subject'.[21] The founding of a subject association was only a first stage in launching
the subject; what was also required was an overall plan aimed
at establishing the subject in the various educational sectors
mentioned in the constitution. At a discussion on geographical
education at the British Association in September 1903, MacKinder
outlined a four-point strategy for establishing the subject:

Firstly, we should encourage University Schools of Geography,
where geographers can be made . . . Secondly, we must persuade at any rate some secondary schools to place the geographical teaching of the whole school in the hands of one
geographically trained master . . . Thirdly, we must thrash
out by discussion and experiment what is the best progressive
method for common acceptance, and upon that method we must
base our schemes of examination. Lastly, the examination
papers must be set by practical geography teachers.[22]

This strategy reads rather like trade union pleas for the closed
shop. The geography teacher is to set the exams and is to choose

exams that are best for the 'common acceptation' of the subject
- there is not even the facade that the pupils' interest should
be the central criteria; the teaching of geography is to be exclusively in the hands of trained geographers and the universities
are to be encouraged to establish schools of geography 'where
geographers can be made'.

In this sense it is clear that the crucial requirement of a university base for geographers to 'be made' can be argued for because
of the need for teachers of the subject in schools. The school
subject therefore provides the platform for bringing about the
creation of a university base where the 'discipline' can be
created by scholars. The importance of the schools in developing
a well-populated university base was recently commented on by a
President of the Geographical Association: 'The recognition of
our subject's status among university disciplines which this
gives together with the costly provision made available for its
study, could never have been achieved without (the) remarkable
stimulus and demand injected from our schools.'[23] That geography was expanding in schools was commented on by numerous
writers. In 1913 W. Maclean Carey noted: 'The teaching of
geography has made great strides within the last ten years.'
He added, however, that it was 'now taking its place as a
definite science', and went on to conclude most unhelpfully that
there was a 'very strong argument in favour of geography being
taught by the chemistry or physics master'.[24]

Carey notwithstanding, the number of specialist geography
teachers continued to grow. In 1919 it was reported that the
Geographical Associated had a membership of over 2,000, which
included 'practically all the recognised teachers of geography
in England and many in Scotland and Ireland'.[25] The Council of
the Geographical Association went on to contend that 'it was
possible for this Association to issue a manifesto on the subject
which has met with practically universal acceptance.[26] This
manifesto stated: 'In teaching geography in schools we seek to
train future citizens to imagine accurately the interaction of
human activities and their topographical conditions'; and added
that 'the mind of the citizen must have a topographical background if he is to keep order in the mass of information which
he accumulates in the course of his life, and in these days the
background must extend over the whole world.'[27]

The benefits accruing from an expanding school geography
were not however without their cost, for partly because it was
labelled as a school subject, geography encountered great
opposition in the universities. David Walker recently wrote of
geography that 'some senior members of our ancient universities
can still be found who dismiss it as a school subject'.[28]

The progress of geography in the university was severely
limited due to the fierce opposition of the other subject groups.
One of the first Chairs of Geography was in the faculty of Arts
at University College, London. In 1903 Professor L.W. Lynde,
by basic training a historian and classical scholar, was appointed.

'He was required to give an undertaking that no instruction in physical geography (including climatology and oceanography) would be given in his department. All such teaching was given in the department of geology, and this restriction still operated even twenty years later . . .'[29]

The first significant development in the university sector had been in 1887 when 'the Royal Geographical Society was successful in getting the University of Oxford to establish a readership in geography'.[30] The readership was offered to Halford John MacKinder. The role of the Royal Geographical Society at this time has been characterised as 'an organised "geographical lobby"'. It was a lobby in which from the beginning MacKinder had played a key role, seeking unsuccessfully to get the Society to sponsor a 'London School of Geography'. In the event the Society offered to help in the creation of a School of Geography at Oxford, which was opened in January 1910, with MacKinder as director. MacKinder staffed the School with A.J. Herbertson and two other lecturers and teaching of the new Oxford Diploma in Geography began. Only four candidates took the first examination but by 1914 there were 41 candidates. Summer schools in geography were also organised and in 1914 200 teachers attended such schools. At these schools the teaching of Herbertson (1865-1915) became highly influential. He wrote textbooks, of which over 1,400,000 were sold; one book, 'Man and His Work', published in 1899, was still in print in the late 1960s. Graves judges that 'his influence on what was taught in British schools was enormous and has since been unsurpassed'.[31]

Meanwhile, however, the problems of establishing geography in other universities were summarised in 1913 by MacKinder when he stated: 'Geography as a university discipline was then all but non-existent.'[32] Speaking over half a century after this difficult period for the subject, Professor Garnett reviewed some of the problems which confronted geography departments in the universities that: 'grew very slowly under a tradition of laissez-faire that strongly reflected the individualistic approaches and widely differing personalities and interests of those diverse scholars who pioneered our subject into being - no-one having received initial training in the new discipline they were professing.' Such idiosyncratic entrepreneurs produced a wide variety of initial modes of geographical training within universities that, 'if not hostile, were not over-friendly to the new upstart subject'.[33] Also speaking of the pioneering venture at University College, R.C. Honeybone recalled other problems encountered in the 1920s: 'Fieldwork was unknown, large scale maps practically non-existent, and the facilities for research severely limited.'[34] The situation at Sheffield University was markedly different. There, since 1908, for nearly 20 years the subject had received 'serious recognition only in the Faculty of Pure Science, and indeed, in the early twenties a hard battle had to be fought to gain appropriate recognition in the Faculty

of Arts.' The department was directed by Dr. (later Professor)
Rudmose Brown – a botanist and scientist by training 'who had
come to know, and again, be much influenced by, the teaching
of A.J. Herbertson. His interest lay in the development of
geography as a science, and he welcomed the University's
initial decision to make the Faculty of Pure Science the subject's
primary home.'[35] Meanwhile at Cambridge, which has produced
'nearly 50% of current holders of chairs in British universities',
there were also problems in this period: the subject was not
examined until 1920.

The Council of the Geographical Association explained the
problems in this way: 'This relation of geography to the humanities and to the Natural Sciences has introduced difficulties in
connection with the examination of students. It does not fit
easily into the examination of the Faculties of Arts or of Science,
or indeed of any other group. No-one of the Faculties can claim
geography as peculiarly its own. There has been a tendency to
solve the difficulty by excluding it from all the Faculties.' The
report added optimistically: 'It is evident from what has been
said that the true solution is to include geography, pass and
honours, in both Arts and Science, as has been done by the
University of Wales.'[36]

By the 1920s, in spite of the problems in universities, school
geography continued its expansion. The organisation of
geographical knowledge was changing from 'classical' patterns
towards a more 'regional' approach. Regionalism followed closely
the work of the French scholar Vidal de la Blache in the previous
decade. In 1927 the Hadow Report stated: 'During the last
twenty-five years the method of teaching geography has notice-
ably changed; perhaps no subject has made a more general
advance.' The Report adds that the main objective of geographical teaching was to develop 'as in the case of history, an
attitude of mind and a mode of thought characteristic of the
subject'.

The success of the efforts to establish geography in schools
is eloquently testified to in the Committee's judgement that 'the
importance of geography as a subject in the curriculum for all
types of post-primary education needs little arguing'. Nonetheless the 'utilitarian reasons' are presented: 'Travel and correspondence have now become general; the British dominions are
to be found in every clime; and these facts alone are sufficient
to ensure that the subject shall have an important place in the
school timetable.' Alongside these reasons the Committee warned
of the dangers of overstressing the utilitarian rationale: 'For
however useful geographical information may be its value must
rest, for the purpose of our reference, on its use as an instrument of education, i.e. as a means of developing the growing
interest of the pupils. In this connection it has proved itself
to be a subject which, when well taught, makes a very strong
appeal to them.'[37]

Nearly a quarter of a century later a Report of the Royal

Geographical Society testifies to the continuing progress for the subject in schools and to its increasing 'academic status'. 'The importance of geography at all levels of education is urged not only by geographers, but by many educationists of standing and experience.' They quote Sir Cyril Norwood, who in 1943 had chaired the Board of Education's Committee which had produced the Norwood Report: 'I therefore want to make the bold claim that geography is an essential part of education whatever forms education may take, and that there can be no question of dropping it in any considered course of study.' Norwood claimed it was 'more important than a foreign language or a science, highly important as these are, for the simple reason . . . that the intelligent person must understand something about the world and the country and the district in which he is set to live his life.' To fully confirm geography's acceptance, the Report notes: 'The steadily increased importance of geography in the grammar schools is reflected by the numbers of those offering the subject in public examinations.'[38]

Yet whilst Sir Cyril Norwood's position on geography in schools appears unequivocal, the Norwood Report in 1943 did point to a number of problems faced by the subject. The Report defined geography as 'the study of man and his environment from selected points of view'. The authors, however, noted that 'natural science, economics, history, the study of local conditions as regards industry and agriculture might also be concerned with environment'. They were concerned with the temptation afforded by 'the expansiveness of geography', for 'environment is a term which is easily expanded to cover every condition and every phase of activity which makes up normal everyday experience'. Hence, 'enthusiasts for geography may be inclined sometimes to extend their range so widely as to swallow up other subjects'; in doing this they 'widen their boundaries so vaguely that definition of purpose is lost, and the distinctive virtues inherent in other studies closely pursued are ignored in a general survey of wide horizons.'[39]

The results of such 'expansiveness' in school geography were later reported by Honeybone, who argued that by the thirties geography 'came more and more to be a "world citizenship" subject, with the citizens detached from their physical environment'. He explains this partly by the spread 'under American influence' of 'a methodology, proclaiming that all education must be related to the everyday experience of children'. But argued that 'when put in the hands of people untrained in geography or trained without a proper sense of geographical synthesis', this frequently meant that 'geography in school started with the life and work of man and made no real attempt to examine his physical environment'. Thus through the work of those teachers untrained or badly trained in the subject, 'by 1939 geography had become grievously out of balance; the geographical synthesis had been abandoned; and the unique educational value of the subject lost in a flurry of social and economic generalizations.'[40]

The central problem, therefore, remained the establishment of departments in universities where 'geographers could be made' and the piecemeal changes in pursuit of pupil relevance and utility controlled and directed. Tudor David maintains that the establishment of geography in the universities 'has not been achieved without a struggle and without a good deal of sotto voce hostility in "high places"'. His sources for this contention are early professors of geography, for instance Professor Frank Debenham, professor of geography at Cambridge, who asserted: 'Teachers of established subject objected to this new omnium gatherum of a study, which threatened to invade their boundaries'.[41]

Likewise Professor Wooldridge argued that geographers were a frustrated university profession because of 'the widespread belief among our colleagues and associates that we lack academic status and intellectual respectability'. He argues that 'what has been conceded is that geography has a limited use in its lower ranges. What is implicitly denied by so many is that it has any valid claim as a higher subject.' Wooldridge, however, hints that acceptance at the lower level is the crucial threshold to cross. 'It has been conceded that if geography is to be taught in schools it must be learned in the universities.'[42] The relevance of the school 'base' to university geography is well illustrated by St Catharine's College, Cambridge. The college has produced so many professors of geography for the country's universities that a conspiracy might be alleged. David Walker disagrees, saying that the reasons for this academic pattern are down to earth. 'St Catharine's was one of the first colleges to offer awards in geography: it established a network of contacts with sixth-form teachers, many of whom later were its own graduates, and with particular schools like the Royal Grammar, Newcastle.' Walker points to the personal nature of subject induction. 'Since the Second World War moreover many of the St Catharine's geographers who went on to become professors, readers and lecturers were taught by one man, Mr. A.A.L. Caesar, now the senior tutor.'[43]

The period following 1945 does seem to have been critical in geography's acceptance and consolidation within the university sector. Professor Alice Garnett explained in 1968 why this period was so important: 'Not until after the Second World War was it widely the case that departments were directed by geographers who had themselves received formal training in the discipline, by which time most of the initial marked differences and contrasts in subject personality had been blurred or obliterated.'[44] At this point, geography departments were established in most universities and the subject had a recognisable core of identity: by 1954 Honebone could write a summary of the final acceptance and establishment of geography as a university discipline:

In the universities, there has been an unparalleled advance in the number of staff and scope of the work in the departments

of geography. In the University of London alone, there are
now six chairs, four of them of relatively recent creation.
Students, both graduates and undergraduates, are greater in
number than ever before. Many of the training colleges and
university departments of education are taking a full part in
this progress; employers are realizing the value of the breadth
of a university training in geography; and the Civil Service
has recently raised the status of geography in its higher
examinations. In fact, on all sides, we can see signs that, at
long last, geography is forcing its complete acceptance as a
major discipline in the universities, and that geographers are
welcomed into commerce, industry and the professions, because
they are well educated men and women . . .[45]

The advances in university geography after the Second World
War partly aided the acceptance of geography as a subject
suitable for the most able children, but problems remained. In
1967 Marchant noted: 'Geography is at last attaining to intellectual
respectability in the academic streams of our secondary schools.'
But added, 'the battle is not quite over', and instanced a girls
grammar school where: 'Geography is at present . . . an alternative to Latin, which means that a number of girls cease to
take it at the end of the third year . . . there is no work available at Advanced Level'; and a boys independent school where
'In the "O" level forms, the subject is taken only by those who
are neither classicists, nor modern linguists, nor scientists. The
sixth form is then drawn from this rather restricted group with
the addition of a few scientists who failed to live up to expectations.'[46] In 1976 the President of the Geographical Association
noted that 'in some public schools geography may still be
regarded as an inferior academic subject'.[47]
One of the problems of the growing reputation and intellectual
rigour of university geography was that it threw the inadequacies
of school geography into higher relief. This growing dichotomy
between school and university geography began to be reflected
in geographers' associations. The Geographical Association
became the forum of school geographers (with a scattering of
university scholars) whilst from the 1950s onwards the Institute
of British Geographers provided the main forum for university
personnel. For behind the rhetoric which sought academic
legitimation and expansion for the subject, school geography
often remained substantially unchanged:

If we analyse the trends of geography teaching during this
century, it appears that, although the type of memorization
has changed, yet memory has always been very markedly the
senior partner in the uneasy alliance of memory and understanding. At one time, there existed the much derided 'capes
and bays'; at another, what we might call 'economic capes and
bays', lists of products related in the flimsiest way to their
environments; at another, the 'pseudo-scientific capes and

bays', the era of isobars and the planetary wind system; and at the present time [1954], we seem to be overemphasizing the 'regional account capes and bays' . . . Frequently, such regional accounts in school are mere feats of memory, with little or no relationship between the various parts.[48]

Two kinds of response developed to the 'capes and bays' critique. Firstly one school of geographers sought to build on the naturalist/fieldwork tradition in geography. A second response originated in the universities partly as a counter to the rapid growth of social sciences such as sociology and economics. This led to definitions of a 'new geography' stressing quantitative methods, model building and social scientific aspirations.

THE FIELDWORK TRADITION IN GEOGRAPHY

The fieldwork element in geography has been present since the earliest days of teaching the subject. Wise has uncovered a range of experiments in teaching geography in this manner in early nineteenth-century English schools. He summarised the methods employed in this way: 'Starting from the home or schoolroom such studies extended outwards to the neighbour-hood, town, district, region, country and eventually to world studies.'[49] The intention then was to broaden out from detailed studies of the child's immediate environment into studies of more extended geographical areas. The pioneering work in English schools and later in German schools influenced the Royal Geographical Society's Inspector of Geographical Education, Dr. J.S. Keltie, in the 1880s. Keltie recorded that the school boards in London, Birmingham, Edinburgh and Glasgow employed and encouraged such methods. The London boards, for instance, had 'A special map of the neighbourhood of each school, a map of the division in which the school is situated, and a map of London and its environs.'[50]

In the twentieth century school teaching of geography has continued to employ local field studies and to extend their use. Often the approach has been most favoured among classes of younger children, notably in primary and elementary schools. The Geographical Association's publication, 'Suggestions for the Teaching of Local Geography', drawn up by the Primary Schools Committee, typifies the approach in its commitment 'to the understanding of the geography of the immediate neighbourhood and . . . its appropriate setting in the larger area to which it belongs.'[51] The emphasis on local geography indicates the dual reappraisal involved in developing more fieldwork in school geography: firstly, more studies out of doors; secondly, greater concentration on the child's immediate environment and neigh-bourhood. The head of the Geography Department at Goldsmith's College, G.J. Cons, pioneered many strategies for training

pupils and students in fieldwork methods. Writing in 1938,
Cons argued that: 'The classroom door is shut; in very many
schools there is little relationship between what is going on in
the classroom, and the busy activities of the real world.'[52] Cons
therefore advocates 'the need for actuality' and in this respect
the then Director of Education for Northumberland is quoted as
saying: 'Geography is the most valuable key-subject of the
school', for it offers 'the chance of a study of the particular
environment of the schoolchild in all its details; its roads,
markets, transport, cost of living, family incomes, houses,
electricity, gas or the absence thereof, and so on, but from
these data the geographic field moves from the locality.'[53]

The establishment of fieldwork geography in the upper ranges
of the secondary school was closely allied with developments in
the universities. As early as 1896 Herbertson had carried out
experimental field classes with school children whilst working
at Heriot-Watt College, Edinburgh. Later at Oxford, he and
H.J. MacKinder, two pioneers of geography teaching, organised
field courses for teachers in the years 1906-14.[54] Their work
derived much from the ideas and writings of Sir Patrick Geddes
(1854-1933) who had founded an 'Outlook Tower' in Edinburgh
for educational scrutiny of the town's environment. In turn,
Geddes' work owed much to the writings of an early French
sociologist, Frederic Le Play (1806-82).[55]

The other external influence which provided a stimulus to
fieldwork in geography was the work of the university field
geologists at the turn of the century. 'It may be said that because
much of the early fieldwork in geography was done by geologists,
who had become interested in landforms, the currently accepted
forms of geographical field work concentrates on the natural
landscape.'[56] In an essay entitled 'Science in Education' written
in 1905, Archibald Geikie advocated training in field observation
so that the student would see 'more than is visible to the unin-
structed man'.[57] More recently, in the period following the
Second World War particularly, fieldwork has been widely
advocated in university geography. The work of Wooldridge
echoes many of the sentiments earlier voiced by Cons in respect
of school studies: 'the ground not the map, is the primary
document'[58] and again, 'over a great range of studies, reality is
in the field'.[59] In 1965 the Board stated that mainly as a result
of the activities of Professor Wooldridge and Geoffrey Hutching:
'fieldwork has progressed far in the last half-century, so that
it is a universally respected approach to the study of geography.
The generation of geographers trained by Wooldridge is today
playing a major part in training yet more geographers in the
same well tried methods.'[60]

The establishment of field study in university geography and
the growing output of field research were associated with new
demands to allow fieldwork a place in the education of academic
secondary school geography pupils: 'Since people like Wooldridge
at London, and others like Linton here in Sheffield were arguing

for it . . . when their students went out into schools they said
"can we do our fieldwork for exams"'.[61] These new initiatives
towards fieldwork for academic students aimed finally to establish
field geography in schools, for as the DES reported in 1972, 'In
spite of constant advocacy by leading teachers for over 40 years,
fieldwork held an uncertain foothold in school geography until
the 1950s.'[62] From this date onwards, progress was rapid and
centred around the development of new exams and new facilities.
'The fieldworking teacher needed the exams to change . . . "A"
levels began to change but at first fieldwork was not compulsory.
In the sixties it began to change . . . when exams changed it
meant you could leave the classroom.'[63] However, to leave the
classroom required an associated development of facilities in the
outside environment. Professional bodies such as the Field
Studies Council, Royal Geographical Society and the Geographical
Association worked to establish facilities for fieldwork. The
former body had in fact been formed in 1943 as the Council for
the Promotion of Field Studies and involved biologists as well as
geographers (c.f. Chapter 10). In 1965 it convened the first
conference on field studies in London. Mr C.A. Tinker of the
Council informed delegates that the demand for places on school
courses was outrunning supply by nearly 100 per cent.[64] The
Geographical Association, which had established a Standing
Committee on Field Studies, completed surveys of facilities
beginning in 1965.

By 1969 fieldwork was clearly well established in many schools.
John Everson confidently noted that: 'it is a truism to state
that the campaign to put fieldwork in the mainstream of school
geography is now over'. He went on to define the progress that
had been made in teaching and examinations:

> Since the war, increasingly, its place has been recognised and
> accepted by most students and teachers. There is now a large
> and growing body of literature describing field techniques
> and areas in Great Britain and abroad in which these tech-
> niques can be used. Examination authorities, such as Oxford
> and Cambridge, Cambridge and Associated Boards, put con-
> siderable emphasis on fieldwork at Advanced level. In these
> and other examinations questions are set which require from
> the student practical experience of work in the field if a
> satisfactory answer is to be written. The C.S.E. boards are
> even keener to promote this type of work and in some cases
> fieldwork is a compulsory part of the examination.[65]

In 1972 the DES survey of schools found that only 8 per cent of
the schools did not carry out fieldwork, whereas 80 per cent
regarded fieldwork as 'important or very important'.[66] The growing interest in fieldwork was also found in the universities. In
1963 Board noted that it had become fashionable 'to include
references to the necessity for fieldwork in the inaugural
addresses by new occupants of chairs of geography'.[67]

In spite of the widespread indicators of acceptance in the
academic sectors of secondary schools and universities, a
number of fundamental problems have remained unresolved.
Partly, the problems of fieldwork derive from practical difficulties which as Everson has conceded are 'legion and daunting'.
'The organiser has to find time to organise and prepare for the
trip; to justify to himself and, more importantly, to others, the
loss of actual school teaching time, especially for classes preparing for public examinations, to find suitable staff for the
work, to keep the costs down . . .'[68] The 1972 survey found
that:

> In 54 per cent of the schools visited the timetable created
> difficulties and the problems appeared to be more severe in
> the grammar than in other types of school. Put in another way,
> fewer than half of the schools possessed sufficient flexibility
> in timetabling to permit educational activities widely acclaimed
> to be valuable for pupils of all shades of ability . . . many
> schools overcome their difficulties by conducting fieldwork at
> weekends or in school holidays.

The report adds, ominously with regard to the ensuing wave of
cuts in educational expenditure, that 'about 42 per cent of the
schools reported difficulties in financing fieldwork'.[69]
   Such problems are also experienced at university and college
level. The DES survey notes that 'many older teachers and some
younger ones received little training in fieldwork techniques at
university or college'.[70] The inadequacies of university fieldwork
were commented on by a lecturer in a well-established department
with a strong national reputation: 'they were trivial . . . aimless
. . . the students took it very lightheartedly and didn't get
much out of it.' Besides the practical problems of organisation
and staffing, fieldwork presented epistemological and presen-
tational difficulties. Significantly, the Presidential Address at
the Geographical Association in 1976 noted that geography
suffered from too many 'woolly' generalisations - there was a
lack of a scientific basis. 'Nowhere is this better illustrated than
in fieldwork, which has long been important in our subject . . .'[71]
   In recent years determined efforts have been made to develop
a model of 'field research' which focuses on the process of
hypothesis formulation and testing, which lead to the provision
of generalisations or theories. As Everson has noted, some
geographers would be worried by this approach, feeling that 'it
might develop an eye for a problem, not an eye for country'
and that 'children will get less thrill and less understanding
than from the former approach'.[72] Similarly, the DES survey
noted: 'Hypothesis testing in the field is a new venture in
school geography . . . it is not surprising that nearly all the
work recorded was confined to older pupils.'[73] In spite of the
difficulties, Everson argues that advocates of the field research
approach 'would say that in this method geographers are operat-

ing in the same way as scientists (and school geographers in the same way as research geographers) and consequently providing general statements which in this form of the study are objective not subjective assessments of the answer.' In this article, Everson significantly goes on to develop an elaborate model for fieldwork titled 'a route to scientific explanation'. Hence fieldwork was seen as needing reform in a similar manner to regional geography and to present a more scientific approach. In school geography the implications of this more scientific approach was that the pupil was to be allowed 'more and more to develop the field research stage of the process as he progresses up the school and grows in appreciation and ability'.[74] But the aspiration for more scientific models of school work remained largely unfulfilled. The DES survey for instance noted that in 1972 only about 15 per cent of schools were using some hypothesis testing in the fields. The most common forms of experience remained 'field teaching and "traditional" fieldwork by pupils'.[75]

THE NEW GEOGRAPHY

'New geography' was a reformulated version of the subject which emerged first in the United States and Sweden. In England this new geography was effectively launched at the Madingley Lectures in 1963. Commenting on this new initiative, E.A. Wrigley contended that regional geography was 'a concept overtaken by the course of historical change'. By this view regional geography 'has been as much a victim of the Industrial Revolution as the peasant, landed society, the horse and the village community, and for the same reason'.[76] To this problem of subject anachronism Chorley and two university geographers proposed an 'immediate solution' through 'building up the neglected geometrical side of the discipline'. They noted:

> Research is already swinging strongly into this field and the problem of implementation may be more acute in the schools than in the universities. There we are continually impressed by the vigour and reforming zeal of 'ginger groups' like the School Mathematics Association [n.b. this presumably refers to the School Mathematics Project] which have shared in a fundamental review of mathematics teaching in schools. There the inertia problems - established textbooks, syllabuses, examinations - are being successfully overcome and a new wave of interest is sweeping through the schools. The need in geography is just as great and we see no good reason why changes here should not yield results equally rewarding.

The messianic nature of their appeal is shown when they argue that it is 'Better that geography should explode in an excess of reform than bask in the watery sunset of its former glories':[77]
    The Madingley Lectures proved a watershed in the evolution

of the subject. Two years before, E.W. Gilbert, in an article on
'The Idea of the Region',[78] had stated that he 'regarded new
geography in the universities as an esoteric cult'.[79] After
Madingley this was no longer the case, as a college lecturer who
was secretary of his local Geographical Association recalled:
'After Madingley my ideas were turned upside down . . . That's
where the turn-around in thinking in geography really started.[80]
But, as Walford later noted, Madingley was 'heady to some,
undrinkable brew to others'.[81]

Chorley and Haggett sought to consolidate the changes they
were advocating, by a new book entitled 'Models in Geography'.[82]
By this time opinions were becoming progressively polarised
about the 'new geography'. Slaymaker wrote in support that
the book was: 'In retrospect, a turning point in the development
of geographical methodology in Britain' and argued that the
publication of this book demonstrated that 'the traditional classi-
ficatory paradigm is inadequate and that in the context of the
"new geography" an irreversible step has been taken to push
us back into the mainstream of scientific activity by way of the
uncomfortable and highly-specialized process of model building'.[83]
Teachers of the subject received less enthusiastic advice from
their journal 'Geography' and its anonymous reviewer, 'P.R.C.':
'What . . . is its object, and to whom is it addressed? These
questions are avoided with perverse skill and in the absence
of guidance, the conviction gradually takes root that, in fact,
the authors are writing for each other! This may explain, though
it does not excuse, the use in some papers of a barbarous and
repulsive jargon.[184]

A year later the President of the Geographical Association
pursued a similar opposition to a more explicit statement of the
fears which new geography engendered. The new systematic
geography, she argued, was 'creating a problem that will
increase in acuteness over the decades ahead for it leads towards
subject fragmentation as fringe specialisms in systematic fields
proliferate and are pursued independently to the neglect of the
very core of our discipline - a core that largely justifies its
existence.'

The tension between academic scholarship 'pushing back the
frontiers of knowledge' and the fragmentation of the 'core' of
the subject has been strongly perceived by geographers. Garnett
felt that geography in the universities was in fact 'so sophisticated' and 'its numerous branches in diverse fields at times so
narrowly specialised' that 'sooner or later the question must
arise as to how much longer the subject can effectively be held
together'.[85] Geographers' paranoia about 'holding the subject
together' has been recurrent and one is reminded of the fears
of the inter-war years about the so-called 'expansiveness of
geography'.

The dangers of fragmentation again impinge on the university
departments where 'geographers are made'. These departments,
Garnett maintained had a duty to unify the subject:

University departments have a duty to ensure that, at least
at the first degree level, the core of our subject is neither
forgotten nor neglected, and that the synthesis of the
specialist fields and their relevance to the core are clearly
appreciated by our undergraduate students. To my mind, it is
only on the foundation of a first degree course structure so
designed that a geographer is basically qualified either to
teach in our Schools or to carry his studies further at a post-
graduate research level.[86]

The relevance of new geography for the teaching of the subject
was also viewed as problematic, particularly in the light of the
experiences in the early twenties when as geographers 'we
worked hard to free our subject from the domination of generalised concepts and principles based all too often on insecure
foundations'. Moreover, 'in the hands of the inexperienced, an
oversimplified model can be a most dangerous tool leading to
facile and stereotyped generalisation and even into new forms of
crude determinism.'[87] Garnett's fears were reiterated a year later
by Professor C.A. Fisher, following an almost identical line of
argument. In perusing geographical periodicals he found much
which seemingly substantiates 'the familiar charge that geography
lacks any central purpose to justify its being regarded as a
single coherent discipline . . .' Hence he feared that 'The light-
hearted prophecy I made in 1959 that we might soon expect to
see the full 57 varieties of geography[88] had since been almost
literally fulfilled, and my personal collection of different
categories of geography that have seriously been put forward
in professional literature now stands at well over half that
number.'[89] In stark contrast to Chorley and Haggett's view of
the excitement of the frontier he states:

> We appear to assume that so long as we keep repeating the
> magic word geography we shall all stand shoulder to shoulder,
> even though we have dispersed ourselves into alien territory
> all the way round the geographical perimeter. To speak
> bluntly, I believe that geography is in serious danger of doing
> precisely this: of over-extending its periphery at the expense
> of its base . . . I fear that in large measure this predilection
> for service at the frontier reflects a lack of conviction in
> what the home base stands for, and a widely prevalent feeling
> among many of our number that the central aims which
> geography grew up to fulfil are hopelessly out of date if not
> entirely meaningless.[90]

Fisher concludes with an exhortation to return to earlier versions
of geography. 'Without suggesting that the "new geography"[91]
is itself a total aberration, I would urge that assessments of its
contribution should be subjected to its own quantitative criteria
and cut down to size. For only then it seems, will geographers
as a whole return to the eminently rewarding task of cultivating

their own well-favoured garden.'[92]
The coverage given to views opposing 'new geography' in the
geography teachers' journal reflected the opinion of many
practising teachers. Peter Hore spent a year investigating the
effects of new geography in the classroom:

> Teachers are not noted for their willing acceptance of new
> ideas. They are essentially practical and conservative people
> and need to be convinced that a new trend, idea or method
> has classroom application before giving it their approval.
> Furthermore they are suspicious of persons in ivory-towered
> universities and colleges of education, who throw out wonder-
> ful suggestions, without testing them in the white heat of a
> classroom composed, say, of thirty aggressive youths from a
> twilight urban area. It is not surprising then, that the waves
> of innovation breaking over the subject are causing concern
> – particularly to those who have coasted along with Eskimos
> and Masai or the Midland Triangle and other regions of the
> world (assuming that they have heard the pounding surf of
> the new geography at all).[93]

At the same time P.R. Thomas asserted that 'the outstanding
feature of established practice in geography teaching in schools'
was 'the persistence of intellectual methods which academic
geographers have progressively rejected'.[94] The dangers were
perceived by many teachers at the time: For example, one
teacher recalled that at this time, 'Geography was in a state of
ferment . . . it was moving too quickly . . . Let alone in the
schools even many of the universities didn't have new geography.'[95] Whilst another noted that, 'This new approach, however
you felt about it, caused a sort of schism . . . both at
university and school level.'[96]
Fears of this schism were expressed in a number of contemporary books. The gap between schools and universities, of
which there is much evidence in previous periods, was thought
particularly worrying: 'Techniques of study are changing more
rapidly in modern geography than at any previous time in the
subject's history. As a result there is a great need for a dialogue
between research workers and those being admitted to the
mysteries of the subject.' In this respect 'Teachers provide the
necessary link; and it is dangerous for the vitality and future
health of geography that some teachers find current developments either incomprehensible or unacceptable.'[97] Rex Walford
made a similar diagnosis, arguing that the 'need for unity within
the subject' was 'more than a practical one of preparing sixth-
formers for their first lectures on campus; it is, I would assert,
a basic requirement for the continued existence of the subject.'[98]
In spite of the opposition of teachers and academics, many of
whom saw regional geography as the 'real geography', there
were strong pressures working in favour of the advocates of new
geography. In the introduction to the book of papers arising

from the 1970 Charney Manor Conference, 'New Directions in
Geography Teaching', Walford summarised the position at the
time. He employed new geography as a term' . . . usually applied
to that loose collection of ideas which revolve around models,
hypotheses, quantitative techniques, concepts and percepts'.
He argued the need for change succinctly, saying that 'If
geography is to survive in the school curriculum it will have to
be more than a convenient examination-pass for those who seek
only to memorise a jumble of facts and sketch-maps.'[99] He added
that 'What is in disrepute is what old geography, haunted by
the spectre of fact-dominated examinations, has turned into.'[100]
David Walker made a similar point in 'Geography', arguing that
traditional geography courses had 'three predominant characteristics which may be considered to be unfortunate': 'firstly a
large content of regional studies; secondly a lack of precision in
accepted statements about inter-relationships between geographical phenomena; and thirdly, very little training in geographical
techniques other than observation, recording and the attempted
drawing of conclusions at an unsophisticated level.' Walker
apportioned the blame for these three faults in this manner: 'The
first of these characteristics seems to be very largely responsible
for the presence of the other two.' Namely, 'a view of geography
well expressed by Hartshorne, "that no universals need to be
evolved, other than the general laws of geography, that all
areas are unique".'[101]

In attacking regional geography, Walker seems to have
correctly elicited one of the central targets of 'new geography'.
P.R. Thomas stated this even more explicitly: 'The fundamental
characteristic of the "new geography" seems not to be, as is
often thought, the use of quantitative methods, but rather
its changed attitude to the region within geographical studies.'
Because of this change 'the study of the particular region as
a unique entity has been superseded by the search for patterns
common to many regions, in which the particular case is only
significant as a source of data used in the process of general-
ization.'[102] But in the late 1960s in spite of warnings about 'the
survival of geography', in many schools geography was
characterised by 'the survival of the regional concept as the
basis of syllabus construction, despite the progressive decline
in the importance of regional geography at most universities and
its virtual disappearance from some.'[103] And despite the contention that 'the quantity and scale of regional studies allowed
by school syllabuses have precluded the teaching of any but the
most rudimentary techniques in geography.'[104]

That fact-dominated regional geography threatened the
survival of the subject could be deduced from a number of contemporary reports. In 1967 the report on 'Society and the
Young School Leaver' noted that its young subjects felt 'at best
apathetic, at worst resentful and rebellious to geography . . .
which seems to him to have nothing to do with the adult world
he is soon to join.' The report adds: 'A frequent cause of failure

seems to be that the course is often based on the traditional belief that there is a body of content for each separate subject which every school leaver should know.' In the least successful courses, it argued, 'this body of knowledge is written into the curriculum without any real consideration of the needs of the boys and girls and without any question of its relevance.'[105]

The threat to geography began to be appreciated at the highest level. A member of the Executive and Honorary Secretary of the Geographical Association recalls: 'Things had gone too far and geography became a too locally based regional thing . . . at the same time the subject began to lose touch with reality . . . geography got a bad name.'[106] A college lecturer, David Gowing, saw the problem facing the subject and argued: 'Pupils feel that present curricula have little relevance to their needs and so their level of motivation and understanding is low. Teachers are concerned that the raising of the school-leaving age and some forms of comprehensive reorganisation may exacerbate these problems.'[107]

Under these pressures new geography made considerable progress. In 1967 Marchant proclaimed: 'After the era of physical geography has come that of mathematical geography',[108] and two years later Professor P.R. Gould proclaimed: 'During the last ten years, geography . . . has exploded. Geographers today are intrigued by the order and regularity they find in the patterns, structures, arrangements, and relationships of man's work on the face of the earth.'[109] More tangible proof of the change was given in the preamble to the new Oxford and Cambridge 'A' level in 1969:

At a high level new methods and techniques are being developed, tested and retained or discarded as appropriate. Inevitably the emphasis shifts from time to time. While we think it totally inappropriate that pupils at school should be forced to follow all the current fashions in geography, some reflection of the changing content of the subject must filter down to Advanced level pupils without upsetting the general stability of the subject. As it now stands the syllabus is not sufficiently flexible to allow this and accordingly the changes detailed (towards 'new geography') are designed to let this happen.[110]

In 1967 the Geographical Association set up a sub-committee to consider the use of models and quantitative techniques in geography teaching.

Even more substantive proof of the change is reluctantly provided in the 1976 Presidential Address to the Geographical Association. Reviewing the chart of DES courses during the years 1970-76, Sheila Jones states: 'It shows quite clearly the current trend. Obviously what some are disposed to call the "Quantitative Revolution" was infiltrating into schools from 1970 to 1973, with applicants heavily outnumbering those who could

actually be accepted for the courses.[111] Likewise the Schools
Council Geography 15-18 Project, in seeking to answer the
question 'Is there really a 'new geography"?', concluded there
had been an important general shift in approaches to the subject:

> geographers have become: (a) more critical of concepts and
> models that had previously been taken for granted, e.g. the
> 'region'; the Davisian cycle, or maps themselves; and hence
> are less ready to rely on 'common sense' and on unquantified
> evaluation of how well models and concepts used in geography
> match the real world. (b) more enterprising in devising new
> models, and in borrowing ideas like systems-analysis, or
> methods of evaluation such as regression analyses from other
> subjects.[112]

In recent years fears about 'new geography' seem to have sub-
sided and a period of consolidation has set in. Of the Cambridge
base of Chorley and Haggett it was recently written, by David
Walker, himself a protagonist:

> The academic revolution of quantification which has battered
> traditional scholarship in fields like economic history and
> linguistics has taken its toll in geography in recent years,
> but the Cambridge department, which Professor Darby took
> in 1966 remains on even keel. The tripos system continues to
> offer a fine balance of specialisation and liberal education.[113]

Perceptions of a subject in crisis have considerably mellowed.
A professor, who is on the Executive Committee and past holder
of a number of positions in the Geographical Association, stated:
'I see geography traditionally as a core to understand why
places are as they are', but said of the present condition of
geography: 'It isn't in flux . . . there is no end to the subject
. . . of course the techniques by which you advance the subject
will change . . . if the present emphasis on quantitative techniques helps our preciseness who could deny that it is an
advance within the subject?'[114] Ultimately the reconciliation with
new geography was closely linked with geography's long
aspiration to be viewed as a science. In a previous decade
Professor Wooldridge had written a book on 'The Geographer as
Scientist'[115] but in 1970 Fitzgerald, reviewing the implications
of new geography for teaching wrote: 'The change which many
think is at the heart of geography is that towards the use of
the scientific method in approaching problems.'[116] Similarly,
M. Yeates argued that geography can be regarded 'as a science
concerned with the rational development and testing of theories
that explain and predict the spatial distribution and location of
various characteristics on the surface of the earth.'[117] At the
21st International Geographic Congress at New Delhi in 1968,
Professor Norton Ginsburg identified social science as the
'fraternity' to aspire to. He saw

the beginnings of a new age for human geography as a fully-fledged member of the social science fraternity . . . the future of geography as a major research discipline will, I submit, be determined on the intellectual battlefields of the universities, where competition and conflict are intense; and where ideas are the hallmark of achievement.

Two presidential addresses confirmed the aspiration to 'scientific' status as a valid intention for geographical research and teaching. In 1968 Professor Garnett saw that there was a 'growing recognition of the role of geography as a space science'.[118] Whilst in 1976 Sheila Jones expressed 'a wish to develop a precision of thought and this is obviously achieved by a more scientific approach to geography . . .' This was because she discerned that too often geographers 'have depended on generalisations and the lack of a scientific basis made many of our studies "woolly"'.[119]

But if by the mid-1970s the teachers of geography had accepted new geography because of its clear benefits in achieving high scientific status within the universities new dissenters were active. In 1977 Peet's 'Radical Geography' summarised some of the problems. The collection was, said Johnson, made up of the essays of scholars 'who have become disillusioned with the "scientific approach" to human geography espoused since the mid-1950s, largely because of the perceived inability of this approach to initiate major social changes.'[120] The tension between prestige and academic progress was taken up in a recent publication 'Change and Tradition: Geography's new Frontiers'. Butterfield, for instance, strongly reaffirms faith in new geography but argues that 'competence in purposeful, yet flexible, scientific method' is needed to hold back the 'pressures of environmental and social relevance and explanation seeking'. In summary:

> Use of quantitative methods has tended to give geography a scientific prestige by association with mathematical techniques, and has led us to believe that we are at least scientific in the techniques that we use. But not all who use a spanner may call themselves mechanics; only those who know how, when and where to use it to dismantle a problem engine may do that. Furthermore, spanners are frequently thrown into the works and to make the problems even more intractable.[121]

The answer was the adoption and teaching of scientific approaches 'not for reasons of prestige or self-justification but as a methodological construct of immense instructional as well as analytical potential for the geographer'. Although an early advocate, one of the first dissenters was David Harvey who in 1973 recognised 'a clear disparity between the sophisticated theoretical and methodological framework we are using and our ability to say anything really meaningful about events as they

unfold around us'.[122] Clearly, having promoted geography as a
science and having thereby earned the associated prestige,
geographers were left with the problems of practically implement-
ing what had been so eloquently promoted.

CONCLUSION

The establishment of geography - 'how geography was rendered
a discipline' - was a protracted, painstaking and fiercely contested process. The story is not one of the translation of an
academic discipline devised by ('dominant') groups of scholars
in universities into a pedagogic version to be used as a school
subject. Rather, the story unfolds in reverse order and can be
seen as a drive from low-status groups at school level to progressively colonise areas within the university sector - thereby
earning the right for scholars in the new field to define knowledge
that could be viewed as a discipline. The process of evolution
for school subjects can be seen not as a pattern of disciplines
'translated' down or of 'domination' downwards but very much
as a process of 'aspiration' upwards.
    To summarise the stages in the evolution of geography: these
offer some support for Layton's tentative model although they
indicate the existence of a stage preceding his stage one. In this
stage, teaching was anything but 'messianic', for the subject
was taught by non-specialists and comprised a 'dreary collection
of geographical facts and figures'. The threshold for 'take-off'
on the route to academic establishment began with MacKinder's
remarkably successful and sustained recipe for the subject's
promotion drawn up in 1903. The strategy reads very much like
trade union pleas for the closed shop: In this case the pressure
group in question was of course the Geographical Association.
In the MacKinder manifesto the geography teacher is to set the
exams and is to choose exams that are best for the 'common
acceptation' of the subject, the teaching of geography is to be
exclusively in the hands of trained geographers and the universities are to be encouraged to establish schools of geography
'where geographers can be made'.
    The strategy offered solutions for the major problems
geography faced in its evolution. Most notable of these was the
idiosyncratic and information-based nature of school geography.
Initially the subject stressed personal, pedagogic and utilitarian
arguments for its inclusion in curricula: 'We seek to train future
citizens', and moreover a citizen 'must have a topographical
background if he is to keep order in the mass of information
which accumulates in the course of his life' (1919). Later the
subject was advocated because 'travel and correspondence have
now become general' (1927). But the result of these utilitarian
and pedagogic emphases was that comments arose as to the
'expansiveness' of the subject and the fact that it became 'more
and more to be a "world citizenship"' (1930s).

The problem was that identified by MacKinder in 1903; geographers needed to be 'made' in the universities then the piecemeal changes in pursuit of school relevance could be controlled and directed. The growth of the subject in the schools provided an overwhelming argument for the subject to be taught in the universities. As Wooldridge noted later: 'It has been conceded that if geography is to be taught in schools it must be learned in universities'. Slowly, therefore, a uniformity in the subject was established to answer those who observed the chameleon nature of the subject's knowledge structure. Alice Garnett noted that it was not until after 1945 that most school departments of geography were directed by specialist-trained geographers, but as a result of this training 'most of the initial marked differences and contrasts in subject personality had been blurred or obliterated'.

The definition of geography through the universities instead of the schools began to replace the pedagogic or utilitarian bias with arguments for academic rigour: and as early as 1927 Hadow had contended that 'the main objective in good geographical teaching is to develop, as in the case of history, an attitude of mind and mode of thought characteristic of the subject'. However, for several decades university geography was plagued both by the image of the subject as essentially for school children and by the idiosyncratic interpretations of the various university departments, especially in respect to fieldwork. Thus while establishment in universities solved the status problems of the subject within schools, within universities themselves the subject's status still remained low. The launching of 'new geography' with aspirations to scientific or social scientific rigour is therefore partly to be understood as a strategy for finally establishing geography's status at the highest level. In this respect the current position of the subject in universities would seem to confirm the success of new geography's push for parity of esteem with other university disciplines.

The aspiration to become an academic subject and the successful promotion employed by geography teachers and educationists, particularly in the work of the Geographical Association, has been clearly evidenced. We know what happened in the evolution of geography: less evidence has been presented as to why this should be so. A clue can be found in Garnett's presidential address to the Geography Association in 1968: a clear link is presented between 'the recognition of our subject's status among university disciplines' and 'the costly provision made available for its study'. Plainly the drive towards higher status is accompanied by opportunities to command larger finance and resources.

Byrne's work has provided data on resource allocation within schools (see Chapter 3). The implications of the preferential treatment of academic subjects for the material self-interest of teachers are clear: better staffing ratios, higher salaries, higher capitation allowances, more graded posts, better career

prospects. The link between academic status and resource allocation provides a major explanatory framework for understanding
the promotion of geography. Basically, if a university base can
be established the subject can be promoted as a scholarly
academic discipline. In schools it follows that the subject will be
'academic', taught to abler students and provided with favourable
finance and resources.

Despite its success in establishing geography as a broadly-
accepted academic discipline, the fears about new geography's
'repulsive jargon' and the dangers it held of 'subject fragmentation' into 'fringe specialisms' are recorded earlier. Above all,
new geography represented an attack by one group of geographers on other groups well establish in schools - the regional
and field geographers. David Walker states quite clearly the
nature of this attack and he and Thomas confirm that regional
geography survived in the majority of school courses. For a time,
the identity of geography was contested by these groups but in
the end new geography achieved a major place in the subject.

In this respect the current position of the subject in universities would seem to confirm the success of new geography's
push for parity of esteem within universities. The direction of
the subject through the new definition emanating from university
scholars was throughout the period scrutinised and co-ordinated
by the Geographical Association. The Association thereby acted
as a mediator between geography as defined by scholars and
geography as traditionally taught in schools. At stages where the
gap between these two widened the Association was always at
hand to warn against too rapid redefinition, to exhort teachers
to change and to encourage retraining in the new definitions of
the subject. Besides defining the internal unity of the subject
at the various levels the Association was alert to definitions of
knowledge by those outside its territory. Environmental studies
posed a particular threat because of its obvious similarity to
field geography and regional geography: two traditions under
attack during the launching of new geography. At this time the
possibilities of a break-up of the subject threatened the survival
of the discipline. But the Geographical Association was on hand
to challenge this low-status 'integrated subject' and to defend
the integrity of its own brand of integrated knowledge that had
been so fiercely promoted for 80 years.

NOTES

1 D. Gregory, 'Ideology, Science and Human Geography'
   (London, Hutchinson, 1978), p. 21.
2 G.S. Robertson, Political Geography and the Empire,
   'Geographical Journal', Vol. 16, pp. 447-57, Quoted ibid.
   Gregory, p. 18.
3 R. Peet, 'Radical Geography: Alternative Viewpoints on
   Contemporary Social Issues' (London, Methuen, 1978), p. 10.

4   Op. cit. Gregory, p. 20.
5   Op. cit. Gregory, p. 17.
6   A von Humboldt, 'Cosmos' (London, 1849).
7   K. Ritter, 'Allgememe Erdkunde' (Berlin, 1862).
8   E.A. Wrigley, Changes in the Philosophy of Geography, in
    R. Chorley and P. Haggett (eds.), 'Frontiers in Geographical
    Teaching' (London, Methuen, 1967), p. 3.
9   Ibid., p. 4.
10 Ibid.
11 J. Brunhes, 'La Geographie Humaine' (Paris, 1925).
12 Wrigley, 'Changes in Philosophy', p. 6.
13 T.G. Rooper, On Methods of Teaching Geography, 'Geogra-
    phical Teacher', Vol. 1 (1901).
14 H.J. MacKinder, On the Scope and Methods of Geography,
    'Proceedings of the Royal Geographical Society', Vol. IX
    (1887).
15 R.J.W. Selleck, 'The New Education: The English Background
    1870-1914' (Melbourne, Pitman, 1968), p. 34.
16 Loc. cit., Rooper, 1901.
17 E.G.A. Holmes 'What Is and What Might Be' (London, Con-
    stable, 1912), p. 107.
18 C. Bird, Limitations and Possibilities of Geographical
    Teaching in Day Schools, 'Geographical Teacher', Vol. 1
    (1901).
19 Inside cover of 'Geography' journal.
20 A. Garnett, Teaching Geography: Some Reflections,
    'Geography', Vol. 54, November 1969, p. 367.
21 For example of inclusion see Joint Matriculation Board
    Calendar, 1918. As a subsidiary subject see Oxford Delegacy
    on Local Examinations Regulations, 1925.
22 H.J. MacKinder, Report of the Discussion on Geographical
    Education at the British Association meeting, September
    1903. 'Geographical Teacher', Vol. 2, 1903, pp. 95-101.
23 Garnet, 'Reflections', p. 387.
24 W. Carey Maclean, The Correlation of Instruction in Physics
    and Geography, 'Geographical Teacher', Vol. 5, 1913.
25 Council of the Geographical Association, The Position of
    Geography, 'Geographical Teacher', Vol. 10, 1919.
26 Ibid.
27 Ibid.
28 D. Walker, The Well-Founded Geographers, 'Times Edu-
    cational Supplement', (28.11.1975), p. 6.
29 Garnett, 'Reflections', p. 388.
30 N.J. Graves, 'Geography in Education' (London, Heinemann,
    1975), p. 28.
31 Ibid.
32 Loc. cit. MacKinder, 1913.
33 Garnett, 'Reflections', pp. 387-8.
34 R.C. Honeybone, Balance in Geography and Education,
    'Geography', Vol. 34, No. 184, 1954.
35 Garnett, 'Reflections', p. 388.

36   Council of Geographical Association (1919).
37   Board of Education, 'Report of the Consultative Committee:
      the Education of the Adolescent' (Hadow Report) (London,
      HMSO, 1927).
38   Royal Geographical Society, 'Geography and "Social Studies"
      in Schools' Education Committee memorandum (1950).
39   Norwood Report, 1943, pp. 101-2.
40   Loc. cit. Honeybone, 1954.
41   T. David, Against Geography, in J. Bale, N. Graves, and
      R. Walford, 'Perspective in Geographical Education'
      (Edinburgh, 1973), pp. 12-13.
42   Ibid., David.
43   Walker, 'Well-rounded Geographers'.
44   Op. cit. Garnett, 'Reflections', p. 368.
45   Loc. cit. Honeybone, 1954.
46   E.C. Marchant, Some Responsibilities of the Teacher of
      Geography, 'Geography', Vol. 3, 1968, p. 133.
47   S.M. Jones, The Challenge of Change in Geography Teach-
      ing, 'Geography' (Nov. 1976), p. 197.
48   Loc. cit. Honeybone, 1954.
49   M.J. Wise, An Early 19th Century Experiment in the Teaching
      of Geography, 'Geography', Vol. 33 (1948), p. 20.
50   J. Scott Keltie, 'Geographical Education: Report to the
      Council of the Royal Geographical Society', Royal Geogra-
      phical Society Supplementary Papers, 1 (1882-5), p. 451.
51   Geographical Association Primary Schools Committee,
      'Suggestions for the Teaching of Local Geography' (n.d.).
52   G.J. Cons and C. Fletcher, 'Actuality in School: an Experi-
      ment in Social Education' (London, Methuen, 1938), pp. 1-2.
53   Ibid. p. 7. Quoting from the report of an address on the
      senior school and its curriculum by H.M. Spink, Director
      of Education for Northumberland.
54   J.F. Archer and T.H. Dalton 'Fieldwork in Geography'
      (London, Batsford, 1968), p. 14.
55   K.S. Wheeler, The Outlook Tower: Birthplace of Environ-
      mental Education, 'Bulletin of the Society for Environmental
      Education', Vol. 2, No. 2, 1970, p. 26.
56   A. Geikie, 'Landscape in History and Other Essays' (London,
      1905), p. 296. Quoted op. cit. C. Board, p. 187.
57   C. Board in Chorley and Haggett (eds.), 'Frontier in
      Geographical Teaching', p. 187.
58   S.W. Wooldridge and W.G. East, 'The Spirit and Purpose of
      Geography' (London, Hutchinson, 2nd ed. 1958), p. 16.
59   S.W. Wooldridge, 'The Spirit and Significance of Fieldwork',
      Address at the Annual Meeting of the Council for the
      Promotion of Field Studies (1948), p. 4.
60   Board, p. 186.
61   Interview, Sheffield Institute of Education, 30.6.76.
62   Department of Education and Science Schools Geography in
      the Changing Curriculum, 'Education Survey 19', (London,
      HMSO, 1974), p. 15.

63 Op. cit. Interview, Sheffield 30.6.76.
64 Op. cit. Archer and Dalton, pp. 14-15.
65 J. Everson, Some Aspects of Teaching Geography Through Fieldwork, 'Geography', Vol. 54, Part 1, January 1969, p. 64.
66 Op. cit. 'Education Survey 19', p. 15.
67 Op. cit. C. Board, p. 187.
68 J. Everson, Fieldwork in School Geography, in R. Walford, (ed.), 'New Directions in Geography Teaching' (London, Longmans, 1973), p. 107.
69 'Education Survey No. 19', p. 17.
70 Ibid., p. 18.
71 S.M. Jones, p. 203.
72 Op. cit. Everson, p. 111.
73 Op. cit. 'Education Survey No. 19', pp. 16-17.
74 Op. cit. Everson, p. 111.
75 Op. cit. 'Education Survey No. 19', p. 16.
76 Op. cit. Wrigley, p. 13.
77 Op. cit. Chorley and Haggett, 'Frontier Movements and the Geographical Tradition', p. 377.
78 E.W. Gilbert, The Idea of the Region, 'Geography', Vol. 45(i), 1961.
79 D. Gowing, A Fresh Look at Objectives, in R. Walford (ed.), 'New Directions in Geography Teaching' (London, Longmans, 1973), p. 153.
80 A. Horton (5.1.77).
81 R. Walford, Models, Simultations and Games, op. cit. (ed.) Walford, p. 95.
82 R.J. Chorley and P. Haggett, 'Models in Geography' (London, Methuen, 1967).
83 O. Slaymaker, Review of Chorley and Haggett: Frontiers in Geographical Teaching, 'Geographical Journal', Vol. 134, Part 2, September 1960.
84 P.R.C., Review of Chorley and Haggett: Frontiers in Geographical Teaching, 'Geography', Vol. 53, Part 4, November 1968.
85 Op. cit. Garnett, pp. 388-9.
86 Ibid., p. 389.
87 Ibid., p. 395.
88 C.A. Fisher, 'The Compleat Geographer', Inaugural Lecture, University of Sheffield (1959), p. 6.
89 C.A. Fisher, Whither Regional Geography? 'Geography', Vol. 55, Part 4, November 1970, pp. 373-4.
90 Ibid., p. 374.
91 To distinguish it from the 'new geography' current at the turn of the century.
92 Op. cit. Fisher, p. 388.
93 P. Hore, A Teacher Looks at the New Geography, op. cit. Walford, p. 132.
94 P.R. Thomas, Education and the New Geography, 'Geography', Vol. 55, Part 3, July 1970, p. 27.

95 Op. cit. Horton, Interview.
96 Interview, 14.12.76, Scraptoft College, Leicester.
97 R. Cooke and J.M. Johnson, 'Trends in Geography'
   (London, 1969).
98 Op. cit. Walford in Walford (ed.), p. 97.
99 Ibid., p. 2.
100 Ibid., p. 3.
101 D. Walker, Teaching the New Oxford and Cambridge Board
    Advanced Level Syllabus, 'Geography', Vol. 54, Part 4,
    November 1969, p. 438.
102 Op. cit. Thomas, p. 275.
103 Ibid., pp. 274-5.
104 Op. cit. Walker, p. 439.
105 'Society and the Young School Leaver', Working Paper
    No. 11 (London, HMSO, 1967), p. 3.
106 W.R.A. Ellis Interview, Sheffield Institute of Education,
    30.6.76.
107 Op. cit. Gowing, pp. 152-3.
108 Op. cit. Marchant, p. 134.
109 P.R. Gould, The New Geography, op. cit. Bale, Graves and
    Walford, pp. 35-6.
110 Oxford and Cambridge Schools Examination Board, 'New
    Syllabus for Advanced Level Geography' (1969).
111 Op. cit. Jones, pp. 197-8.
112 Schools Council, 'A New Professionalism for a Changing
    Geography' (London, December 1973), p. 3.
113 Op. cit. Walker, p. 6.
114 Interview, Department of Geography, Leicester University,
    14.12.76.
115 S.W. Wooldridge, 'The Geographer as Scientist (London, 1956).
116 B.P. Fitzgerald, Scientific Method, Quantitative Techniques
    and the Teaching of Geography, op. cit. Walford (ed.),
    p. 85.
117 M.H. Yeates, 'An Introduction to Quantitative Analysis in
    Economic Geography' (New York, McGraw Hill, 1968), p. 1.
118 Garnett, 'Reflections', p. 391.
119 S. Jones, 'Challenge of Change', p. 203.
120 R. Peet, 'Radical Geography' (London, Methuen, 1978).
121 G.R. Butterfield, The Scientific Method in Geography in
    R. Lee (ed.), 'Change and Tradition: Geography's New
    Frontiers' (Queen Mary College, London, 1977), p. 13.
122 D. Harvey, 'Social Justice and the City' (London, Arnold,
    1973), p. 128.

The origins of rural studies are both conceptually and chrono-
logically widely spread. It is possible to distinguish two
paramount themes, neither of which contributed exclusively to
the development of rural studies, and parts of which were
important in the development of biology and geography. Firstly
were those advocates who stressed the utilitarian aspects of
education allied to husbandry and agriculture. For instance, in
1651 Samuel Hartlib proposed in his 'Essay for Advancement of
Husbandry Learning' that the science of husbandry should be
taught to apprentices.[1] Later, alongside Britain's agricultural
revolution in the eighteenth and early nineteenth centuries a
number of private schools began to teach agriculture. In the
early nineteenth century a school at Tulketh Hall near Preston,
run by G. Edmundson, included the subject, as did A. Nesbitt's
school at Lambeth, then situated in London's rural environs.[2]

The second group advocated the use of the rural environment
as part of an educational method: they were concerned with
the pedagogic potential of such work. Rousseau summarised the
arguments in his book 'Emile', written in 1767. He believed
that nature should teach the child, not the classroom teacher
with his formal methods. The pedagogic implications of
Rousseau's thesis were first explored practically in 1799 by
Pestalozzi in his school Burgdorf in Switzerland, and later by
Froebel and Herbart in Germany.

In England the major influence was seen in the elementary
schools and in their curricula where the utilitarian rather than
pedagogic tradition was followed. The tradition emerged in the
schools of industry set up in the last decade of the eighteenth
century and related to the Poor Law system.[3] The curriculum
of these schools included gardening and simple agricultural
operations amongst other activities, such as tailoring and
cobbling for the boys and lace-making for the girls. They were
seen as vocational schools for the poorer classes.[4]

The curricula of the schools for industry were partly adopted
in the early monitorial schools set up by educationists like Joseph
Lancaster. Utilitarian intention is evidenced in the reports of
school inspectors appointed by the Board of Education to visit
schools in receipt of grants. Mr Tremenhearne reported in
1843 that in a Winkfield school: '. . . the garden work would
seem to invite familiar lectures on the simple points of natural
history which would lend a new interest to labour.'[5] In the later
nineteenth century the use of 'nature study' in addition to school

gardening was advocated by people such as T.H. Huxley and Matthew Arnold. Such advocates moved beyond utilitarian considerations and were concerned with nature study as an educational method, a separate epistemology, and drew their inspiration from German writing and practice. In 1869 T.H. Huxley said 'Let every child be instructed in those general views of the phenomena of Nature for which we have no exact English name . . . "Erdkunde" - earth knowledge - that is to say a general knowledge of the earth and what is on it, in it and about it.'[6] Similarly in 1876 Matthew Arnold had remarked that he would like to see ' . . . what the Germans call Naturkunde - knowledge of the facts and laws of nature - added as a class subject.'[7]

Both Arnold and Huxley were concerned to establish nature study as a foundation for more scientific investigation. Huxley felt that after the 'preliminary opening of the eyes to the great spectacle of the daily progress of Nature' and given familiarity with the 'three R's' the child should pass on to 'what is, in a strict sense, physical science'. Huxley saw physical science as composed of botany and physics: 'Every educational advantage which training in physical science can give is obtainable from the proper study of these two . . . and I should be contented for the present if they, added to our "Erdkunde", furnished the whole of the scientific curriculum of the school'.[8] Similarly, Arnold argued that children should be taught about 'the system of nature': 'Children . . . are taught something about the form and motion of the earth, about the causes of night and day and the seasons. But why are they taught nothing of the causes, for instance, of rain and dew, which are at least as easy to explain to them and not less interesting.'[9]

The arguments for nature study as a foundation for the teaching and learning of science were taken up in a number of government reports. In 1895, for instance, the Bryce Commission reported that 'Ample provision must be made in schools for scientific teaching, beginning if possible with natural history and the other sciences of observation and working up to chemistry and physics.'[10] In the last two decades of the nineteenth century the 'nature study' advocates and the utilitarian tradition of school gardening gained support from the fairly rapid conversion of agriculturalists. Selleck notes that there was 'evidence of an expectation that education might contribute to the solution of the problems of the agricultural industry in ways that were similar to those by which it had assisted other industry.' He felt that this expectation ' . . . manifested itself in a number of ways: the introduction of nature study into the curriculum, the attempt to improve rural education, the tendency to experiment with courses in the principles of agriculture, the popularisation of the "school journey", the pressure to start school museums.'[11] Recommendations for a change in school curricula began to appear in parliamentary reports. For instance, in 1882 the Technical Instruction Commission recommended that: 'In rural schools instruction in the principles and facts of agriculture, after suitable introductory object lessons, shall be made obligatory in the upper standards.'[12] In 1883 the subject, Principles of Agriculture, appeared for the first time in official lists and seven years later the Code of the Education Department recommended 'alternative courses which could be applied to rural schools'.[13] From this point on there seems to have been rapid growth, for Hudspeth reports that in 1897 school gardening was 'introduced as part of a general education rather than being used in a purely utilitarian manner', and when in 1900 the system of block grants to replace subject grants was introduced, gardening still carried a separate grant; in 1902, for instance, this grant was earned by 4,359 children in 289 schools.[14] The expansion Hudspeth refers to was partly a result of the efforts of the Agricultural Education Committee, formed in 1899, which campaigned actively and with some success. In 1900, for instance, the Board of Education issued a circular advising teachers to: ' . . . lose no opportunity of giving their scholars an intelligent knowledge of the surroundings of ordinary rural life and of showing them how to observe the processes of Nature for themselves.'[15] In spite of the interest shown by the Board of Education in 1904, when the secondary school curriculum was established by the issuing of the 'regulations', rural studies along with other utilitarian subjects with a working class orientation, was omitted. Rural education though was still taken seriously within the elementary sector with emphasis on those pupils not expected to proceed to the secondary stage. In keeping with this view secondary examinations (known from 1917 as 'school certificates') did not include rural studies.

Sample courses in rural education for elementary schools were prepared. In 1905 the Board of Education's 'Handbook of Suggestions for Teachers' produced a guide to school gardening, and in 1908 a pamphlet entitled 'Suggestions of Rural Education' offered specimen courses in nature study, gardening and rural economy intended to replace earlier draft courses prepared in 1901 and 1902.

The publication of a memorandum on the Principles and Methods of Rural Education by the Board of Education in 1911 stressed that the movement to implement rural education was designed to make teaching in rural schools ' . . . more practical, and to give it a more distinctly rural bias; to base it upon what is familiar to country children, and to direct it so that they may become handy and observant in their country surroundings.'[16] The Board of Education's statistics evidence a substantial growth in school gardens:

1904-5	551 schools
1907-8	1,171 schools
1911-12	2,458 schools

In the latter year 20 'departments' of gardening or rural education

are recorded.[17] Further, some counties had appointed expert
instructors to organise horticulture teaching in schools, and
other counties offered help for teachers to go on courses of
instruction at colleges and institutes of agriculture and horticulture.[18] Alongside these developments 'nature study' began
to spread into many elementary schools. In 1902 a nature study
exhibition in London stimulated the growth of the subject and
in the same year a Nature Study Society was formed which still
exists.

The pre-war growth of rural studies in school was summarised
as ' . . . an attempt to use education to further the interests
of rural industry in ways similar to those in which it was being
used in the city'.[19] The most obvious method of supporting rural
industry was to retain the labour force that emerged at the age
of 13 from the elementary schools. Many of these children
joined the 'drift from the land' which seriously threatened the
viability of the rural economy. Fabian Ware argued that developing an interest in his natural environment through education
'would not only make a better worker of the agriculturalist, but
would strengthen him morally against, at any rate, the lower
attractions of town life'.[20] The case for rural education was arti-
culated in Parliament by Sir Carne Rasch. His concern for education was one of reluctant involvement: 'To speak plainly, I
detest it so far as I am concerned. I am simply here as an
agricultural member, principally to keep the rates down and
particularly the rates for education.'[21] In another debate Rasch
had posed the question, 'What do Honourable Members think of
agricultural labourers' children? . . . Do they imagine that when
they leave school they turn into professors or Members of
Parliament?' and answered it asserting 'They do not want your
higher education: they do not want your curriculum or whatever
Hon. Members choose to call it . . .'[22] From here the argument
leads plainly to the need for studies particularly designed for
rural children.

During the 1914-18 war the country required home food to be
produced wherever possible. As a result, the war gave an
impetus to school gardening and the keeping of Livestock. The
Board of Education produced a circular called 'Public Elementary
Schools and the Supply of Food in Wartime'. This circular
asserted that 'Public opinion is in favour of the development in
rural schools of practical interests'.[23] In the period following the
war there is evidence of rural curricula being viewed and presented by the Board of Education not only as a general influence
in rural schools but also as a separate subject. In 1922 the
Board stated that 'teachers should regard their subject as rural
science'. The circular of that year develops the linkage between
rural studies and science first tentatively explored by F.E.
Green's 'A First Book of Rural Science' published in 1913: 'Study
of cultivated plants and the practice of their cultivation open up
so many by-paths of investigation that it is very likely to produce here and there among pupils that intelligent wonder and

curiosity which lie at the root of scientific research.[24] The link-age was also developed by the Thompson Committee on 'The Position of Natural Science in the Educational System' in 1918:

> There is general agreement amongst science teachers that the best preparation for the study of science at secondary school is a course of nature study up to the age of twelve. This course should be of as practical a character as possible and should aim at arousing an interest in natural phenomena and developing the powers of observation. Full use should be made of the opportunities afforded by the school garden to make the pupils acquainted with the spirit of scientific investigation.[25]

In the circular on 'Rural Education' of May 1925 the Board of Education again stressed links with science, asserting: 'It should be possible for the country child to learn something of the fundamental principles of mechanics, to make some study of air, water, heat and light with a view to understanding the processes of plant and animal life, and to apply simple tests in the examination of soils.' This circular, which was the precursor of a very influential Board pamphlet, set out the background to the new central initiative to establish rural education:

> The Board have on previous occasions made it clear to Local Education Authorities by means of Circulars, Pamphlets, Memoranda etc. that they consider it of great importance that the teaching in rural schools should be associated closely with the environment of the children; and much has been done in the course of the last fifteen or twenty years, especially through the development of instruction in Gardening and other forms of practical work . . . it appears desirable at the present time to emphasise afresh the principle that the education given in rural schools should be ultimately related to rural conditions of life.[26]

In defining the implications for syllabus design of 'rural edu-cation' the Board followed along guidelines laid down in 1922 in a book by Gunton and Hawkes. These two rural studies teachers envisaged their subject as 'the Hub of the Curriculum Wheel'. All the subjects of the curriculum were to be taught within a rural, practical context.[27] Similarly, the Board considered the importance of a rural bias in elementary science, arithmetic, geography, history, English, manual instruction and domestic subjects.

In Hertfordshire the aims of rural education were pursued in a 'Suggested Syllabus of Rural Education' for 'Older Children of both Sexes in Public Elementary Schools'. The syllabus was approved by the County Education Committee at a meeting on 7 January 1927 and was then circulated to schools.[28] In 1929 an HMS Inspector prepared a report on the workings of the syllabus, which concluded: 'Perhaps the chief value of the "syllabus" has been the encouragement of the right outlook among rural teachers towards their special problem.' The syllabus presented ' . . . a new situation which gave confidence to many Head Teachers who were in sympathy with the doctrine but were timorous of launching out.'[29] In 1929, 33 Hertfordshire elementary schools were involved in experiments related to the syllabus. The report deals with the 'Effect on Ordinary School Subjects'. Whilst all subjects were affected, in certain schools, apart from the general improvement in 'Handwork and Gardening', the most successful linkage, as in past initiatives, was with elementary science and nature study. 'This section of the syllabus is developing very well indeed, and the opportunities afforded by the farm, the garden and the countryside for observational work and simple deductions are being well utilized.' Hence the report notes: 'The school garden is being regarded more and more as a laboratory for experiments.'[30] The responsibility for contextualising the 'ordinary' subjects of the curriculum in such a rural and practical manner was seen as mainly that of the headmaster, who 'should so co-ordinate the outdoor and observational work with the ordinary subjects of the curriculum that the former becomes the starting point from which the more generalised instruction proceeds.'[31] As well as the inspector's report, the results of the Hertfordshire scheme were also commented on in the locality. At the re-opening of the Merchant Taylors' School at Ashwell, the Chairman of the Education Committee made a clear statement of the Council's views which was reported in the local press: 'they particularly regretted . . . the way the urban centres were growing more and more and the rural districts losing their population to the towns, and they felt that the scheme would help keep people in the rural areas.'[32] Carson records that in Hertfordshire, there was opposition to the scheme: 'There is no doubt that working people in the villages resented this attempt to keep them in their place, however good the motives, and the writer has frequently come across the deep suspicion of rural studies held by farmworking families who, above all, did not want their sons trained to stay on the land.'[33]

Nationally, opposition to the scheme was summarised in a book by Margaret Ashby on 'The Country School'. In the villages she investigated, only 40 per cent of the boys stayed on the land, and only 10 per cent of the girls worked on the land or married agricultural workers. As a doctor she especially noted the effects of poverty on rural children and posed the question, 'Is a rural bias justified morally?' and answered that 'Economic forces are infinitely stronger than school and unless we are certain that these forces favour a rural career for the children, it is plainly wrong for the school to press them in that direction.' She adds conclusively: 'If the rural labourer's child appreciated the story of his own class any tendency he might have to leave the country would be reinforced.'[34] Undoubtedly, awareness of the opposition to their schemes

caused a new emphasis to be given to the Board of Education's
'Education and the Countryside' published in 1934. This time
the Board argued that their pamphlet was 'not concerned
primarily with the vocational training of those who will earn
their livelihood in the country districts', but with the 'various
ways in which schools are making the environment of their
pupils contribute to the fashioning of a good general education.'[135] Besides, the pamphlet argued, rural life was improving
rapidly and figures were provided to substantiate a view that
the drift from the land was less significant than had been
widely thought.

Significant progress in the establishment of 'rural studies
organisers' in many counties is reported in the pamphlet: 'In
most counties, some officer, usually well qualified in horticulture, is available to give expert advice on school gardening
problems. The amount of time devoted to this varies from county
to county and depends largely upon the value attached by the
authority to practical work in rural schools.'[136] In fact the value
attached to practical rural education was subsequently changed
by the 1944 Education Act and the ensuing reorganisation of
the educational system. Some indications of a change in the
official Board of Education view can be discerned before this
date. In 1943 the Report of the Committee of the Secondary
School Examinations Council appointed by the President of the
Board of Education noted, with regard to natural science:

> The framing of all courses and the choice of illustrative
> material should in our opinion be influenced so far as may be
> feasible by the environment of the school. Yet that influence
> should not be so great as to cause the syllabus to become
> 'specialised'; we urge this particularly with regard to natural
> science in rural schools, for we do not think it in the interest
> of agriculture or rural industries themselves that the teach-
> ing in schools should be directed too closely to these ends.[37]

The Board's exhortations regarding specialisation were soon to
prove abortive.

RURAL STUDIES SINCE THE 1944 EDUCATION ACT

After the Second World War two influences were particularly
important in redefining rural studies. Firstly, 'stimulated by
the thinking that had produced the 1944 Education Act and the
secondary modern schools, teachers began to search again in
our rural heritage for whatever' might be used educationally to
advantage.'[138] Alongside this search 'the effect of the 1944 Act
was to alter the school organisation so that teaching in secondary
schools became largely specialist in nature.'[139] At first, the
changes in secondary organisation did not radically alter the
inter-war potential which rural studies had exhibited. Teachers

and educationists continued in search for new educational
methods of using the rural environment, and certain schools
continued in focusing their whole curriculum around investigations of this environment. In 1950 A.B. Allen saw rural
studies at the centre of the curriculum in country schools:

> Taking agriculture and horticulture as our foundation subjects,
> we see the interrelationship within the curriculum. Agriculture
> leads into elementary science, general biology, nature study,
> world history and world geography. It also leads into math-
> ematics with its costing problems, mensuration and balance
> sheets. Horticulture leads into elementary science (and so is
> linked with agriculture), and local history.[40]

At the same time the Central Advisory Council for Education was
exhorting teachers: 'The first and rather obvious point is that
what a school teaches should be connected with the environment.
That is, the curriculum should be so designed as to interpret
the environment to the boys and girls who are growing up in
it.'[41] In some of the early secondary modern schools this vision
of rural studies as the 'curriculum hub' connecting school to
environment and life had a marked influence. In 1949, A.J.
Fuller, a keen gardener, was given the headship of Wrotham
Secondary School in Kent. He appointed R. Colton to teach
sciences and S. Carson to teach rural science. The new school
consisted of three huts in a field. Carson taught 4F - i.e.
Fourth Year Farming. There were also 4P (Practical) and 4A
(Academic). However, since there were no examinations the
farming class often attracted some of the brightest pupils.
Recruitment often took place through the Young Farmer's Club.
'There was a less rigid division between school and community.'
The agricultural apprenticeship scheme had just started: 'The
best boys, the most able, who today would be in the sixth form,
went into farming gladly. Good farms, good employers!' Carson
built the activities of the class around the rural environment.
'I think the inspiration probably came from Fuller.' 'I had a
strong feeling that education wasn't just book learning . . . it
involved commonsense applied to a problem.'

Carson had 4F for all subjects except science, which Colton
taught, and woodwork. 'I taught them maths, English, history,
etc. All tied in completely with the rural environment . . . for
example maths I based as much as possible on the farm activities.
In fact I used a series of books which were popular then called
"Rural Arithmetic".' In English: 'We were fairly poorly off for
books in those days frankly, so we read a lot of literature
associated with the countryside . . . a lot of English was
straightforwardly connected with the farm.'

As the tripartite system of education gradually emerged in the
form of new school buildings and modified curricula, it became
clear that rural studies and gardening were only developing in
the secondary modern schools. In 1952 a questionnaire survey

of gardening and rural studies teachers in Kent produced, with three exceptions, the reply from grammar and technical schools of 'subjects not taught', whilst in 63 of the 65 secondary modern schools the subject was given an important position in the curriculum.[42]

By this time, however, secondary modern schools were increasingly concerning themselves with external examinations. The effect on Carson's scheme in Wrotham was echoed in other schools which had sought to build the curriculum around the rural environment: 'The advent of external examinations gradually prevented the more capable children from taking part and eventually led the scheme to be aimed at the less able children only.'[43] When Carson moved to Royston Secondary School in Hertfordshire in 1954 he noted the changing atmosphere in secondary modern schools. The adviser, Geoff Whitby, had run an elementary school in the 1950s at Ashwell in Hertfordshire which had epitomised the 'hub of the curriculum' vision of rural studies. However, the head of Royston, Mr. Young, had little time for such a view.

> He didn't see it as rural education in that sense because he was already thinking ahead to raising the standards of this school to what would eventually be C.S.E. The classes were streamed. I only ever got the lowest of the three streams. While at first I could do what I liked with that bottom stream and I did the same sort of thing as in Kent, over the next few years this was whittled away from me as more specialism invaded the curriculum, and these kids eventually spent practically no time running the farm.[44]

A similar point was made in an article by Mervyn Pritchard, a St Albans headmaster who later chaired the School Council Working Party on Rural Studies:

> There appear to be two extremes of thought in secondary modern schools - (a) a concentration on external examinations (b) those who won't have them at any price. In those schools where the brighter pupils are examined it is unusual to find rural science as one of the subjects taken and as the pupils concentrate more and more narrowly on their examination subjects, it is unusual to find rural science used as a social subject such as craft, art or music may be.
> Even where pupils are not examined there appears to be a concentration of the teaching of the subject in streams of classes of duller children.[45]

Pritchard's working party later summed up this phase: 'The old concept of the subject predominantly as gardening, often gardening for the backward boys only, did not die easily'.[46] Not only did it not die easily; subsequent events were to prove this practical version was alive and well decades later.

In 1957 the Herfordshire Association of Teachers of Gardening
and Rural Subjects, worried by the loss of status and influence
of the subject, carried out a similar survey to the Kent one.
This time, significantly, questionnaires were sent only to
secondary modern schools. The financial treatment of rural
studies showed clearly the priorities of the secondary modern
headmasters: 'It is surprising to learn . . . that some schools
allow the rural science department no money at all while others
are so small that the financial pinch entails great worry to the
teacher.'[47] Of the 39 schools that returned questionnaires, 15
had no classroom allotted for rural studies.[48]

Of the 53 teachers involved, 26 were unqualified in gardening
or rural studies[49] and the general 'image' of rural studies
teachers is elegantly caught in the illustration overleaf. Not
only was the status of the rural studies teacher questionable
but his isolation on the staff was often confirmed by placing the
rural studies facilities in a distant corner of the school grounds.

The concern of rural studies teachers at the deteriorating
status and position of their subject led to a variety of responses
in the latter part of the 1950s. Mervyn Pritchard exhorted: 'As
often as possible, the rural studies teacher should mix with his
colleagues, even if he has to kick off muddy gum boots to drink
his cup of tea. Much useful interchange of knowledge and
information is carried out among the staffroom gossip. Informal
discussion of school policy can be helped along judiciously by
the rural studies teacher. Frequent contact can convince our
colleagues of one's normality and value.'[50] Apart from such
exhortations, some teachers were concerned to develop a
'Philosophy of rural studies'. In 1954 Carson and Colton produced
a paper which appeared in the Kent Association Journal, and
later in 1957, in the Lincolnshire 'Rural Science News'. It was a
systematic attempt to think through a subject philosophy, a first,
embryonic attempt to define a subject, and one equipped with a
contemporary rationale. They argued: 'For this study to justify
its inclusion in the school curriculum, it must be shown to play
a vital part in developing a fully educated citizen.'[51] Carson and
Colton were editors of the Kent Association of Teachers of
Gardening and Rural Science Journal. The 'Rural Science'
appendage was added at Carson's insistence when the Association
was formed in 1949.[52] The Association was predated by an
ephemeral association of rural science teachers in 1925, and by
a small association in Nottingham founded in 1940, and the
Manchester Teachers' Gardening Circle founded in 1941.[53] By
1954 the Kent Journal was beginning to define a philosophy for
rural studies and soon after claimed, 'this Association has constantly sought parity of esteem with the rest of the curriculum
for all rural studies'.[54]

The teachers' changing perception of their work is reflected
in the changes in the name of the Kent Association: in 1958
they changed their name from 'the Kent Association of Teachers
of Gardening and Rural Science' to 'The Kent Association of

Teachers of Rural Science'; in 1959 this changed to 'The Kent
Teachers' Rural Studies Association'. Their Journal proclaimed:
'Rural studies embraces all subjects which we know on the timetable as nature study, gardening, rural science and farming',[55]
a sign that a new phase in claiming curriculum territory and
promoting the subject was underway.

— "The Rural Science Teacher must take part in
activities which are the heart of the
organisation of the school Society" —

THE GROWTH OF SUBJECT ASSOCIATIONS

In February 1956, R.F. Morgan wrote in the Kent Journal that
efforts were being made to contact 'similar organisations to our
own with a view to exchanging ideas and one day of forming an

association on a national basis'. At the time he reported that apart from Kent, only Middlesex and Nottinghamshire had flourishing associations. 'Devonshire had a Rural Science Teachers' Association but it has now been absorbed by the Science Teachers' Association.' Dorset, Essex, Shropshire and the West Riding of Yorkshire were all keen to form associations.[56] More significantly, R. Colton, who had just left Kent to become Rural Studies Organiser in the Holland division of Lincolnshire, was about to form an association there. S. Carson, who had recently moved to Hertfordshire, formed an Association of Teachers of Gardening and Rural Subjects at a meeting in January 1957: 'The object of that [forming the association] was really to raise the status of rural studies and get the facilities for the subject which other subjects got . . . but the situation was never there to achieve any more than that it was specialism in a school and should be adequately supported.'

Carson's final sentence here summarises the situation which rural studies had come to occupy by 1957. As the Kent Journal noted, 'with the building of large secondary schools within the last few years, full-time specialists are needed.'[57] Rural studies was just one of a range of specialisms in the secondary modern schools. Moreover it was of low status and historically poorly organised.

Carson saw that rural studies had to 'adapt or perish'. In a world of examinable specialist subjects the advocation of rural studies as an all-pervasive educational approach was no longer feasible.

By this time I'd really given up hope of getting rural studies seen in the way I'd taught it in Kent. Then I saw it as a specialist subject which had weak links.
My alternative vision . . . was that a lot of kids don't learn through paper and pencil and that we do far too much of this. A lot of kids could achieve success and use all the mental skills that we talk about in the classroom such as analysing and comparing through physical activities . . . With the farm it was a completely renewing set of problems and the fact that it was a farm was incidental. You were thinking in educational terms of process with these kids.
That's the sort of dreams I was well aware of giving up and I talked about it a number of times. I've always felt dissatisfied since and I've met many teachers who'd come across the same realisation - not in such explicit terms as they'd never had the chance of doing it, whereas I had. I meet them now in schools.

In 1958 Carson took over from Geoff Whitby as the organiser for rural education in Hertfordshire. He pursued his belief that to survive, rural studies had to be defined and organised as a subject. 'I visited the secondary school teachers whom I knew through the association, and stimulated them to get themselves

organised to try and get any kids other than the least able, to
get them better facilities in their schools. . . . "If you're not
given a proper classroom, refuse to teach this subject in any old
place and as adviser call me in" was what I told my teachers . . .
If it rained, they all just sat in the bicycle shed.' The problems
in raising standards in Hertfordshire convinced Carson and his
Hertfordshire colleagues that Richard Morgan's tentative plans
for a National Association, first mooted in 1956, represented 'a
way to raise the standard and status of rural studies because
we decided that unless it was raised nationally we wouldn't be
able to do it in Hertfordshire.' In July 1960 Carson called a
meeting of County Rural Studies Associations at High Leigh
Conference Centre in Hertfordshire. The delegates were welcomed by the Hertfordshire County Education Officer, S.T.
Broad. In October 1960 the Conference decided to form a
National Association by affiliating County Associations at a fee
of £5 per year. Six counties affiliated in this manner - Hertfordshire, Nottinghamshire, Essex, Northumberland, West Riding of
Yorkshire and Middlesex. Conference saw an 'urgent need to
institute an enquiry into the provision made by various counties
and the drawing up of guidance on the teaching of the subject
as has recently been done in their own subjects by the Maths
Association and the Science Masters' Association.'[58]
    In the first National Journal it was noted that the committee of
the Association would 'take every opportunity to promote the
teaching of rural studies'. The 1961 Journal also stated in 'The
Constitution':

> The aim of this association shall be 'to develop and coordinate
> rural studies'. Rural studies includes nature study, natural
> history pursuits of all kinds, the study of farming and the
> activities of the countryside, as taught in primary and
> secondary schools. Rural studies should be regarded as an art,
> a science and a craft; a subject as well as a method of teach-
> ing. It has unique educational, cultural and recreational
> significance.[59]

By 1961 eleven new County Rural Studies Associations had been
formed and affiliated; The Association continued to expand
throughout the decade and by 1970 had added 12 new affiliated
county associations.

THE ESTABLISHMENT OF SECONDARY MODERN SCHOOLS
AND THE ADVENT OF CSE

The examinations situation found in the National Associations'
1962 survey was characterised by a 'confusing variety'.[60] A
total of 188 schools took 'O' levels in such papers as biology,
rural biology and agricultural science but others sat exams set
by the College of Preceptors, the City and Guilds and a variety

of other external bodies. Ninety-one schools entered pupils for 'area or other local teacher-controlled examinations'.[61] At this time the CSE was about to be introduced and the report speculated that 'the proportion involved in examinations will no doubt rise'.[62] However, the report added, rural studies teachers 'are by nature opposed to the competitive and restrictive aspects of examinations in schools, and for this reason have only accepted the position reluctantly. The National Association with the aid of many county associations, has spent a good deal of time and effort on experimenting with new types of evaluation designed to encourage original courses in schools.'[63] The reluctance of rural studies teachers was evident from the very beginning of the moves towards CSE. In 1959, in a report on the first year of the North Hertfordshire Certificate of Education in Rural Science, Mr W.A. Dove mentioned the problems pupils had with the examination: 'Keeping in mind the hard fact that few "A" stream boys take gardening' he said that 'the panel decided that the exam should consist of a theory paper so compiled that weakness in the use of the English language would not be a heavy handicap.' Concluding his report, Dove commented, 'I think this exam was a successful experiment . . . if we must have exams in the secondary modern school.'[64]

The spread of the CSE drew attention to the dilemma that faced advocates of rural studies. A good deal of the energies of the associations centred on gaining more facilities, time and better qualified staff for the subject. But in the increasingly exam-conscious secondary moderns little success could be hoped for in a non-examinable subject. To break out of the cycle of deprivation faced by the subject the only way forward seemed to be in defining an examinable area. By 1962 Carson had realised the cul-de-sac which the National Association's efforts had entered:

> We never forgot our aims were to see this subject get taught to *all* children . . . that facilities should be better, etc. Then it became increasingly obvious to me and one or two others, that it wasn't going to get anywhere! That however many good ideals we might have and however much people like Comber[65] might stimulate us and say what good we were doing; in fact it was not going to be realised.

As a result the Association initiated a major experiment by which to test a new rural studies exam. The experiment was reported in the Herts. journal which said that following a meeting of representatives of rural study associations, the panel of HM Inspectors for rural studies and Dr Wrigley of the Curriculum Study Group of the Ministry of Education, a joint experiment was conducted in schools in North Hertfordshire, Nottinghamshire, Staffordshire, Lincolnshire and East Sussex 'to test the validity of our examination scheme. This is being evaluated by the Ministry of Education's Study Group'.[66]

Sean Carson was involved in the experiment: 'It was an attempt to find out whether exams were a good thing. We were trying to find out whether we should remain outside or whether we should have anything to do with them.'

The moves to devise an examination in the subject posed a number of problems for rural studies. For behind the rhetoric of the advocates and subject associations, and apart from a few innovatory schools and teachers, most rural studies teachers continued to base their work on gardening. The subject's essentially practical assignments were not easily evaluated by written examinations. The draft report on the experimental examinations commented that to date: 'Few examinations included much practical work and rarely was there any assessment of the candidate's practical ability and achievement over a period of time.'[67] These examinations produced 'unfavourable backwash effects in the teaching of rural studies': 'In order to produce candidates who would be successful in the written examination teachers felt that they had to concentrate on written work to the neglect of practical activities which are the essential features of rural studies.'[68] Of the new CSEs in rural studies that were being introduced in 1966 the report commented: 'Rural studies teachers were stimulated by the prospect of an external examination at fifth year level, but were concerned lest the written papers of the traditional form of examination should come to dominate examinations in rural studies and so influence detrimentally the nature of the course.'[69]

By this time it was clear that a number of rural studies teachers felt that the worst of these fears about accepting examinations were being fulfilled. A teacher at Bass Hill Secondary School in Hertfordshire wrote:

> What has been forgotten in our exuberance to thrust forward rural studies as an examinable subject is the mainspring of its very creation. This is the joy, experience, and most of all, the practical and useful scientific logic which is gained during the release from far-sighted concepts which many other subjects tend to involve themselves in.

He saw rural studies as particularly related to its main clientele in the non-examination streams of secondary moderns: 'Many will agree with me in saying that the children who gain most of all from rural studies are the academically less able.' This group were adversely affected by the kind of examinations which had been introduced: 'Once again we can see the unwanted children of lower intelligence being made servants of the juggernaut of documented evidence, the inflated examination.' He concluded:

> True education is not for every man the scrap of paper he leaves school with. Dare we as teachers admit this? Dare we risk our existence by forcibly expressing our views on this? While we pause after the first phase of our acceptance, are we

to rely on exams for all, to prove ourselves worthy of the
kindly eye of the state?[70]

The questions this teacher asked were at the time being answered
by his rural studies colleagues. In 1962 Carson and Colton had
written: 'To our minds, there would be very much less value in
the subject if it were taught merely as an assemblage of facts
concerning plants and animals.'[71] Yet reluctantly Carson ultimately accepted examinations. For him the reasons were clear:

Sean Carson: Because if you didn't you wouldn't get any
money, any status, any intelligent kids.
Ivor Goodson: Did you ever think 'this is going to be a big
problem, the beginning of something . . .'
Sean Carson: No, I didn't see that as clearly as I maybe
should have done. I just thought 'if you're outside this you've
had it in schools'. It was already happening inside some
schools. Where a [rural studies] teacher was leaving, they
didn't fill the place, because they gave it to someone in the
examination set up.
Ivor Goodson: So you had to climb aboard that?
Sean Carson: Yes, or rural studies would have definitely
disappeared.

The correspondence relating to the draft report on the experimental rural studies exams implies that the overwhelming concern
of those involved was with the 'existence' and status of the
subject. Speaking of the publication of the draft report in
bulletin form, Mervyn Pritchard wrote: 'The problem remains
whether the Bulletin in its new form will enhance the prestige
of rural studies';[72] and Richard Morgan, Secretary of the
National Association, worried that the report '. . . has played
down our case considerably and seems deliberately to have
reduced the impact of rural studies as a subject'.[73] The concerns
of Pritchard and Morgan imply that by 1966-7 rural studies
teachers, having largely accepted the inevitability of an examination in their subject, were worried by the image thus presented. The Rural Studies Association had developed a definition
of the subject as a broadly-based, potentially scientific discipline.
When teachers came to draw up syllabuses related to their practice the predominance of gardening was clearly illustrated:
'Once you began to write a syllabus it became obvious. As soon
as you enter the exam market it becomes obvious what is actually
happening in school.' Yet the close scrutiny of the subject
engendered by the syllabus definition required for examinations
as well as illustrating that most teaching focused on horticultural
training, also offered the opportunity to work out more broad-
based definitions. A number of rural studies teachers, initially
working with CSE began to seize this opportunity, developing
new courses and questioning the horticultural tradition on which
rural studies had come to be based. This initiative was to form

the basis of the rural studies response to environmental education which is considered in Part Three.

THE EVOLUTION OF RURAL STUDIES

The History of rural studies, particularly in the twentieth
century, indicates the close connection between the changing
patterns and 'arenas' of the educational system and the way in
which rural studies are defined and promoted. In the elementary
schools, rural studies was often seen as a major influence per-
vading the curriculum, the 'hub of the curriculum wheel'. This
was especially the case in those rural areas where a specific
brand of rural education was promoted, with strong utilitarian
or pedagogic emphases. At this stage in its development the
links between rural studies, the educational system and the
changing national economy were clearly exhibited.

In the period following the 1944 Education Act as the new
tripartite system slowly developed the character of rural studies
depended largely on local circumstances and initiatives. By the
early 1950s, however, it became clear that the subject was only
taking root in the secondary modern sector. The 1952 Kent
questionnaire gives detailed evidence of a subject often taught
only to the less able boys, inadequately equipped with toolsheds,
storing space and classrooms and with substantial numbers of
the teachers involved inadequately qualified or unqualified in
the subject. The picture of a low-status subject was not only
confirmed, but exacerbated by the growth of specialised curricula
and examinations in secondary modern schools. In this new
situation the subject was faced not only with status problems,
but with actual survival problems. Carson talks of even the
activities with the less able being 'whittled away from one as
more and more specialism invaded the curriculum'. Pritchard
noted how 'in those schools where the brighter pupils are
examined it is unusual to find rural science as one of the subjects
taken'. Increasingly as secondary modern schools became more
examination conscious, rural studies disappeared or was seen as
a very low priority area of the curriculum. The resources of
the school were aimed at those subjects which were examinable,
and through which the school could build up a record of examination successes.

In the mid-fifties, faced with status and survival problems
some rural studies teachers began to appreciate the urgent need
to organise themselves into a subject association - a pattern
followed by those subjects successfully embodied in grammar
and secondary modern curricula and examinations. The object
of forming the association was seen by the prime mover, Carson,
as being 'to raise the status of rural studies and get the facilities
for the subject which the other subjects got' - a cry echoed by
the Kent Association three years earlier: this association has
constantly sought parity of esteem with the rest of the cur-

riculum for all rural studies.

The new subject association saw as its prime motive the development of school facilities for the subject and improved supply and training of subject teachers. The growth of CSE also ensured that the subject association had to face the need for rural studies examinations. This involved changing much of the rhetoric with which rural studies had been promoted in earlier periods and a number of dedicated subject teachers spoke out against this development.

In the early stages the oscillation between the utilitarian and pedagogic arguments for the subject was continuous, but 'academic' arguments were never seriously entertained or deployed because the subject never attained Layton's stage 2. However, the growth in importance of external examinations introduced for the first time an academic dimension. Despite opposition which recognised the threat to the utilitarian and pedagogic advantages of the subject, the association went ahead with framing examinations because as Carson said 'if you didn't you would not get any money, any status, any intelligent kids'.

The stragegy involved substantial difficulties: for the first time rural studies had publicly to announce and formally define its content. Whilst opening up new risks to the subject in the fight for survival and status, new strategies and potentialities began to emerge among the more ambitious subject advocates, which led the subject away from its utilitarian and pedagogic traditions.

NOTES

1 S. Hartlib, Essay on Advancement of Husbandry Learning (1651), quoted in J.W. Adamson, 'Pioneers of Modern Education 1600-1700' (Cambridge University Press, 1951), pp. 130-31.
2 W.H. Hudspeth, 'The History of the Teaching of Biological Subjects including Nature Study in English Schools since 1600' (M.Ed. thesis, University of Durham, 1962), pp. 69-70.
3 The Poor Law Act was passed in 1834.
4 S. Carson, 'The Use of Content and Effective Objectives in Rural Studies Courses' (M.Ed. thesis, University of Manchester, 1967), p. 4.
5 Minutes of the Committee in Council on Education 1842-43, Board of Education, pp. 545-6, quoted op. cit. Carson, p. 15.
6 T.H. Huxley, A Liberal Education and where to find it, in his 'Collected Essays', Vol. III (London, Macmillan, 1905), pp. 123-35.
7 M. Arnold, 'Reports on Elementary Schools 1852-1882' (London, Macmillan, 1889), p. 191.
8 Huxley, 'Collected Essays', pp. 123-5.
9 Arnold Reports on Elementary Schools, p. 191.
10 Board of Education, 'Report of the Royal Commission on

Secondary Education' (HMSO, 1895), p. 284.
11 R.T.W. Selleck, 'The New Education', p. 128.
12 'Second Report of the Royal Commissioners on Technical Instruction' (London, HMSO, 1884), Vol. 1, p. 537, quoted op. cit. Selleck, pp. 128-9.
13 Selleck, 'The New Education', p. 129.
14 Hudspeth, 'History of Biological Subjects', p. 224.
15 Board of Education, 'The Curriculum of the Rural School', Circular 435, April 1900, quoted op. cit. Selleck, p. 129.
16 Board of Education, 'Memorandum on the Principles and Methods of Rural Education' 1911, p. 7.
17 Board of Education, 'Report for 1904-1939' (London, HMSO, 1939).
18 Board of Education, 'Report for 1910-1911' (London, HMSO, 1911).
19 Selleck, 'The New Education', p. 150.
20 F. Ware, 'Educational Reform' (London, Methuen, 1900), p. 62.
21 'British Parliamentary Debates,' Fourth Series, 1906, Vol. CLVI, col. 1562.
22 'British Parliamentary Debates', Fourth Series, 1902, Vol. CVII, col. 935.
23 Board of Education, 'Public Elementary Schools and the Supply of Food in Wartime' (London, HMSO, 1916), p. 12.
24 Board of Education, 'Suggestions for the Consideration of Teachers and Others Concerned in the Work of Public Elementary Schools - The Teaching of Gardening', Circular 1293 (London, HMSO, 1922).
25 Board of Education, 'Report of the Committee on the Position of Natural Science in the Educational System of Great Britain' (London, HMSO, 1918), pp. 60-61.
26 Board of Education, 'Rural Education', Circular 1365, 28 May 1925 (London, HMSO), and 'Rural Education: Adaptation of Instruction to the Needs of Rural Areas', Educational Pamphlets, No. 46 (London, HMSO, 1926), p. 6.
27 H.W. Gunton and C.W. Hawkes, 'School Gardening and Handwork' (Pitman, London, 1922).
28 Hertfordshire County Council, 'Suggested Syllabus for Rural Education for Older Children of Both Sexes in Public Elementary Schools', No. 1467, C.P. 222, 1926-1927.
29 Hertfordshire County Council 'H.M.'s Inspectors' Report upon the Working of the Rural Education Syllabus in Public Elementary Schools', No. 1581, C.P. 19, 1929-1930, p. 1.
30 Ibid., p. 4.
31 Herfordshire Syllabus, 1926, p. 2.
32 Ashwell's Important Place in Education, 'Hertfordshire Express', 18 October 1933.
33 Carson M. Ed., p. 37.
34 Dr M.K. Ashby 'The Country School' (Oxford University Press, 1929), p. 171.
35 Board of Education 'Education and the Countryside', Pamphlet

No. 38 (London, HMSO, 1934), p. 5.
36 Ibid., p. 10.
37 Norwood Report, p. 108.
38 S. Carson and R. Colton, 'The Teaching of Rural Studies' (London, Edward Arnold, 1962), p. 3.
39 Schools Council Working Paper 24, 'Rural Studies in Secondary Schools' (London, Evans/Methuen Education, 1969), p. 5.
40 A.B. Allen, 'Rural Education' (London, Allman and Son, 1950), p. 16.
41 Report of the Central Advisory Council for Education (England), 'School and Life' (London, HMSO, 1947), p. 35.
42 'Journal of the Kent Association of Teachers of Gardening and Rural Science', April 1953, pp. 4-6.
43 Carson M. Ed., p. 48.
44 'Journal of the Kent Teachers Rural Studies Association', No. 17, May 1961, p. 3.
45 M. Pritchard, The Rural Science Teacher in the School Society, 'Journal of the Hertfordshire Association of Gardening and Rural Subjects', No. 2, September 1957, p. 4.
46 Schools Council Working Paper 24, p. 5.
47 Pritchard, 'The Rural Science Teacher', p. 5.
48 'Report on Rural Subjects and Gardening in Secondary Schools in Hertfordshire', 1957 (mimeo).
49 Ibid., p. 5.
50 Ibid.
51 'The Kent Association of Teachers of Gardening and Rural Science Journal', No. 4, 1954. Also appeared in 'Rural Science News', Vol. 10, No. 1, January 1957.
52 Carson, M. Ed. thesis, p. 25.
53 Ibid., p. 53.
54 'Kent Association of Teachers of Gardening and Rural Science Journal', No. 10, September 1957, p. 7.
55 'Kent Journal', No. 13, March 1959, p. 1.
56 'Kent Journal', No. 7, February 1956, p. 22.
57 'Kent Journal', No. 12, September 1958, p. 1.
58 S. Carson, The National Rural Studies Association, 'Journal of the Hertfordshire Association of Teachers of Gardening and Rural Subjects', No. 8, October 1960, p. 21.
59 'National Rural Studies Association Journal', 1961, p. 5.
60 'Rural Studies: A Survey of Facilities' (London, Pergamon, 1963), p. 33.
61 Ibid., p. 32.
62 Ibid., p. 33.
63 Ibid.
64 W.A. Dove, Report on the North Hertfordshire Certificate of Education in Rural Science, 'Journal of Hertfordshire Association of Teachers of Gardening and Rural Subjects', No. 5, April 1959, pp. 40-41.
65 L.C. Comber, HMI with responsibility for rural education.
66 The Certificate of Secondary Education, 'Hertfordshire Teachers' Rural Studies Association Journal', October, 1963.

67 The Certificate of Secondary Education Experimental
Examination - Rural Studies Draft Report, 1966 (not published by Schools Council).
68 Ibid.
69 Ibid.
70 P.L. Quant, Rural Studies and the Newsom Child, 'Hertfordshire Rural Studies Association Journal', April 1967, p. 12.
71 S. Carson and R. Colton, 'Teaching of Rural Studies', p. 4.
72 M. Pritchard, letter to A.J. Prince, 7 October 1966.
73 R. Morgan letter to M. Pritchard, 8 October 1966.

PART THREE

Relationships Between Subjects: The Territorial Nature of Subject Conflict

7 'CLIMATES OF OPINION' WITH RESPECT TO EDUCATION

AND THE ENVIRONMENT, 1960-1975

As we have seen notions of 'environment' already existed in each of the three subjects whose fortunes we are following, in geography and biology through the fieldwork tradition and in rural studies if it could survive the transition to an exam-oriented curriculum. However, in the 1960s the 'environment' began to emerge as a major idea in its own right and to influence policy making in a number of ways. At this time a separate 'Department of the Environment' was designated by the government in response to a growing public concern with environmental matters; and by the end of the decade Max Nicholson was able to declare without seeming precipitous: 'It has been said that the one thing in the world which is invincible is an idea whose time has come. Such an idea in these days is the care of man's environment.'[1] In reviewing the influence of such a powerful idea it will be useful to note the different levels of the education system at which ideas can arise and be taken up and implemented. Some ideas, for instance, can influence thinking at an international level both through the activities of international agencies and through press and television. The idea of a Ministry of the Environment was not of British origin, and environmental legislation has always been influenced by international comparisons. Though the decentralised pattern of government and the language difference between countries has made it particularly difficult for educational ideas to penetrate from Europe, professional links across the Atlantic have always been significant. Curriculum development, educational technology, and more recently, accountability have all gathered strength in North American before becoming significant in Britain.

However, for ideas to be taken up and promoted at national level they have to be seen as relevant and capable of being adapted to specific national contexts. Curriculum development was transformed into a teacher-based activity when it encountered the greater power and status of the British teaching profession, and accountability may well meet a similar fate. New ideas cannot easily be implemented at national level in Britain, though as we shall see later they can be rejected if they challenge the hegemony of the subject-based examination systems. They have to be translated down to the local level or school level. At the local level we meet the people who have direct contact with schools without being part of them - advisers, teacher centre wardens, college and university lecturers - and the 'cosmoplitan' heads and senior teachers who seem to share membership of the local professional community with their more specific school responsibilities. It would appear to be among such groups that the fads and fashions of the educational world are manufactured, sold and exchanged.

Then at the school level, also, ideas get invented, imported, metamorphose and die. Parlett's notions of 'ideas in currency', invented to describe the nature of policy discussions in an American college, seems equally appropriate to the English secondary school. These ideas: 'Circulate around the college and . . . represent components of the informal system of college thinking. Ideas in currency are working hypotheses, constructions of reality, mini-descriptions and so forth. They represent a series of almost perceptual categories that permit ordering of experience. However, they also act as expectations and often these are self-confirming.'[12] One year political battles within a school may focus on the young school leaver, while another year it may be assessment or the pastoral system of third-year options. External ideas which suit the 'problem of the moment' may get taken up and adapted to fit the interests of the dominant coalition, while other ideas of equal validity get ignored.

This section of the book examines the fate of environmental education between 1965 and 1975; and seeks to interpret its significance for curriculum conflict in general. It therefore concerns itself with how notions of the 'environment' entered into policy discussions at all four levels - international, national, local and school - and with the interaction between these distinct but mutually influential areas.

THE INTERNATIONAL BACKGROUND TO THE EMERGENCE OF ENVIRONMENTAL EDUCATION

The first efforts to broaden international awareness about the environment were taken by the United Nations in the favourable climate for certain aspects of world co-operation which followed the Second World War. In 1949 the United Nations convened a 'Scientific Conference on the Conservation and Utilisation of Resources'. In the same year UNESCO sponsored the foundation of the International Union for the Conservation of Nature.

In the period following these developments a series of conferences, programmes and activities was initiated, and two decades later, in 1971, the British HMI responsible for environmental education judged that for his area the most important of all the international movements was the United Nations 'with its in-built machinery of UNESCO that bears the world-wide responsibility for environmental care'.[3] UNESCO had set up a specialised Ecology and Conservation Sector in 1961 and in 1968 marked the beginning of a new wave of international activity with respect to the environment by holding the 'Biosphere Conference' in Paris. It was later claimed that at this Conference 'perhaps for the first time, world awareness of environmental education was fully evidenced'.[4] The educational programme that was advocated focused on the following needs: to develop environmental study material for educational curricula at all levels, to promote technical training and to stimulate global awareness of environmental problems.

In detail the educational programme suggested that regional surveys should be carried out; ecological components should be introduced into the present educational programmes; specialists should be trained in environmental sciences in universities and colleges of education; environmental studies in primary and secondary schools should be stimulated; national training and research centres should be set up.[5]

As a result of these recommendations the European Committee for the Conservation of Nature and Natural Resources was set up and subsequently organised the European Conference in Strasbourg in 1970. The influence of this Conference which launched 'European Conservation Year' is mentioned in 'A letter to Europeans' from the Secretary General of the Council of Europe which adequately captures the contemporary perceptions of environmental crisis:

> Pollution is here for us all to see, smell and taste. Water is often unfit to drink. Smoke and fumes attack our lungs. Our nervous systems are under severe strain from noise. Waste products, some practically indestructible, build up faster and faster. In many places soil is eroded away. Landscapes are spoiled and the variety of wildlife gets less every day. All this is happening throughout the world, but more than anywhere in our own densely populated continent. If it goes on much longer, Europe will be uninhabitable. This is not scaremongering. We are facing hard facts: facts discussed by all our nations at a conference organised in Strasbourg last February.[6]

In the same year, 1970, an International Working Meeting on Environmental Education in the School Curriculum was held in Foresta Institute, Carson City, Nevada, USA. The meeting accepted the following definition of environmental education: 'Environmental education is the process of recognising values and clarifying concepts in order to develop skills and attitudes necessary to understand and appreciate the interrelatedness among man, his culture and his biophysical surroundings'. The report suggested 'to the governments and their responsible educational authorities as well as to the national education organisations' that: 'through a reform of the total curriculum' environmental education should be introduced 'as an obligatory and integrated component of the school educational system at all levels' and further that 'national environmental legislation be used to include obligatory environmental education at all levels.'[7] Following the Nevada meeting a European working conference on Environmental Conservation Education was convened

in Zurich between 15-18 December 1971. The objectives of the
conference were: to assemble for the first time at a European
level, specialists working in the field of environmental education,
'in order to exchange information, to clarify concepts and to
formulate specific recommendations for projects and programmes
related to primary and secondary education, teacher training,
higher education and out of school education.'[8] In his opening
address Mr Frank Nicholls, Deputy Director General of IUCN,
explained that the IUCN decided to hold the conference in the
belief that education is of vital importance in the world environmental crisis, 'both in creating environmentally aware attitudes
throughout the general population and in producing the environmental specialists and other professionals needed to deal with the
complex problems facing mankind.'[9]

The first keynote lecture, given by Dr Tom Pritchard of the
British Nature Conservancy, reiterated the points introduced
by Nicholls. Pritchard considered many of the measures taken
in the name of environmental conservation to be merely palliative
and attributed this to a deficiency in the system which did not
allow the existing expertise to be applied by the planners and
decision makers.

Thus he envisaged a dual function for environmental education
both as a 'vocational training for specialists' and as a means of
'creating public awareness about environmental affairs, with the
ultimate aim of realising the conservation of natural resources
and stimulating enjoyment of the environment.'[10] Pritchard's
comments on the incorporation of environmental education are of
interest because some of the insights derive from his participation
in the contemporary debate on this subject in England.

Within the formal school system, environmental education
could be incorporated into existing subject areas or be taught
as a subject in its own right. At the primary level, the child's
interest was easily stimulated through the concept of contact
with and discovery of its environment, and through the use of
innovative teaching methods. This unity of approach was difficult
to maintain at the secondary level since the subject areas were
arbitrarily prescribed, and, at the higher secondary level,
environmental education was usually available only as a specialisation. Pritchard concluded that: 'Most important of all, in the
context of widespread reform of educational systems, was the
recognition of environmental education as a priority area by the
responsible authorities.'[11]

A second keynote lecture by Dr J. Cerovsky raised similar
questions with respect to 'Comprehensive Programmes of
Environmental Education'. He argued that the most appropriate
method was the promotion of interdisciplinary infiltration of
environmental teaching and education in all subjects. He added
that 'Introduction of a special subject of "environmental studies"
should principally be accepted and encouraged, but not regarded
as the only and final stage of development.'[12]

To summarise the educational strategy favoured by the Working

Sector the Report adds: 'Whichever design is chosen the pedagogic methods followed in Environmental Education should require all pupils to be engaged in field work, in first hand investigation and in open discussion of problems. Teachers should act as partners rather than authorities in the learning process.'[13] The flavour of these international conferences was essentially exhortatory, and most of the currently fashionable educational ideas were hitched to the environment 'bandwagon'. Nevertheless, international interest in the environment persisted beyond the optimism of the late sixties.

Following the European Working Conference the General Assembly of the United Nations convened a conference on the Human Environment, held in June 1972. This time, significantly, the Conference was 'action-oriented' rather than limited to restating the well-known problems because by 1970 'it was clear that the world was already paying attention to the problem. In government councils, in the Press, in schools and universities, threats to the environment had become a major topic of discussion in many countries.'[14]

THE NATIONAL BACKGROUND TO THE EMERGENCE OF ENVIRONMENTAL EDUCATION

The chronology of environmental consciousness in England strongly follows that in the international community. Thus the first important development was in 1949 when the Nature Conservancy was founded. Conservation was defined as 'a philosophy for action based on ecology', and the Nature Conservancy advocated that 'we must . . . guide our actions so that they are in harmony with ecological processes'. The Conservancy noted that 'Pollution is a sign of our failure to conserve properly when we produce waste beyond the capacity of nature to render it harmless.'[15] Later the Nature Conservancy became part of the National Environment Research Council which was established by Royal Charter in 1965. In its first report the Council stated that 'because countryside and its wildlife is highly vulnerable to the impact of human pressures of many kinds, including the needs of agriculture, industry, urban development and recreation, it is important to obtain a proper understanding of the natural heritage.'[16]

In part the role of the Nature Conservancy had been adopted by the Council for Nature even before its amalgamation with the Natural Environment Research Council. The Council for Nature was founded in 1958 as a co-ordinating body for over 450 organisations and bodies representing naturalists of all interests. A year after its foundation the Council formed the Conservation Corps (now called the British Trust for Conservation Volunteers). In 1966 the Conservation Society was formed, the society considering its central aim to be: to persuade people to 'live within the renewable resources of the Earth and not beyond their limits'.[17] In 1969 the conservationist lobby was further strength-

ened by the forming of the Committee for Environmental Conservation. The Committee includes 14 national conservation groups
and seeks to consider all matters of national importance affecting
the environment.

One of the members of the Committee is the Duke of Edinburgh,
who had been responsible for the most significant of all the
national initiatives with respect to the environment. In 1963 it
became apparent, partly as a result of the 'Observer' wild life
exhibition held that year, that there was an absence of national
leadership with respect to the countryside environment. This
weakness was noted by the Duke of Edinburgh who initiated a
study conference entitled 'The Countryside in 1970' from which
it was hoped would come machinery for removing the conflicting
factions in the conservation movement, and give it a common
purpose for the future.[18]

The first study conference was held in 1963 and representatives
from more than 90 national organisations were assembled and
were encouraged to learn about one another's interests and to
move towards a common understanding. Partly to facilitate this
co-operation, 12 working groups were set up to concentrate on
what were identified as the main issues. Jack Longland, later to
become Chairman of the Council for Environmental Education,
saw the catalytic role of the conference for environmental education:

> The first conference in 1963 recognised the important part
> that education must play in promoting an appreciation of the
> environment and an understanding of the problems arising
> from the conflicts between the many different interests con-
> cerned with the environment. Whilst it is true that the
> presentation of the traditional school subjects did not ignore
> the environment, there had by 1963 been no more than the
> beginnings of studies of the environment as a whole.[19]

The first study conference took a decision to call a special
conference, which subsequently met at Keele University in
March 1965 to: 'appraise the implications for the formal education
system of the issues raised at the 1963 Student Conference'.[20]

The conference made a number of conclusions and recommendations concerning education and the environment which developed
from a primary belief that: 'Positive educational methods are
needed to encourage awareness and appreciation of the natural
environment as well as responsibility for its trusteeship by every
citizen.' And also asserted that: 'The countryside is a rich
source of inspiration and teaching material which can contribute
substantially to education at all levels; field studies provide a
valuable means of using and developing this educational resource'.[21]
The conference recommended that: 'Fundamental and operational
education research, with participation by teachers, should be
intensified to determine more exactly the content of environmental
education and methods of teaching best suited to modern needs.'[22]

The 'Countryside in 1970' Conference undoubtedly influenced government policy, if only because of the presence of ministers at the meetings. In 1970 the Prime Minister, Edward Heath, stated that: 'The protection of our lovely countryside and our glorious coast, the prevention of pollution of our rivers and of the air we breathe, must be one of the highest priorities of the seventies.'[23] A Department of the Environment was set up to assume responsibility in England and Wales for all functions which affect the physical environment. A White Paper, 'The Protection of the Environment', was presented to Parliament in May 1970. It asserted: 'Government can and must give a lead but success will depend on an increasingly informed and active public opinion.'[24] A Royal Commission on Environmental Pollution was also set up in February 1970 and in its first report noted that 'public opinion must be mobilised'.[25]

The culmination of the environmental lobby's effort was the third 'Countryside in 1970' Conference in October of that year. The Secretary of the Standing Committee stated:

> Environmental education is variously defined . . . The essentials are clear: to help individuals . . . to understand the main features of their physical environment, their inter-relationships with it, and the requirements for its management: to instil a sense of personal responsibility and active concern for the condition of their surroundings and to encourage enthusiasm for and enjoyment of the environment.[26]

The importance of the international initiatives described earlier for the national development of environmental education became evident in the 1970s. The National Association of Environmental Education and the Council for Environmental Education both accepted and promoted the definition of environmental education provided by the Nevada Conference.

Interestingly, in view of its influence, the United Kingdom was the only major country not officially represented. The DES refused either to grant the National Association the money to travel to the Conference or give it official representative status. However, both the National Association's Statement of Aims and the final Environmental Studies 'A' level drew widely on the working party recommendations from the Zurich Conference.

LOCAL DEVELOPMENTS IN THE PROMOTION OF ENVIRONMENTAL EDUCATION

Besides the conference and government agencies and reports which advocated environmental education, a number of other initiatives focused specifically on promoting its growth.

At the Keele Conference it became clear that a number of teachers, most notably the biologists, were closely scrutinising the potential use of field studies of the environment in teaching their subject. The work of these pioneers was somewhat optimistically described in a speech by Jack Longland, subsequently to become Chairman of the Council for Environmental Education: 'The windows of many classrooms have been flung wide open. Parallel with this, teaching-subjects are beginning to be judged by their relevance to each other and to the world outside. The life and work of the schools have begun to flood out of doors.'[127] In the years following Keele a number of authors and advocates continued to press the case for environmental education. Garth Christian, for instance, wrote an influential article. 'Education for the environment' and a book 'Tomorrow's Countryside' in 1966, both arguing for more environmental education.[28] In the same year a grant was given to Leicester Museum by the Carnegie United Kingdom Trust to launch a research project on field studies education.

In June 1967 the Association Examing Board circulated tentative proposals to schools sitting its exams. The response indicated that 'there is a nucleus of about 30 schools interested enough seriously to consider the adoption of the proposed new subject'. The new subject reflected 'the need today for a syllabus which will enable the pupil to explore the concept of "environment", and in particular the natural or rural environment, in a way which has relevance to both the rural and urban child'. The intention was that 'the studies should lead to an understanding of the countryside as a whole, as a basic natural resource, along the lines advocated in the "Countryside in 1970" Conferences'. On the question of the title for the proposed new subject the AEB circular reported: 'Considerable discussion has already taken place regarding a title for the proposed syllabus, and the suggestion is that "Environmental Studies" is the most apt title.'[29]

Keith Wheeler puts the emergence of a climate of opinion favourable to environmental education as slightly later: 'In retrospect 1968 can be regarded as the year when the somewhat ill-defined, but potent concept of environmental education made its first real impact on the thinking of teachers'.[30] In March 1968 a co-ordinating body responsible for environmental education was established under the chairmanship of Jack Longland. This body, the Council for Environmental Education, was 'established to advance education in the importance of the environment and the status of man therein'.

At the same time a conference, held from 29-31 March 1968, was organised by G.C. Martin and a decision was taken to form a Society for Environmental Education.[31] The speaker at the conference dinner, Dr Dyos, claimed environmental studies to be the 'most revolutionary form of educational study. It could develop an understanding and critical awareness among pupils which could lead them to care for the environment.'[32] The environmental educationists of SEE and within the Colleges of Education were overwhelmingly geographers and biologists.[33] The two prime movers of SEE, for instance, George Martin and

Keith Wheeler, were both geographers. By the late 1960s it was these subject specialists who looked set to promote environmental education. However, although their arguments were beginning to carry weight they had to be translated to the school level. This meant facing questions such as 'Who will teach it?', 'To which pupils?' and 'For which exam?' It was over these issues that the respective fortunes of the subjects in schools depended and over which the ensuing battle was to be fought. Although the argument at the public level tended to be in terms of high-flown aims, the realities of subject power at the school level were never far beneath the surface. Indeed the evidence presented in the chapters that follow is remarkable for the high visbility of these conflicts, which one might have expected to have been more thoroughly camouflaged.

ENVIRONMENTAL EDUCATION AT SCHOOL LEVEL

At school level a number of categories of environmental education emerged. Two main varieties can be discerned. The first was to be found in the broadly-conceived environmental studies 'faculties' which developed in the humanities and science sections of comprehensive schools. The faculties were often introduced for managerial as well as academic reasons; for in the new large-size comprehensive middle management structures offered the opportunity for delegating a range of organisational tasks. Alongside this managerial impetus contemporary curriculum initiatives like the Goldsmiths IDE course and the Humanities Curriculum Project stressed the epistemological reasons favouring new integrated departments.

Whilst new faculties were organised around integrating themes, of which the environment was a leading choice in the late sixties, the teaching personnel were composed of traditional subject specialists. In the environmental studies faculties on the humanities side, geographers predominated, and in those on the science side, biologists. But geography and biology continued to thrive and the number of traditional geography and biology departments continued to hugely outnumber the innovative faculties. Moreover very few environmental studies training courses were developed and even those that existed were training non-graduates who went largely into primary and middle schools. As a result the teachers in environmental studies faculties continued to view their careers largely in terms of their original specialist discipline: there were no reasons, other than ideological, for changing allegiance.

The second variety of environmental education was developed in a range of new environmental studies departments which originated in existing rural studies departments. The moving force in these initiatives were the rural studies teachers, most notably in Hertfordshire where the largest number of environmental studies posts and departments were created. The reasons

for the concern of rural studies teachers can be fairly clearly
seen for, as we showed in Chapter 6, their very survival
within schools was threatened and as a result their main protagonists closely scrutinised the opportunities offered by the
changing climates of educational opinion. As early as 1963,
Carson had warned that rural studies must adapt to the 'changing climate' or perish. Rural studies teachers, he asserted, had
two duties, 'one to their classes and one to the educational
climate in which they worked'.[34] Of the latter he noted later
that educationists 'were constantly saying "you should be
teaching environmental studies". It was part of the climate of
opinion at the time.'

Of course, Carson represented only one sub-group within
rural studies, although he was also a moving force behind the
Rural Studies Association. The re-definition of rural studies
towards environmental studies was to be bitterly contested and
the questions of teachers' livelihoods and the associated survival
of the subject were to be the major considerations.

NOTES

1   M. Nicholson, 'The Environmental Revolution' (Harmonds-
    worth, Penguin 1972), p. 17.
2   M. Parlett, 'The Wellesley Milieu' (Oxford, 1975), mimeo.
3   K. Beal, The Background to Environmental Education in
    Environmental Studies in the All Ability School, 'Report of
    a Conference of Secondary Heads and Teachers held at
    Offley Place, Hertfordshire, 28th November – 2nd December,
    1971', p. 34.
4   International Union for Conservation of Nature and Natural
    Resources, 'Commission on Education: Report on Objectives,
    Actions, Organisation and Structures Working Programme',
    August 1971, (IUCN, 1971).
5   Beal Report, p. 34.
6   'A letter to Europeans from the Council of Europe',
    December 1970.
7   International Union for Conservation of Nature and Natural
    Resources, 'Final Report, International Working Meeting
    on Environmental Education in the School Curriculum',
    September 1970, USA (IUCN, 1970).
8   International Union for Conservation of Nature and Natural
    Resources, 'Final Report, European Working Conference on
    Environmental Conservation Education, Supplementary
    Paper', No. 34, Switzerland 1972 (IUCN), p. 1.
9   Ibid., p. 2.
10 Ibid., p. 4.
11 Ibid.
12 'Final Report of European Working Conference', 1972, p. 6.
13 Ibid.

14 'New Challenge for the United Nations', UN Office of Public Information, 1971 (quoted in Project Environment Report, No. 2, January 1972).
15 'Twenty One Years of Conservation' (London, Nature Conservancy, 1970).
16 Natural Environment Research Council, 'Report 1965–66' (London, HMSO, 1967).
17 Conservation Society, 'Philosophy, Aims and Proposed Action', (London, The Conservation Society, 1970).
18 G. Martin and K. Wheeler (eds.), 'Insights into Environmental Education' (Edinburgh, Oliver and Boyd, 1975), pp. 7–8.
19 J. Longland, 'Education and the Environment', a talk reproduced in transcript by permission of the Association of Agriculture, 78 Buckingham Gate, London SW1 (n.d.).
20 'The Countryside in 1970, Proceedings of the Conference on Education', University of Keele, Staffordshire, 26–28 March 1965 (London, Nature Conservancy, 1965), p. 5.
21 Ibid., p. 33.
22 Ibid., p. 34.
23 'Countryside in 1970, Proceedings of the Third Conference, October 1970' (London, Royal Society of Arts, 1970).
24 'The Protection of the Environment' (London, HMSO, 1970).
25 'Royal Commission on Environmental Pollution, First Report' (London, HMSO, 1971).
26 Proceedings of the Third Conference, 1970.
27 Proceedings 1965, p. 10.
28 G. Christian, Education for the Environment, 'Quarterly, Review, April 1966; G. Christian, 'Tomorrow's Countryside' (London, Murray, 1966).
29 'A.E.B. Circular to Schools', June 1967.
30 G.C. Martin and K. Wheeler (ed.), 'Insights into Environmental Education' (London, 1965), p. 8. Council for Environmental Constitution.
31 I.F. Rolls, Environmental Studies: A New Synthesis, 'Education for Teaching', Spring 1969, p. 21.
32 'Society for Environmental Education Bulletin', Vol. 1, No. 1, Autumn 1968, p. 3.
33 B. Barret, The Society in Retrospect, 'SEE', Vol. VIII, No. 2, 1976.
34 S. Carson, The Changing Climate, 'NRSA Journal' 1963, pp. 14–15.

8   REDEFINING RURAL STUDIES:

THE GENESIS OF ENVIRONMENTAL STUDIES

By the second half of the 1960s, groups seeking to promote their subject or discipline and the associated interests of their membership were faced by a rapidly changing situation. The accelerating pace of comprehensive reorganisation, the growth of curriculum reform movements and the emergence of 'the environment' as a major source of concern presented a complex new arena for the subject groups to operate within.

The differing patterns of assertion, evolution and consolidation between the three groups considered herein meant that they acted in starkly different ways. The geographers had by this time, following nearly a century of assertion and change, established their subject within the secondary school curriculum. In the universities the subject was approaching final acceptance and its academic rigour was presented and promoted by new initiatives to make the subject more quantitative, theoretical and scientific. The establishment of the subject at the tertiary level represented the final consolidatory stage in Layton's three-stage model of subject evolution. In such a situation, new conditions which encouraged integration, interdisciplinarity and more environmental and local study were likely to elicit minimal adjustment rather than maximal change. Geographers were in the position of defending those strategies which had achieved the establishment of their subject and the consolidation of their own special interests.

Biologists had begun their struggle for acceptance at around the same time as the geographers and after nearly a century of assertion had made rapid progress in the fifties and sixties. The subject had become established in the universities and was near to final broad-based acceptance in the secondary schools. The major source of biology's successful promotion was the claim to be a 'hard science' with rigorous methods and theories. The new conditions encouraged those elements which biologists had progressively reduced in pursuit of hard scientific status. Environmental and field studies represented the softer, less methodical and scientific side of biology, as did initiatives towards integration and interdisciplinarity. Defence of biology's status as a science required minimal adjustment to the new conditions rather than a readiness to embrace the new possibilities.

In contrast to biology and geography, rural studies remained a school subject confined within one sector of the secondary school curriculum. Rural studies was a low-status subject offered

124

to those secondary school pupils defined as less able. In 1963
Sean Carson wrote that:

> Rural studies does not exist in a vacuum. It is influenced by
> what happens in other subjects and by the relative importance
> accorded to them, as well as by the orientation of educational
> programmes generally . . .
> During the next few years considerable changes are likely,
> both in the framework of our school system, and in the
> curricula within schools, and if rural studies is to retain its
> influence, then those schools who believe in the subject must
> be clear about their aims and ready to adapt their methods to
> new conditions.[1]

Confined within the secondary modern school sector rural studies
was especially vulnerable to comprehensive reorganisation. In
1966 the NRSA Journal carried its first report on 'The Place of
Rural Studies in the Comprehensive System', produced by a
working party set up at the spring 1966 Conference of Wiltshire
Teachers of Rural Studies. After reviewing the rapid spread of
comprehensive schools throughout the country the Wiltshire
teachers proclaimed that rural studies 'has much to offer as a
subject in its own right in the comprehensive system of education'.[2]

Within the report there is some evidence that the Wiltshire
teachers were extremely concerned about the fate of their
subject in the comprehensive school. The change to comprehensives was taking place against a background of decline in the
subject which had begun in some areas in the late 1950s.[3] By
the early 1960s Sean Carson saw the decline setting in in
Hertfordshire in certain schools 'where a teacher was leaving,
they didn't fill the place, because they gave it to someone in
the examination set up'. By 1966 the Wiltshire teachers were
advising: 'The urgent necessity is for us to persuade teachers
and education authorities that the omission of the facilities for
teaching rural studies in new schools and in buildings which are
being adapted to a comprehensive form of education would be a
mistake.'[4] The problem was partly explained by the fact that:
'as many of the new heads of comprehensive schools were being
appointed from grammar school backgrounds these heads had
little or no experience of the value of rural studies in the education of the secondary child.'[5]

The teachers themselves saw clear evidence of broad-based
decline and by November 1967 one was writing of a 'general air
of defeatism among rural studies teachers'.[6] A Hertfordshire
teacher recalled this period:

> A few years back, rural studies was being phased out . . . it
> was getting itself a poor name . . . it was . . . you know,
> losing face . . . it was being regarded as not the subject we
> want in this up-and-going day and age. And we had awful

difficulty in getting examining boards and universities to
accept it at 'O' level and 'A' level . . . mainly because of its
content . . . I could see that I was going to have to phase out
rural studies because the demand for it in the school was
going down . . . it was being squeezed out in the timetable
and the demand for it at options level in the fourth year was
going down.[7]

Not only was rural studies less in demand but those areas of
the curriculum where the subject may have expanded were being
taken over by other subject specialists. In the comprehensives
rural studies was often not included or was being confined to the
'less able'. Following the Keele Conference and the Nuffield
projects, biologists and geographers began to gain control of
'field studies' of the environment. At the tertiary level, as has
been noted, similar specialists had begun to define 'environmental studies'.

In a position of rapidly falling demand and closing options,
rural studies was faced with extinction, certainly in those
counties where comprehensive education was rapidly pursued.
Carson in Hertfordshire was convinced that rural studies 'would
rapidly have disappeared' and Topham saw that by 1969 rural
studies 'was finished'.

Faced with extinction in the emerging comprehensive schools
and lacking any university base, rural studies advocates were
clearly at the stage where new ideas had to be embraced and
mobilised 'as a potential means of establishing a new intellectual
identity and particularly a new occupational role'.[8] The new
ideas available included 'integration', 'relevance' and 'team
teaching' as well as 'the environment'. All were equally advocated
and embraced. The 1969 rural studies teachers' annual general
meeting adopted the following resolution, that: 'Vigorous steps
be taken by rural studies organisations to show what their
departments have to offer in the form of relevant, valuable,
integrated work. Practical courses to be run with team teaching
moves to dispel the inferiority complex so many rural studies
teachers show . . .'[9]. In a similar vein the Chairman's report
advocated that: 'In the reorganisation of schools we should
grasp the opportunity to assert ourselves to lead the way with
team teaching and integrated courses to make sure that our
subject is well established.'[10]

The adoption of the rhetoric of integration, interdisciplinarity
and team teaching did little, however, to define a new intellectual
and occupational identity. The major problems were the low-
status image of rural studies, its inadequacy as an intellectual
synthesis and the failure to provide examinations which might
rectify these two deficiencies. The definition or acquisition of
new intellectual content and the construction of new high-
status examinations syllabuses offered a strategy which sought
to transform the prospects of rural studies.

The two-pronged strategy can be analysed in detail in the

period following 1965: (1) Attempts to re-define and re-direct rural studies can be clearly discerned in the conflict over the name given to the subject. (2) Attempts to increase the status and intellectual rigour of the subject can be analysed by scrutinising the new examination initiatives. Symbolically advocates like Carson spoke of the need for a new 'discipline', thereby hinting at the high-status normally conferred through the intellectual pursuits of subject scholars in universities.

REDEFINING RURAL STUDIES: 1965-9

In 1955, a lone advocate, C.C. Lewis, warned that 'for want of a name the battle might be lost'[11] in arguing for a new title for the subject. The name which Perry chose to replace rural studies was 'Lifecology', 'which I hope conveys the impression of the study of the interdependence of man and all living things with a wide variety of habitats'.[12]

The initial response of most of the members of the National Association to the arguments put forward by Perry, and to the need for reappraisal so clearly indicated at the Keele Conference in 1965, was to call for a greater promotion and consolidation of the subject. Carson argued for the exclusiveness of the subject saying that biology and geography should not deal with environmental education because 'to the teacher in secondary school the terms represent a subject with clearly defined limitations'. He concluded: 'We are left with the alternatives "environmental studies, or science" and "rural studies, or science".[13] Having dismissed the science appendage ('nor ought there to be any magic for us in the word science') this left a clear choice between 'environmental studies' and 'rural studies'. On their relative merits Carson was firm: 'The term "environmental studies" is almost unknown outside a few colleges and has no clear definition within schools or universities.'

The case for 'rural studies' provides a useful summary of the subject's position in 1965: there were 37 county associations of teachers in Rural Studies Associations; a rural studies course existed in half the secondary moderns in England and Wales; there were CSE examinations in the subject in all boards; about 36 rural studies advisers were employed in LEAs; and five colleges of education ran three-year courses to train rural studies specialists.[14]

The rapid changes following Carson's article in 1965 led a number of rural studies teachers to begin 'redefinition' of their subject in the schools. At the same time Carson in his research at Manchester from 1966-7 was seeking to establish what certain groups and individuals thought should be taught in schools with particular reference to rural studies. He sent questionnaires to people 'widely representative of all the interests reflecting the needs of society in relation to the countryside'.[15]

Alongside his efforts to define the various countryside groups'
requirements of the subject Carson also sought to establish
what were the views and practice of rural studies teachers. His
research shows a very different perception of the subject from
the two groups. The countryside groups saw the major objectives as being: 'to promote an understanding of the countryside
and man's relation to his natural environment and to wild life'.
Other important objectives were: 'the development of aesthetic
appreciation, the encouragement of creativity, giving children
a realisation of the value of a contact with nature or developing
acceptable social behaviour.'[16] All these objectives were under-
represented among rural studies teachers whilst one objective,
'to develop skills and standards of craftsmanship in gardening
or other rural crafts', was 'heavily over-represented in schools'
and in CSE syllabuses. Carson noted that 'During the interviews
for the validity check some teachers remarked that they had not
realised that they had been paying so much attention to this
objective.'[17]

Carson's research showed that the innovatory efforts of a
few teachers, and his own efforts to redefine the subject, were
far removed from the practice of most rural studies teachers.
The National Association was faced by this basic dilemma with
any strategies to change the occupational identity of the
membership. This dilemma was instanced in the Council meeting
of the Association held in Newark on 10 February 1968. One
item referred to the proposed new AEB environmental studies
'O' level. The minutes report that Sean Carson felt that there
was 'too much "sociology" in the proposed paper'[18] and there
was some discussion by members of Council upon the degree of
sociology which could be included and which a teacher trained
for rural studies could be expected to teach. At Newark, Policy
Committee considered the possibility of changing the name of the
association - possibly to environmental studies, for in the next
month both the Council and the Society for Environmental
Education were formed. Policy Committee 'considered the
question of changing the name of "rural studies" following the
comments at Conference and press reports of these comments',
but recommended that 'no change should be considered but that
the work we do under the title of "rural studies" will determine
its status.'[19] Council agreed, noting:

that while there was some opposition to the name it would be
folly to bow to it. The term was accepted by all the C.S.E.
boards, many colleges of education, at least nine universities
which were offering it in the B. Ed. context and by at least
one 'A' level board. [This presumably refers to the negotiations
then under way with the Northern Universities Board - see
Chapter 9]. In addition it was hoped that an 'O' level board
would accept the name shortly.[20]

Evidence of a volte face within weeks of the Newark decision was contained in a circular, dated 8 March, sent by Richard Morgan to all members of Policy Committee: 'Following a recent conversation with Mr. M. Pritchard I have decided that it may be to our advantage to invite him to attend our next meeting on 16th March at Tamworth.'[121] At this time Mervyn Pritchard was active as Chairman of the Schools Council Working Party on Rural Studies. The Working Party had been set up in November 1965 by the Schools Council following discussions with the National Rural Studies Association. It met eleven times under Pritchard, who was headmaster of Redbourn Secondary School, St Albans. Its report was presented to Council in June 1968 but we can assume Pritchard had a fairly clear view of the likely conclusions by the time of the Tamworth gathering. The results of the Tamworth meeting were recorded in a confidential minute. It was decided: 'that we support Mr. Pritchard in his idea that a Standing Committee at Schools Council level ought to be set up and that the Standing Committee should be named "rural and environmental studies"', and 'that we accept the definition of rural studies in the terms: "The study of the environment in and around the school . . ."'[122] The next meeting of Policy Committee in May agreed to the change of name because of 'the formation of the Council for Environmental Education, the rise in the number of environmental studies courses in Colleges of Education, the resistance of examination boards to the name rural studies, and the impression that the word that commands most respect is "environmental".'[123] In June the Schools Council Working Party report on Rural Studies was submitted and argued that: 'The realisation of the full potential of rural studies has become a matter of great educational importance. Because rural studies has such a wide bearing on many aspects of life its limits are not easy to define nor are its values so clear-cut as those of some subjects.'[124] The Working Party 'felt the need, as a prerequisite to define the subject as currently taught'. The definition is precisely the same as that adopted by the NRSA Policy Committee in March upon Pritchard's recommendation: 'Rural studies is the study of the environment in and around the school with particular reference to animals and plants important to man and leading to an understanding of man's interaction with the countryside.[125]

The discussion on the change of name took place in the various County Associations. A letter from the West Riding branch to the General Secretary in November summarised a number of the problems which emerged. Firstly, the branch was not sure whether the change of name referred to 'the rural studies movement' or the subject of rural studies. If it was the former, 'the N.R.S.A. [should] offer a choice of either "rural studies" or "environmental studies"' presumably as subject names for secondary school courses.[26] This recommendation was subsequently accepted by Policy Committee.[27] Secondly, the branch was worried by the claim for exclusive responsibility for environmental studies which might be implied by the change of name.

In August the Association held its conference in Hertford where there were several discussions, 'often very heated', about the proposed change of name. In September, at the annual general meeting, the proposal to change the title was moved by the General Secretary and Sean Carson, who had recently changed his title in Hertfordshire to 'Adviser for Environmental Education'. The motion was passed by 12 votes to 7, with 2 abstentions.[28] Carson recalls: 'there was a bitter division at this 1969 Conference and the meetings that followed. It was the first time the spirit of comradeship had disintegrated since 1960.'

Thus the title was changed to the National Rural and Environmental Studies Association. Three years later the process of transformation was completed and the National Association of Environmental Education emerged. Writing in mid-1971 in the Association Journal the Chairman, Philip Neal, had presaged the change in the editorial and hinted at the aspiration for parity with other well-established school subject associations:

> I believe we must grasp the nettle firmly – perhaps we should have had the courage to go the whole way recently – had we dropped 'rural' from our title we may well have had more members now. We are the association of teachers concerned with the environment. Let us state this clearly . . . Does 'Association for Environmental Education' express exactly what we do . . . Does it not parallel the Association for Science Education, the Association for Physical Education?[29]

THE NEED FOR A DISCIPLINE

Although initiatives aiming to change the National Association's name were formally distinguished from attempts to change the identity of the subject, such re-definitions were advocated in the same period. On one point, those advocating change were unanimous: what was needed was not a new 'emphasis' or 'subject' but a 'discipline'. The rhetorical requirement of 'a discipline' symbolised the dual purpose of redefinition: a new synthesis of knowledge but also one which afforded higher status and could be offered to a new clientele covering a broader ability spectrum.

Sean Carson, whose research at Manchester was particularly concerned with the new CSE, began in the autumn of 1966 to perceive the need for 'a discipline' of rural studies for the following reasons:

> The lack of a clear definition of an area of study as a discipline has often been a difficulty for local authorities in deciding what facilities to provide and more recently in having rural studies courses at colleges of education accepted for the

degree of B.Ed. by some universities. It has been one of the reasons for the fact that no 'A' level course in rural studies exists at present.[30]

Further, in commenting on the Report of the Study Group on Education and Field Biology, he noted: 'Because rural studies was not recognised as a discipline at any academic level, even at 'O' level, the Group were prevented from giving it serious consideration.'[31]
Carson's judgements were passed on to the Schools Council Working Party on Rural Studies who reiterated them in the report to the Council of June 1968. The working party perceived 'the need for a scholarly discipline'. The discipline would spread 'across the present system of specialisation' and might 'take the form of an integrated course of study based upon environmental experience in which rural studies has a part to play.'[32]
The most common pattern for defining new 'disciplines' of knowledge in the essentially hierarchical education system in England has been through the work of university scholars. Unfortunately at this time there was very little academic activity in this field for the rural studies advocates to build upon. Reviewing the university scene in 1972 Marsden noted that: 'Courses labelled "environmental studies" tend to have an individualistic flavour and a distinctly "applied" quality.'[33] The first 'environment' course was precisely of this applied kind: the School of Environmental Science at East Anglia University. The School was proposed in 1960 but had to wait seven years whilst the basic sciences of chemistry, biology, mathematics and physics were first established. Similar courses have more recently been established elsewhere by scientists at new universities, for instance the University of Ulster in Coleraine and more limited developments at Sussex. Courses have also been developed at Sheffield and at Exeter a course on 'environmental chemical engineering' has been introduced.
The idiosyncratic applied courses developed in universities offered no hope of an overarching definition of an 'environmental' discipline. The pattern was similar in the colleges of education. Paterson found that the courses were 'clearly individualistic and doubtfully defined' and to confirm this he noted the fact that environmental studies has to be discovered under a number of different names: 'Although environmental studies is the commonest title, environmental sciences, contemporary and environmental studies, social and environmental studies and environmental education itself also exist.' Paterson felt that this lack of common identity was 'not necessarily a mistake': 'If all were clearly the same the subject might be more fully recognised by the conventionally minded yet each variation in the title indicates nuances of subject matter and general ethos. These are the products of those who teach the subject and who, for the most part, actually initiated the courses.'[34]

The approach in the colleges was markedly different to developments in the schools. The first main level 'environmental studies' course was established in 1961. Three years later Leicester College opened two annexes and a Department of Environmental Studies was formed and manned by three full-time members of staff working as a team to cover the various aspects of the course. The work at Leicester was dominated by geographers and Paterson judged the most common source of environmental courses to be 'by idealism out of geography'.[35] Biologists were a second group actively involved in many college courses on the environment. Rural studies, the background of most school pioneers, was grossly under-represented. Paterson felt that: 'It is significant to note . . . the paucity of rural studies tutors whose own broad areas directly overlap and possibly include much of currently accepted environmental studies.' Few of the colleges used gardens, greenhouses or animals. One college possessed a fully equipped rural studies unit but the environmental studies department stated it 'is not much used'.[36]

In fact the developments in the colleges often followed, certainly in a chronological sense, work in secondary schools. Paterson noted that many colleges stated among the aims of their courses a desire to 'fit into the modern climate of education'. This he suggested reflected the fact 'that the schools are already calling for teachers of environmental studies, that they are educationally ahead of the colleges'.[37]

The main difference between the schools and colleges was in the position of the rural studies teachers. In the colleges they were not faced with imminent extinction because of comprehensive reorganisation (though of course there was a substantial long-term threat to their position thereby implied). In addition only five colleges specialised in rural studies in 1963.[38]

Even in those colleges which taught rural studies the overlap with practice in schools was patchy. In June 1976 Alexander and Carson, in a report on College of Education syllabuses, noted that the results of their enquiry 'showed what many in the schools have already felt to be true, that is, that college courses too often bear little relation to what is required of teachers in school and are now urgently in need of review.' Reporting on the adverse correlations between school and college courses, they state: 'If the premise is accepted that the college courses should reflect the accepted definition of rural studies then this result is important because it shows that, in fact, most courses are very different from the ideal.[39] The confusions to which Alexander and Carson point were still evident two years later when a report by lecturers in rural studies in colleges posed the question: 'To what extent should the aims of courses in rural studies in colleges be different from those of courses in schools?' and 'what are the aims of rural studies in schools which provide the basis for the courses in colleges?'[40] The report concluded that the role of the subject in primary and secondary

schools 'needs to be redefined or at least updated. The aims of
the subject at school and college level could then be clarified.'[41]
Such overdue clarification has not been undertaken since 1970.
In an article called 'Whither Rural Studies?' Mylechreest argued
in December 1975 that 'although a definition of environmental
education in the school curriculum was agreed in 1970 there is
no such agreement for higher education'. He concluded: 'The
continued provision of rural studies specialists is therefore of
vital importance.' The argument is persuasively self-fulfilling -
since no 'new specialist environmental studies teachers' are
trained, 'The rural studies teacher can make a distinct contribution which is necessary for interdisciplinary environmental
studies.'[42]

As a new disciplinary definition of environmental studies was
not forthcoming from the scholars in the higher education sector,
the process of definition had to be undertaken at the secondary
level. One of the pioneers of the 'A' level syllabus later claimed
that the process of curriculum development undertaken 'is
schools-based and is the result of initiatives taken together by
practising teachers with the support of their local authority.
Such self-generated work offers a viable way of developing an
area of the curriculum.'[43] Thus in the schools-based model the
academic discipline is developed because classroom teachers perceive the need for a new area of knowledge and then set about
involving academics in its construction.

The perception of such a need among rural studies teachers
can be discerned from the beginning of 1967. In February 1967,
Mervyn Pritchard, as secretary of the 'Research and Development sub-committee' of the National Rural Studies Association,
reported that: 'There was some difficulty in impressing the
intellectual content of the subject', and that the sub-committee:
'wanted to discover how rural studies experience can help
students with gaining entry to colleges of education, and what
value post "O" level qualification in rural studies would have for
this purpose.' In the discussion which followed this report John
Pullen, HMI, said, 'Several questions required answering',
among them: 'Do we consider an "A" level course should be
included in rural studies? What do we do about the reaction,
"We do not want people with 'A' level in rural studies". What
parts of rural studies should be treated as aspects of other
disciplines?' At the same meeting policy committee reported that
a sub-committee had been formed 'to find existing curricula for
able children leading to at least "O" level in the rural studies
field' and 'to produce evidence that there is a need for rural
studies up to "O" level i.e. to show that the subject is of
benefit to able pupils.'[44]

In March a 'statement of evidence' was presented by the
National Association to the Schools Council Working Party on
Rural Studies. The definition of rural studies advocated was
almost identical to that established in Carson's Manchester
research: 'The study of the landscape, its topography, geology

and pedology, the ecological relationship of the plants and animals naturally present, together with the study of man's control of this natural environment through agriculture, horticulture and forestry.'[45] In advocating this definition of rural studies and adding as an objective 'The development of an awareness and appreciation of the natural surroundings' the National Association contended that there was a growing demand for examinations at 'O' and 'A' level in rural studies. 'We are certain that if such examinations are introduced they will be used increasingly.' Finally they asserted that the content which they had defined 'provides a unified and clear area of study and a valuable academic discipline'.[46]

At this time a small group of HM inspectors interested in rural studies, among them John Pullen, also saw a need for a discipline of rural studies in schools. They argued in an article published in October 1967 that, broadly interpreted, 'rural studies in school should mean that pupils will have experienced work which calls for disciplined study to acquire a structured body of knowledge about the countryside, entering into many of the familiar subjects of the curriculum.'[47] The HMIs saw such rural studies work as potentially examinable at 'A' level.

Work now being attempted at many schools could justifiably claim to reach this level. It is true that some schools with strongly developed rural studies courses find, as one might expect, that older pupils turn very naturally and successfully to 'A' level courses in chemistry, biology and geography and often gain university entrance on the standards they have achieved. Nevertheless the time appears to be ripe for the introduction of 'A' level courses in agriculture, agricultural science, and in the wider field of rural studies.[48]

The changeover to comprehensives precipitated a number of teachers who had previously worked with CSE to define rural studies at 'O' level and 'A' level. The 1968 NRSA Journal noted that schools in Yorkshire, Nottinghamshire and Hertfordshire were campaigning for such exams.[49] Reporting on 'rural studies in the comprehensive school', Topham argued that 'rural studies should be so organised within the comprehensive school that no child, boy or girl, of whatever ability, is denied the opportunity to participate'.[50] The rural studies teachers in a comprehensive school should aim to offer: (a) a course leading to an 'O' level GCE; (b) a course leading to CSE; (c) an integral course; (d) to participate in a general studies course; (e) a course leading to the 'A' level GCE, and when established to a certificate of further secondary education. Consequently, 'in a large comprehensive school one can envisage generous allocation of staff to the department'.[51]

The perennial dilemma of rural studies advocates is again illustrated when having argued so cogently for a variety of examinations in the subject, Topham stated: 'I firmly believe

that success in examinations is not really indicative of the value
of any subject, and this is especially true of rural studies'.
His opinion was anticipated by a comment from P.L. Quant in
April 1967:

> There is no doubt that in our efforts to maintain our status
> in the looming inevitability of the comprehensive school –
> indeed our very existence – we have dragged the 'Science is
> our Leader' concept out of the cut and thrust of rural studies
> teaching to replace it by a syllabus of scientific detail which
> is chaining us down.[52]

The Schools Council Working Party on rural studies met
between November 1965 and June 1968 when its report was
presented to the Council (the working party's brief was 'to
examine rural studies in secondary schools').[53] One of the paramount problems facing teachers of the subject was dealt with in
the section on 'status':

> The position varies greatly but there is no doubt that a sub-
> stantial proportion of rural studies teachers do find them-
> selves in a difficult position because of the demanding nature
> of the task, the lack of ancillary help, and the attitude which
> regards the subject as a sublimating exercise for the less able.[54]

Elsewhere the report noted: 'The old concept of the subject
predominantly as gardening, often gardening for the backward
boys only, did not die easily.'[55] The remedy for this situation
was clearly perceived. 'Examinations in rural studies have helped
to improve the image of the subject and to give it a certain status
in the eyes of the pupils and their parents. Acceptable "A" levels
could raise the status still further.'[56]

The working party had produced a strong recommendation that
the Schools Council 'should set up a curriculum development
project to establish patterns of curricula in rural studies acceptable to all secondary schools'. The Report noted that 'the
Council has agreed that a proposal for a curriculum development
project in rural studies should be drawn up for its consideration'.[57] The lobbying of the Council by the working party and
sympathetic HMIs seems to have ensured fairly rapid consideration
of the need for a curriculum development project. What is significant is that whilst the brief of updating rural studies remained
a central if implicit part of the project the title was changed in
line with the new name and aspirations of the Rural Studies
Association. 'Project Environment' began in April 1970 and was
staffed by two leading members of the association: Ron Colton,
director, and Richard Morgan, deputy director.

From the beginning the project worked very closely with
representatives and agencies of the Rural Studies Association.
The most significant partnership was probably with the Joint

Working Party on Environmental Education. This body was convened in 1971 under the guidance of David Alexander. Alexander,
an ex-rural studies teacher, was adviser in Bedfordshire and
was General Secretary of the National Association at the stage
of its transition from NRESA to NAEE. In a memorandum to the
working party the Project Environment team posed the dilemma
faced by rural studies representatives in claiming the new
subject area:

> The question is, should the Joint Working Party pursue the
> matter of the type of updated courses in Colleges of Education
> which the existing rural science and rural studies departments
> should provide in their subject role in the wider cause of
> environmental education? Or should it widen its brief . . .
> into those physical and sociological aspects of the environment
> which geographers, historians, and sociologists and others
> might rightly claim were more central to their disciplines and
> look at the whole of environmental education? In a nutshell,
> the choice is between the up-to-date area which is succeeding
> rural studies and environmental education in its whole-
> curriculum concept.[58]

CONCLUSION

The position of rural studies in the mid-sixties meant that the
teachers of the subject were faced with a rapid decline in its
intellectual and occupational acceptability. In such a situation
(following Ben-David and Collins hypothesis) it can be seen
from the movement to change the name of the subject just how
enthusiastic some of the subject's practitioners were to embrace
a new intellectual and occupational identity.
From this crisis situation advocates of a new approach to the
subject were able to gain support not only for the definition of
a new intellectual and occupational identity, but also for a
strategy to change the status of the subject. To survive in the
newly emerging comprehensive schools, the subject needed to
be taught as an 'O' and 'A' level examination. By establishing
such examinations, the way would be prepared for rural studies
teachers to argue for more school finance and resources and to
consolidate their departmental territory inside the school. It
was for these reasons that a committee was set up specifically
'to produce evidence that there is a need for rural studies up
to 'O' level, i.e. to show that the subject is of benefit to able
pupils'.
The pursuit of academic status, however, highlighted the
conflict inside the subject which had surfaced when examinations
were first mooted. Topham and Quant both expressed the feel-
ings of a substantial body of rural studies teachers that their
work was ill-suited to academic examinations. The feasibility
project to establish if rural studies was examinable at CSE had

likewise worried about the 'unfavourable backwash effects' of
written examinations for the teachers of the subject. The split
over whether the subject should be titled rural studies or
environmental studies was very much a split between the early
emphasis on pedagogic and utilitarian traditions, and the new
move to embrace the academic tradition. This conflict was
reflected in the split within the subject which was evident at
the meeting of 14 June. Particularly among rural studies groups
in the north of England there was great 'emotional attachment'
to rural studies. The 1969 Conference again showed there was a
'bitter division' and that the 'spirit of comradeship had disintegrated'. Subject association's meetings provided the area
within which the various sub-groups and factions sought to
promote their particular versions of the subject. The influence
of examination board policy was presented as a major reason
for changing the title of the subject to 'environmental studies'.

The passage to higher status followed certain aspects of
Layton's model, particularly the movement away from utilitarian
and child-centred aspirations. In other respects, however, the
pattern was markedly different. The movement to Layton's stage 2
did not proceed as he envisaged. 'The tradition of scholarly
work' could not emerge without the establishment of scholarly
communities at the tertiary level. Although certain groups were
established, notably in the new universities, connections with
the teachers in schools only occurred in one-off events such as
the Offley Conference (see Chapter 9). The central problem was
that at the tertiary level the main scholars were from geographical
and scientific backgrounds; although attracted to 'environmental'
problems, they seldom saw 'environmental studies' as the means
of establishing new intellectual and occupational identities.
Indeed, in a flourishing tertiary sector there was little need
for occupational redefinition.

Even with those agencies and institutions directly concerned
with influencing or training personnel for the school sector,
considerable differences of allegiance were evident. Project
Environment's progress was enormously affected by the fact that
the Director left in the middle of the three-year period to take
a job in America. As a leading member of NAEE noted: 'We missed
a real chance to develop a decent academic version of environmental studies . . . chances like that don't come twice and I
think he's got a hell of a lot to answer for'.[59] Most of the
'environmental studies' advocates in the colleges of education
were actually main specialists in either geography or biology.
Hence bodies like the Society for Environmental Education worked
primarily in opposition to any claims from rural studies specialists that their work was synonymous with environmental
education.

NOTES

1 S.M. Carson 'The Changing Climate', 1963, p. 14.
2 'N.R.S.A. Journal', 1966, pp. 31-2.
3 See, for instance, reports in the 'Journal of the Kent
   Association of Teachers of Rural Science', No. 12, September
   1958, p. 3.
4 'N.R.S.A. Journal', 1966, p. 36.
5 'N.R.S.A. Policy Committee Report to Council', 17.6.67.
6 George Wing to Sean Carson, 12.11.75.
7 Interview with Gordon Battey, a Hertfordshire teacher,
   8.11.75.
8 'Ben-David and Collins', p. 45.
9 National Rural Studies Association Annual General Meeting
   Report, 6 September 1969, Resolution 2.
10 Ibid., Chairman's Report (W.T. Brock of Hertfordshire).
11 'Kent Association of Teachers of Gardening and Rural
   Science', No. 6, June 1955, p. 22.
12 G.A. Perry, What's in a Name?, 'N.R.S.A. Journal', 1964-5,
   pp. 32-3.
13 S. Carson, Rural Studies: the case for the name, 'NRSA
   Journal, 1964-5, pp. 33-7.
14 S. Carson M.Ed., p. 72.
15 Ibid., p. 269.
16 Ibid.
17 Op. cit. Carson, p. 72.
18 N.R.S.A. Policy Committee Minutes, 10.2.68.
19 N.R.S.A. Council Meeting Minutes, 10.2.68.
20 N.R.S.A. Policy Committee circular, 8.3.68.
21 N.R.S.A. Policy Committee Minutes, 16.3.68.
22 N.R.S.A. Policy Committee Minutes, 25.5.68.
23 N.R.S.A. Policy Committee circular, June 1968.
24 'Schools Council Working Paper 24: Rural Studies in Secondary Schools' (London, 1969), p. 6.
25 Ibid., p. 6.
26 Ibid., p. 7.
27 Letter from West Riding Rural Studies Association to R.
   Morgan, 14 November 1968.
28 General Secretary's circular, June 1967.
29 N.R.S.A. Minutes of A.G.M., 6.9.69. For: Bedfordshire,
   Buckinghamshire, Birmingham, Cambridgeshire, East Riding,
   Essex, Hertfordshire, Nottinghamshire, Oxfordshire,
   Shropshire, Wiltshire, individual members. Against: Cumber-
   land, Westmorland, East Suffolk, Lancashire, Manchester,
   Staffordshire, West Riding, Worcestershire. Abstentions:
   Lindsey, Glamorgan.
30 The National Association, 'Journal of the National Rural and
   Environmental Studies Association', 1971.
31 Carson M. Ed., p. 135.
32 Ibid., p. 61.
33 Working Paper No. 24, p. 19.

34 W.E. Marsden, Environmental Studies Courses in Colleges of Education, 'Journal of Curriculum Studies', Vol. 3.
35 A. Paterson, 'Main Courses in Environmental Education in College', mimeo (pages unnumbered), 197 .
36 Ibid.
37 Ibid.
38 Ibid.
39 'Rural Studies, A Survey of Facilities 1963', p. 36.
40 S. Carson and D. Alexander Analysis of Some Colleges of Education syllabuses of Courses in Rural Studies, NRSA Policy Committee Research Sub-committee, June 1968.
41 'Report of the Working Party of the R.E.S. Section of the A.T.C.D.E.', 1970, p. 15.
42 Ibid., p. 22.
43 M. Mylechreest, Whither Rural Studies?, 'School Science Review', December 1975, Vol. 57, No. 199, pp. 276-84.
44 S. Carson (ed.) 'Environmental Studies, the Construction of an "A" Level Syllabus' (Slough, N.F.E.R., 1971), pp. 7-8.
45 N.R.S.A. File Minutes of Meeting on 11.2.67.
46 Carson, M. Ed., p. 369.
47 'N.R.S.A. Journal', 1968, p. 38.
48 Rural Studies in Schools, 'Trends in Education', October (London, DES, 1967), p. 31.
49 Ibid., pp. 30-31.
50 'N.R.S.A. Journal, 1968, p. 44.
51 Ibid., p. 45.
52 Ibid., p. 46.
53 P.L. Quant, 1967, p. 12.
54 Working Paper 24, p. 4.
55 Ibid., p. 15.
56 Ibid., p. 5.
57 Ibid., p. 12.
58 Ibid., p. 3.
59 Interview with NAEE Executive committee member, Leeds Conference, 30, August 1975.

SCHOOLS-BASED INITIATIVES

In the period of changeover to the comprehensive system after
1964 several schools began to offer rural studies courses in
their sixth forms. As a result a number of rural studies teachers
drew up courses which were potentially of 'A' level standard.[1]
    The first approach to an examination board was made by the
Regis School at Tettenhall in Staffordshire. The effort proved
abortive and in November 1967 it was reported that 'Tettenhall
submitted their "A" level syllabus to the Northern Universities
Board and had it refused'.[2]
    A more successful approach was made by the Shephalbury
School, a school in the process of becoming a comprehensive
situated in the Hertfordshire new town of Stevenage. The Head
of Rural Studies at Shephalbury, Paul Topham, had trained in
biology and horticulture at King Alfred's College, Winchester.
His first post in 1959 was at Berkeley Secondary Modern school
in the New Forest, where he was in charge of rural studies. In
1963 he moved to Shephalbury. Topham saw his work at
Shephalbury up until 1966 as a 'questioning period' in considering the potential role of rural studies in the comprehensive
school. By and large he considered rural studies teachers were:
'entertaining the troops because nobody else could manage
them'. Apart from social control of deviant pupils he considered
that the teachers of the subject 'were not getting anything out
of a traditional rural studies course that you could justify if you
were called to account for what you were teaching'.
    Having judged traditional rural studies to be largely redundant
in the comprehensive school Topham felt 'we had then to work
out something we did consider a viable proposition'. In an 'all-
ability' school he felt such viability was dependent on broadening the base of the subject to involve the ablest students. He
began to work out a new definition of the subject in a general
studies course, based on the environment, which he taught in
the sixth form.
    Topham's course was extremely successful in the school,
where he had now become Head of Upper School. On 22 November
the Head contacted an examining board to enquire about the
possibility of getting Topham's course validated as an 'A' level.
At this time some exam boards, notably the Associated Examining
Board, were considering an 'O' level in the subject. One headmaster noted after his enquiry that he was given 'the impression

that the Board would be very interested in the production of
this syllabus'.[3]

As a result on 1 February 1967 Topham circulated a number
of universities, colleges and professional bodies to elicit their
views about content for an 'A' level in rural studies. He was
particularly concerned to define the syllabus in 'the applied
ecology field'. When these views were received Topham produced
the first draft of an 'A' level which asserted: 'The aim of the
syllabus is to provide the scientific understanding required to
enable the candidate to understand man's control of his environment, and the conflicts which arise as a result of expanding
requirements and the consequent need for conservation.'
Significantly the draft added that 'The syllabus relates biology
to physics and chemistry which it is assumed will have been
studied previously or concurrently.'[4]

The 'A' level consisted of two parts: part 1 had two theory
papers on the Physical Environment and the Living Environment;
the second part of the examination proposed a 'submission for
examination of a record of original research including fieldwork'.

In June the first draft of the 'A' level was sent round to a
number of universities and examining boards for comment. A
number of problems were raised. A geography professor
commented: 'So much of this appears to be geography as it is
now conceived that I am surprised that the word only appears
once in the draft'[5]; whilst a university biologist thought that 'it
would be very difficult to teach it in a genuinely scientific way
at school level'.[6]

The examining board forwarded the syllabus to one of their
advisers. He found the syllabus 'very difficult to evaluate since
the headings are so broad and generalised'. He added 'my
impression is that it may be rather thin, but I do not know
exactly how far the author intends to go'.[7] He also commented
on discontinuities between parts 1 and 2 and of the original
research in the latter part said: 'My fear is that these projects
will be simply descriptive; I suggest that they should be firmly
rooted in a theoretical body of knowledge.'[8] The second draft of
the syllabus replaced scientific 'understanding' with 'knowledge'
in the section on aims and the reference to biology, physics
and chemistry was deleted. Although the section on 'The Living
Environment' was re-titled 'Biological Systems' other changes
took account of the discontinuities between part 1 and 2 to which
the adviser had drawn attention.[9] Once again Topham circulated
his draft proposals.

This time Sean Carson, who had just completed his M. Ed.
at Manchester and was again acting as adviser in Hertfordshire,
was asked to comment. His work at Manchester had led to a
definition of rural studies in many ways similar to Topham's,
but until now they had worked independently. Carson had
defined rural studies as covering 'The Study of the Landscape',
'The ecological relationship of the plants and animals naturally
present' and 'the study of man's control of this natural environ-

ment through agriculture, horticulture and forestry'.[10]

Carson returned 'some suggested amendments': 'Basic biology, and geography should be omitted from this paper but instead a note should be included saying that the candidate should have sufficient basis in these subjects to develop the ecological relationships that are the concern of rural studies.'[11] He considered that the section on biological systems should be re-titled: 'We are not replacing biology but extending it. Suggest "the natural environment" as this is the term used in various definitions of rural studies.'[12] Carson's experience of the 'politics' of syllabus construction acquired in his roles within the National Association were evident in two comments: 'The official definition of rural studies as used in the N.R.S.A. evidence to the Schools Council would be a better statement of aims than the one here, and would have additional validity.' And his conclusion to the letter: 'I think the above changes would give the paper a better balance, it would not tread on the toes of geography and biology but build on the same foundations as the newly defined discipline of rural studies.'[13]

Following submission of a third draft of the 'A' level to the Examining Board on 21 August, Topham was informed that the Board 'has now formally approved your proposed Advanced Level Syllabus in rural studies'. The letter added: 'You will wish to know that concern was expressed at the extensive nature of the syllabus and the question was raised as to whether or not this would lead to superficial teaching.'[14] Nonetheless the letter confirms that the 'A' level would be forwarded to Schools Council for approval.

In fact the 'A' level was not sent on to Schools Council and in July 1968 a Board official wrote in response to an enquiry from Topham that the board would prefer to consider the 'A' level in detail when it had finalised its own syllabuses.[15] In January 1969 a new Standing Advisory Committee for Environmental Subjects reviewed the syllabus and recommended it as an experimental syllabus which could not be offered with geography or biology.[16]

After submission to Schools Council by this committee six months ensued until Topham phoned the Board to request written details of the Council's response. A Board official replied:

> I attended the sub-committee at which your proposals were considered and approved in principle. This approval was subsequently confirmed in the published minutes of the sub-committee . . . however, I have been told that the decision of the sub-committee is merely a recommendation to a senior committee and we are not, therefore, free to go forward.[17]

Five months later it would appear that Schools Council had referred the matter back to the Board. A board official informed Topham:

I would now like to confirm that the Board's Advisory
Committe for Environmental Subjects recently gave further
consideration to your proposed special syllabus in rural
studies. The Committee confirmed their approval of the
principle of an examination of rural studies at 'A' level but
agreed that the current proposed syllabus was not suitable
for a course leading to such an examination. They felt that
the syllabus was too wide (i.e. gave details of too great a
breadth of subject material) to allow a sufficient study in
depth for an 'A' level examination. It is, therefore, suggested
that the syllabus should now be re-drafted with a reduction
in the total subject matter coverage.[18]

In preparing for a meeting with the Board to consider his redraft Topham was later offered a list of 'major points which will
need consideration.'

The content of the syllabus is too extensive to allow the study
in depth normally expected at 'A' level . . .
The formal written examination papers should indicate the
depth of treatment of the syllabus. Those submitted in
January 1969 indicated an insufficient depth of study for 'A'
level.
It would be advisable for the syllabus to originate from the
particular environment of the school and to develop from this
course.
It should be verified that success in an advanced level examination in rural studies would be acceptable as a qualification
for university entrance.
The question of the degree of overlap between rural studies
and other subjects must be considered. The degree of overlap would probably require the exclusion of any concurrent
presentation of biological subjects and geography.[19]

THE HERTFORDSHIRE 'A' LEVEL

In August 1969 Paul Topham left Shephalbury to become an
advisory teacher in environmental education under Sean Carson.
Upon his joining the county staff Topham and Carson discussed
the future of rural studies in the county: 'We more or less
agreed that we should really do environmental studies and we
would like to make a complete changeover, though be realistic
and realise not everyone would join in.' The changeover to
environmental studies was for two reasons: Firstly, the National
Association, in dialogue with Mervyn Pritchard of the Schools
Council Rural Studies Group, had already advised that environmental studies should be recognised and promoted by rural
studies teachers; secondly in circulating his draft 'A' level in
rural studies, Topham had: 'taken advice from various people,
biologists, geographers and so on in universities and basically

they were saying we were talking about a broader aspect and
that perhaps we should use the word "environment".' Carson and
Topham decided upon a strategy to implement the changeover
to environmental studies in the Hertfordshire secondary schools.
They concluded that: 'probably the best way to establish environmental studies would be at the highest academic level that
could be established in schools.'

Paul Topham was somewhat ambivalent about the new undertaking which inevitably superceded his Shephalbury initiatives:
'I would like to have seen this piece of work as a school-based
"A" level, if only to show that a school can put an "A" level up
and get it accepted.' He felt that what was particularly significant about the Shephalbury scheme 'was the fact that we were
trying to tailor a course to the needs of the kids and not
have to meet the requirements of other people's courses.' The
Hertfordshire initiatives began in the final months of 1969 with
a series of evening meetings with teachers to discuss the
possibilities for teaching the new subject. By now Topham
thought: 'that we had got to prove that environmental studies
was something that the most able of students could achieve and
to do something with it . . . if you started off there all the
expertise and finance that you put into it will benefit the rest -
your teaching ratio goes up, etc. and everyone else benefits -
the side effects that people don't mention sometimes.'

Sean Carson adds a number of reasons for the founding of
the working party of Hertfordshire teachers:

> In talking to Paul, we decided that the only way to make pro-
> gress was . . . to draw up an examination even though it
> meant entering the examination racket . . . We decided that
> the exam was essential because otherwise you couldn't be
> equal with any other subject. Another thing was the compre-
> hensive education was coming in. Once that came in, no
> teacher who didn't teach in the fifth or sixth form was going
> to count for twopence. So you had to have an 'A' level for
> teachers to aim at.

Initially, the working party consisted of a group of headmasters and sixth form teachers drawn almost exclusively from
12 Hertfordshire schools interested in teaching environmental
studies at 'A' level. In early 1970 the group met to redraft
Topham's 'A' level which had recently been rejected for the
third time by the Examining Board. On 23 February, Carson
began a new set of negotiations with the Board: submitting the
new syllabus 'on behalf of a consortium of schools in Hertfordshire . . .'

Carson explained that as a result of the working party's
deliberations, Topham's syllabus had been 'completely redesigned'. It was divided into four sections: (i) physical
environment; (ii) biological systems: (iii) productive systems;
and (iv) the changing environment. It was to be taught in 'an

integrated manner with practical studies throughout' with '40 per cent of the marks given for records of fieldwork throughout the course.' Carson concluded hopefully that 'as the content of the syllabus has not been appreciably changed and we understand that the previous paper was agreed in principle by at least one of the Schools Council Committees we look forward to this paper being adopted as early as possible.'[20]

The Associated Examining Board rapidly judged the new submission and it would appear that on 10 March Carson was unofficially informed that the submission was unsuccessful. On 3 June he informed his Chief Education Officer that he was writing to the Examining Board to try to elicit the basis for their comments on 10 March.

At this point the County Education Officer decided to call a conference to which were invited university teachers, representatives of the examination boards, colleges of education, professional bodies, HMI, the Schools Council, the representatives of the Hertfordshire head teachers and sixth form teachers who had started to meet as a working party to reconsider the syllabus.[21] The initiator of the conference idea was Sean Carson:

> I went to see our County Education Officer . . . said what we'd like to do . . . that we couldn't get any satisfactory answer from exam boards about things we put up . . . universities wouldn't accept rural studies, and didn't know what they were supposed to accept.
> Could we have a conference, I would write to universities, head teachers etc. and try to get from them what sort of thing we should be doing and the okay to do it. So that is what we did, we set the conference up.

The Offley Conference

Aims and Objectives

The conference met at Offley in Hertfordshire from 23 to 25 October 1970. In convening the conference it is clear that the advocates of environmental studies in Hertfordshire followed Carson in hoping that the sponsorship of the univerisities and other professional groups could be engaged to overcome opposition to the new subject. A local head stated: 'This may possibly be an historic occasion. It is not very often that a new discipline is injected into the English system of education.'[22] Another headmaster felt that 'There are those who are themselves regarded as academically acceptable who might produce an acceptable syllabus'.[23] The aims of the conference were outlined by its convenor, Mr S.T. Broad, the Hertfordshire County Education Officer: 'This conference has been called to do a job of work. We hope, as a result, to have an area of study called environmental studies or environmental science, clearly outlined, that will have the authority of this conference behind it and

which we can present with confidence to schools and examination
boards.'[24] The source of the 'authority of this conference' was
hinted at later: 'Some agreed core is essential to any further
advance . . . it must lead to an "A" level examination acceptable
for university entrance.'[25] The power which universities had in
determining 'A' level acceptability was dealt with in Carson's
introductory speech; Referring to earlier pioneers of 'A' levels
in rural studies, he stated:

> Often they were asked 'what evidence have you that univer-
> sities would accept candidates with this sort of "A" level',
> and on making enquiries to universities the reply was 'show
> us the successful candidates and we will tell you'. A chicken
> and egg situation. Finally it was decided to contact the univer-
> sities direct and see whether there was sufficient interest and
> agreement on the subject for an attempt to be made to break
> the deadlock. Hence this conference.[26]

A later speaker was even more explicit about his perception of
who controlled the content of the 'A' level when he said 'In
crude terms we must consult the customer and get his ideas
of what the product should look like in detail.'[27] The reasons
for schools accepting the universities' hegemony were clearly
enunciated by Mr Broad. 'It is essential for schools now that
there should be "A" level courses acceptable for university
entrance. For courses to succeed in sixth forms it is important
for them to have academic respectability and validity and this is
often represented by examinations.'[28]
Later in the discussion Professor Hunter, using a broadened
concept of 'the customer', dealt with some of the potential
problems:

> I am convinced of the value of environmental studies on edu-
> cational grounds but there is the difficulty of convincing the
> customer. The problem is that the customers, and in particular
> the Civil Service, are specialists. They don't want people
> with a general picture except for a very few at the top and
> these normally arrive there in the course of their professional
> experience.[29]

M.H. Edwin of the DES commented that: 'What is coming out of
our discussion is the familiar tension between school courses
based on pupils' needs and courses which meet university
requirements';[30] and developing this theme, Mr Hartrop of
Durham University Education Department then reminded the
conference 'that the real customers are the pupils who will take
this course'.[31]
In summarising one of the group discussions Professor Hunter
alluded to an emerging dichotomy:

> We must decide whether we are aiming in the schools at a

syllabus to satisfy university entrance requirements or one
on educational grounds. Although a course aimed mainly at
educational value may be highly desirable, there is a danger
of environmental sciences being put in a similar category as
general studies. If this then has to serve as a university
entrance requirement, I think university selection committees
will be reluctant to accept it in assessing a student's ability
for a university place.[32]

Syllabus Discussion

The Offley Conference, having begun with the introductions by
Mr S.T. Broad and Sean Carson and the report of the Hertfordshire teachers' working party, was organised around a series of
papers and study groups, each followed by group discussions.
Dr R. Best spoke on 'Problems of the Countryside', Professor
Newbould on 'World Conservation Problems', and J.D. Fladmark
on 'The Urban and Social Environment'. Study groups considered 'A Sociological Approach', 'A Biological Approach',
'World Conservation Problems' and 'Man and his Environment'.
The idea of the specialist papers and study groups was to focus
discussion on specific themes, but the original transcripts
indicate that the participants were mainly concerned with certain
fundamental issues. One group leader reported: 'I have no
guidelines for a syllabus to offer' because 'members obstinately
insisted that far more fundamental questions had to be answered
before you could get down to an actual syllabus.'[33] Two recurrent
features in the discussions were firstly, the concern for the
boundaries of the knowledge to be defined and secondly, the
search for unifying themes or concepts for the new 'A' level
subject. Sean Carson had in fact exhorted the conference to
consider these questions in the first session: 'Definition of the
concepts is important, and delineation of the boundaries. This
will be your main task at this conference. Some things must
finish up outside our boundaries if only for reasons of the
limited time available in schools.'[34] Before the study groups he
added: 'The Chairmen of the groups will bring you up against
the hard facts and I draw attention to the necessity for establishing boundaries early in the conference.'[35]
    The participants who gave most consideration to boundary
problems at the conference were the representatives of the
university science and geography departments. In his introduction, Mr P. Jackson, a Hertfordshire headmaster, had
referred to the biologists and geographers as 'the heavy-weight
group'! Their comments bear elegant testimony to Esland's
perspective on 'subject communities': 'They are exponents of
English, Maths, or whatever; they have been initiated into the
problems and procedures of a community which appear to them
as plausible and self-evident.'[36]
    Professor Newbould discussed the entry requirements for his
School of Biological Studies at Ulster with regard to boundaries:

'Will "A" level environmental studies substitute for biology?' he
asked. 'I am not clear about this. Biology and geography "A"
levels will continue to be the main intake, but how will this new
subject adjust to existing subjects? It might be necessary to
adjust the boundaries between subjects.'[37] The following speaker,
Dr Healey of King's College Zoology Department, added: 'I
assume a course with a geographical basis with biology included.
I agree that boundaries need careful definition.'[38] Later Newbould hinted that when boundary negotiations were completed
a new subject community might emerge: 'We would also hope to
produce teachers who would teach environmental studies in
schools, and thus that the circle would be completed.'[39]
Geographers were also very concerned about the boundaries of
the proposed new subject. A number of speakers were evidently
worried about the degree of 'overlap', but a solution was proposed by Dr Douglas of Hull University, who stated: 'To have a
scheme of environmental studies which is different from
geography, such as wide-ranging environmental studies of the
local area or part of your immediate school hinterland would
create a new field of study which doesn't overlap too much with
geography.'[40] Mr Hartop of Durham University Education
Department asserted that: 'The way in which geography is
developing now includes almost everything now suggested in the
environmental studies syllabus. Parts of geography could be
expanded to consume almost everything.'[41]

Another speaker, Mr Pritchard, who had chaired the Schools
Council working party on rural studies, commented on the
problem posed by subject representatives on exam. board
committees: 'the Boards analyse such a syllabus only in geographical content, or they go before a biological committee and they
examine them only for biological content. Each of these complains
that there is not sufficient for their own discipline'.[42] Professor
Newbould, in conceding that 'we have to draw boundaries', saw
that 'the one essential is to have lines drawn logically'.[43] As
a partial solution to the problem of 'the breadth and depth
implicit in the subject of environmental studies',[44] he suggested
that 'a strong unifying theme'[45] was needed. (Newbould recommended that the theme should be 'Energy'.)

The search for a unifying criterion was connected with the
procedures of examination construction. Jackson commented
somewhat invertedly:

> To develop a subject for which the present examination system
> is not structured, requires both naive students and irrespons-
> ible teachers. As long as examinations are the status symbol
> in the sixth form, we must make it possible to pursue their
> (environmental) studies without handicap.[46]

Miss B. Hopkins of the University of London Schools Examination
Board asserted: 'We must look for unity in construction in the
syllabus',[47] and Mr G.J. Neal of Schools Council added: 'This

criterion is one by which acceptance is governed. The elements
of unity and of depth of study are regarded as important. You
cannot take one particular subject in isolation from the examination as a whole, they must have some degree of comparability.[148]
That the 'essential unity' of environmental studies as a new 'A'
level subject was regarded as problematic by some was implied
in the final discussion. The confrontation between Mr Lucia of
the Associated Examining Board and Mr Broad of Hertfordshire
was to prove prophetic:

Mr Lucia: We have had a syllabus put forward to us, as you
know, for environmental studies and have approved it at
'O(A)' level. I think, however, that we must look carefully
at some of the reasons for examining environmental studies. I
did not find impressive the arguments that, say history and
mathematics are available at both 'A' and 'O' levels. These
are subjects which are taught in infant, primary and secondary
schools and they take on very different aspects in these different areas. I think I am right in saying that the problem is one
of definition. This conference must ask itself the question -
what is it that we see as fundamentally an 'A' level discipline
and does the subject 'environmental studies' satisfy our
criteria? I understand the London, Oxford, N.J.M.B. and
Cambridge Boards have 'O' level syllabuses either for general
use or as special papers. Our problem here is concerned with
the paper of an 'A' level syllabus. We find ourselves, as did
the Chairman of one of the four groups, referring to the fact
that an 'A' level syllabus should be 2/3 science - is this
generally acceptable? We shall not be able to decide whether
environmental studies is appropriate for 'A' level examining
until we have sorted out our aims and objectives and decided
what part of the sixth form is likely to be involved and why
they want this particular examination.
Mr Broad: Yes, perhaps because you have not been here during
the Conference you have missed some of the explanations. The way
in which we started off was to say that none of the company here
was unaware of the need for conservation. We accepted that as
a nation we have almost the entire mass of the people in
positions of authority, superbly ignorant in these fields and
yet wielding enormous power. We thought that it would be a
good idea that these people should not be so ignorant and
that in fact the people who were going out from our schools
and universities should not be without any knowledge of the
problem of environmental control at all. We realised that the
supply of teachers either from universities or colleges of
education who should be basically knowledgeable in these
matters was essential. Everybody here accepts the need for
the 'A' level course, without which we cannot begin to deal with
the problems. If Britain isn't able to deal with the problem what
other country can? It is urgent that something should be done
and that we ought not to be choking over gnats at this stage.[149]

Significant in this discussion is Mr Lucia's comment which
introduces the link between the search for boundaries and
unifying criteria and the need for an 'A' level examination to be
'a discipline': 'What is it that we see as fundamentally an "A"
level discipline and does the subject "environmental studies"
satisfy our criteria?' Once again this reaffirmed the sort of
criteria used by examining boards and the need for an overarching definition of a 'discipline'. This would have most
academic acceptability if developed by university scholars, but
in Hertfordshire it was to be developed in detail largely by
practising teachers.

The Hertfordshire Working Party

Aims of the Working Party

The maintenance of the momentum after the Offley Conference
was provided by an initiative in Hertfordshire promoted by
Sean Carson. Clearly the local follow-up to Offley had to take
place rapidly so as to maximise the prestige and status afforded
by such a large gathering of academics and educationists.
Carson decided the best way to follow up Offley was by convening a working party composed of a range of teachers whose
specialist subject reflected the main content areas of the envisaged syllabus. The group met in December 1970 with a clear
brief 'to prepare an "A" level syllabus, based on the views of
the conference, for submission to a number of examination
boards'. This objective was pursued in the hope that an
examination board would adopt the syllabus and thus make
it possible for schools everywhere to devote sixth form time and
teaching to environmental studies. The working party was made
up of specialists in those disciplines Carson and Topham adjudged
relevant; notably biology, physics, geography, history and
social anthropology. The participants were all practising
teachers freed from their teaching duties on the relevant days
to work at the Hertford Teaching Centre. They were aided by
Dr J. Kitching of Durham University, Miss B. Hopkins of the
University of London Schools Examinations Department, Dr
Healey of King's College, London, Mrs J. Riley of Manchester
University and Mr J. Sykes of the Town Planning Institute.

The teachers were expected to develop the sections of the
syllabus where their specialist disciplines contributed. But
'Sean laid it down at the beginning of the working party that
all comments by separate subject specialists on their subject
must be phrased in ways understood by the full team . . . and
the relationships between subjects had to be developed.'

Other requirements for an 'A' level syllabus were clarified in
the early period of the working party's meetings. A telephone
memo which seems to be from an examination board exists for
early February 1971.[50] This memo and other information, much
of it gathered at Offley, allowed Carson to define in March 'a

number of clear functions' for an 'A' level syllabus. He claimed 'the working party have had these in mind throughout':

> Firstly, the examination must be recognised by a number of university faculties as a qualification for entry.
> Secondly, universities generally must recognise the course as a discipline of sufficient rigour to indicate intellectual quality of the successful candidate . . .
> Thirdly, an 'A' level pass must offer career opportunities at non-graduate level . . .
> Fourthly, an 'A' level syllabus must offer a course that is relevant to modern needs, educationally worthwhile and which has a logical unity of purpose . . .
> Fifthly, the introduction of a new course at this level must offer new educational methods (which will involve students deeply) and new examination methods which will assess achievements in these activities if it is to justify its inclusion as distinct from (and not instead of traditional subjects) . . .
> Finally, the course has to be a practical possibility in schools . . .[51]

The requirements that the course 'has to be a practical possibility in schools' seems weakest when viewed in terms of who would teach the course. As we have noted, the main constituency among teachers was likely to be the rural studies teachers - a group of teachers largely trained for, and associated with, 'non-academic' pupils. Carson and Topham set out with a predilection for geography and biology and consequently asked geographers and biologists to join the working group. These specialists tended to see the exercise in terms of the 'gains and losses' for their specialist subject. Hence the factual content derived from these traditional disciplines was actively promoted. As a result the 'A' level emerged with a strong bias in favour of the more 'academic' geographical and biological content. As a result viability of the course within schools depended heavily on the involvement of these specialists in teaching the course. As we have seen, the self-interest of such specialists often ran counter to involvement in such integrated courses. Carson's syllabus, whilst intellectually justifiable, faced major problems of political viability.

CONCLUSION

The Hertfordshire initiatives promoted by Carson and Topham followed from their belief that 'the best way to establish environmental studies would be at the highest academic level'. The practical appeal of this strategy was that teaching ratios and resources would both improve if the able students were to be offered an academic examination. Both Carson and Topham believed that 'the only way to make progress was to get in on the examination racket' and with the emergence of comprehensive schools they saw that 'no teacher who didn't teach in the fifth and sixth form was going to count for tuppence!'

The initial negotiations with examination boards having proved abortive, Carson decided to organise a conference of academics and headmasters to 'try to get from them what sort of things we should be doing', and the 'okay to do it'. The plan 'to gain the consent and sponsorship of the universities' was supported by the Hertfordshire Chief Education Officer and by local headmasters. One of the latter noted that 'there are those who are themselves regarded as academically acceptable who might produce an acceptable syllabus'. The nature of university influence over 'A' level examinations is clearly evidenced, although the tension between the academic tradition and pupil needs is signified in the comments of Edwin, Hartrop and Hunter.

What is, however, very clear is that university personnel were far from unanimous in their response to this new area of knowledge. Following Young, one would expect that the dominant interest groups within universities would firmly reject the initiative as indeed many of them did. But the significant point is that Carson was able to select a range of supporters from within the universities who were willing to act as promoters of the new subject. In this way the conference represented an attempt to reverse the normal hierarchical control of examination syllabuses by the universities in selecting university personnel who were actively on the side of this new contender for academic status. At the same time, the concern with 'boundaries' at the conference implicitly conceded the territorial concerns of most geographers and biologists (evidenced best in the early reactions to Topham's syllabus). Such opposition was normally channelled into contesting the claim of environmental studies to be a discipline, thereby fighting on ground where traditional academic subjects were strongest. Similarly the opposition of the examination boards was based on the sort of points raised by Lucia about whether environmental studies was 'fundamentally an "A" level discipline'. By invoking the academic tradition in this manner, Lucia was contesting Carson's strategy of establishing academic credibility by an organised display of university support.

NOTES

1 Speaking of these courses a group of HMIS felt they could 'justifiably claim' 'A' level status, op. cit. 'Trends in Education', October 1967, p. 30.
2 George Wing Letter to Sean Carson, 27.11.67.
3 Internal memo, Shephalbury School.
4 Rural Studies 'A' level: First Draft, Shephalbury County Secondary School.
5 Letter, 27.7.67, personal file.

6   Letter, 6.2.67, personal file.
7   Letter, 20.7.67, personal file.
8   Ibid.
9   Rural Studies 'A' level, Second Draft, Shephalbury County Secondary School.
10 Carson, M.Ed., p. 369.
11 Letter, August 1967.
12 Ibid.
13 Ibid.
14 Letter, 20.11.67.
15 Letter, 26.7.68.
16 Letter, 18.2.69.
17 Letter, 23.6.69.
18 Letter, 4.11.69.
19 Letter, 12.1.70.
20 S. Carson to P.D. Neale, Secretary to the Board, 23.2.70.
21 S. Carson to S.T. Broad, Internal memo, 3.6.70.
22 S. Carson (ed.), 'Environmental Studies, The Construction of an "A" level Syllabus' (Slough, NFER, 1971), p. 6.
23 'A level Environmental Studies', Report on a Conference held in Hertfordshire on 23rd-25th October 1970 (Hertfordshire County Council, mimeo), 1970, p. 12.
24 Ibid., p. 54.
25 Ibid., p. 3.
26 Ibid., p. 4.
27 Ibid., p. 8.
28 Ibid., p. 11.
29 Ibid., p. 3.
30 Ibid., p. 14.
31 Ibid., p. 15.
32 Ibid., p. 16.
33 Ibid., p. 56.
34 Offley Report, p. 55.
35 Ibid., p. 29.
36 Ibid., p. 50.
37 Ibid., p. 9.
38 Course E282, Unit 2, p. 7 (section written by G. Esland).
39 Offley Report, p. 13.
40 Ibid.
41 Ibid., p. 15.
42 Ibid., p. 29.
43 Ibid., p. 17.
44 Ibid., p. 29.
45 Ibid., p. 40.
46 Ibid., p. 31.
47 Ibid., p. 32.
48 Ibid., p. 11.
49 Ibid., p. 30.
50 Hertfordshire 'A' level file.
51 Carson, 'Environmental Studies' pp. 76-7.

GEOGRAPHY AND ENVIRONMENTAL STUDIES

The Emergence of Environmental Studies

The first reactions to the emergence of environmental studies from geographers came in 1950. At the time, the Royal Geographical Society was preoccupied with the threat of social studies, but in the memorandum on that subject attention was drawn to the associated dangers of environmental studies. Concern focused on the growth of environmental studies in training colleges, though the report noted: 'Under the name of "social studies" this new subject is being increasingly taught in schools.' In the colleges, environmental studies were replacing geography courses and ' . . . as a result, the number of teachers in training who study geography beyond the stage they reached at school is reduced to the small percentage taking "advanced" geography.' The report recognised a further danger, that: 'Student teachers may misunderstand the special purpose of this course of "environmental studies" in their own training, and regard it as another "subject" suitable for the primary or secondary modern school.'[1]

In fact geographers' fears that trainee teachers would not be successfully socialised into their subject proved premature. The advance of environmental studies really began in the second half of the 1960s and for a time geographers remained more concerned with successors to social studies such as 'IDE' and 'humanities'.[2] In the presidential address to the Geographical Association in 1967, E.C. Marchant typified the normal response of geographers to such integrated work. '"We geographers", they say, "have built up our subject into a discipline which is at last treated with academic respect: now we are asked to undermine it with superficiality, propaganda - and pictures of water taps".'[3] A year later, the President, Alice Garnett, criticised geographers' responses:

> We rightly acclaim our discipline as a unique 'bridging subject' and as a keystone in educational curricula, so concerned within itself with the integration of knowledge that, surely, geographers should be the first to express interest in taking a lead in such interdisciplinary trends. Yet at times I have gained an impression that the reverse seems to be the case.[4]

The uncertainty about responses to IDE and humanities integrated courses was discussed by the Executive Committee in 1969, but new worries were voiced: 'at the omission or exclusion of geography from some current integrations of subjects in secondary schools'. The minutes then noted that 'there were no specific findings to report back' but that in the meantime 'correspondence with members has shown their fears concerning the threat to geography involved in the growth of environmental studies in schools, colleges and universities. There was a matter worthy of deeper consideration.'[5] Some members felt that even discussing this would be: 'tantamount to admitting the validity of environmental studies or would indicate a measure of approval.'[6]

In addition to the legacy of geographers' responses to the 'threat' of integrated studies stretching back half a century, the reaction to environmental studies was complicated by a further factor. In earlier sections the internal dissent among geographers with reference to 'new geography' is recorded. In large measure the opposition came from those with a 'regional' or 'fieldwork' orientation in their training and practice. The close relationship of regional geography and the fieldwork tradition was reflected in the work of Professor S.W. Wooldridge. He argued that the aim of geographical fieldwork is 'regional synthesis',[7] and in his obituary in 'Geography' it was recorded by M.J. Wise, later an advocate of close links with environmental studies, that: 'Above all, geography was for him regional geography.'[8]

In 1966 Professor C.A. Fisher read a paper to the Research Committee of the Royal Geographical Society - it was later published in extended form under the title 'Whither Regional Geography?' Fisher argued that geographical research was in serious danger of 'over-extending its periphery at the expense of neglecting its base'.[9] For Fisher the 'traditional core of geography' was regional study as against the 'new', systematic geography, but he noted: 'While systematic geography now flourishes like the Biblical bay tree, regional geography (however defined) appears to be declining and even withering away.' Fisher added some details of this decline of regional geography: '. . . not only has there been a noticeable decrease in the importance attached to it in the university syllabus, but this process is apparently also spreading to the schools'. He noted the announcement that the Southern Universities Joint Board 'O' level geography examination for 1970 would include no paper in regional geography.[10]

The increasingly threatened supports of regional geography were therefore faced with the pervasive challenge of new geography alongside the more traditional challenge of integrated studies currently epitomised by environmental studies. For once the internal threat seems to have been deemed greater than the external dangers represented by the emergence of environmental studies. The obituary of Professor P.W. Bryan, an eminent regionalist, records that in 1967: 'Only twelve months before his

death and already a sick man' he attended a 'strenuous full-day
conference at Leicester University on environmental studies.
He probably felt that this term expressed more clearly his own
life's work and ambitions as a geographer.'[11] Similarly, in 1970,
P.R. Thomas asserted in 'Geography' that:

> The tendency towards an environmentalist approach to explan-
> ation in school geography is at least partly due to the survival
> of the regional concept as the basis for syllabus construction,
> despite the progressive decline in the importance of regional
> geography at most universities and its virtual disappearance
> from some.[12]

But the alliance between regional geography and environmental
studies was not to last. Partly this was because after 1970 the
'new geography' tradition began to lose impetus and became
increasingly assimilated into traditional patterns of geography.
A college lecturer felt 'the new geographers became less violent
. . . they flushed regions out but then accepted regionalism back
in not as facts . . . but as a spirit and concept.' He noted a
further conclusive reason for ending the alliance: 'The crisis in
geography caused traditional geographers to flee into environmental studies . . . they wanted a refuge to go on teaching as
they were teaching . . . but they were overtaken by the
environmental crisis and the rapid growth in environmental
studies that followed it . . .'[13] The increasing convergence of
new, systematic geography and regional and field geography,
together with the rapid growth of the new subject of environmental studies, once again helped unite geographers in their
opposition to the perceived external challenge.

The Geographers' Reaction 1970-1975

The initiatives from Hertfordshire, led by rural studies teachers,
to promote environmental studies as a new school subject and
'scholarly discipline', culminated in the Offley Conference of
1970. The spokesmen for geography at the conference reflected
the growing concern. Dr Douglas, for instance, sought to define
environmental studies in a way that would not 'overlap too much'
with geography.[14] Indeed commenting on the claims the geographers made, Mr Hartrop, in a manner reminiscent of the Norwood
Reports' complaints at the 'expansiveness of geography' nearly
30 years before, commented that 'parts of geography could be
expanded to consume almost everything'.[15]

The reasons for the geographers' reaction can partly be
deduced from the evidence of a sample survey of secondary
schools carried out by HM inspectors in 1971/2.[16] They found
that whilst in grammar schools only one 'combined studies' course
had replaced geography (one out of 44 schools), in secondary
modern schools 40 schools out of 104 had replaced geography by
such courses, and in comprehensive schools 20 out of 59 schools.[17]

That the geographers were intensely worried by the threat
of Hertfordshire teachers defining an 'A' level in environmental
studies was illustrated when Sean Carson went to speak to the
Geographical Association at this time.

I was invited to go and speak on environmental studies . . .
There was a really good start when the chairman said 'I'm
Chairman of this meeting but I can't adopt a neutral attitude
on something I feel so strongly about . . .
Then I made my spiel about geography not being God-given
religion, but a range of knowledge we had assembled to our
convenience and there was no reason why we shouldn't
reassemble it in any other form. This (i.e. environmental
studies) was another form in which it might be reassembled
and just because you had learnt things in a different tradition,
there's no reason why you should go on repeating so other
people repeat it after you . . .'

After his speech "There broke out shouting and rude remarks
and the Chairman made very little effort to control it . . . they
said I was out to destroy geography. I remember thinking 'its
like facing a Congressional Inquiry'."
The geographers' official reaction to environmental studies was
summarised in a presidential address to the Geographical
Association on January 1973 by Mr A.D. Nicholls. His speech
began by asserting, somewhat wishfully: 'It is not surprising
that in the minds of most teachers, environmental studies should
be associated with geography'. Having thereby hinted at the
thrust of his argument, he later stated: 'The definitions given
by well-known geographers to provide answers to the question
"What is geography?" might equally well be used to answer the
question. "What are environmental studies?"' And similarly, with
a sideswipe at 'new geography': 'In the first decade of this
century the founding fathers of the then "new" geography came
from many and varied disciplines. Their original choice of
discipline would make an admirable list of environmental
studies.'[18] Nicholls' views were undoubtedly shared by most
geographers; one college of education lecturer remembers that
at this time: 'At an early environmental studies meeting we felt
that geography had been doing it for years and we said so . . .'[19]
Tony Fyson also claimed that: 'On a pragmatic level a new
subject dealing with the environment is still going to leave a lot
of geography teachers claiming that their traditional fare is the
true way to approach the topic'; and that 'on an academic level
it is possible to argue that geography . . . can develop to
include the aims of the environmental studies lobby'.[20]
Nicholls' second argument turned on the need for 'a subject';
again he drew on a long tradition. In 1913 Dr J.F. Unstead had
argued against MacKinder's advocation of a combined subject, saying that a subject is an organised body of knowledge and that: 'in
geography, the facts do hang together.'[21] Unstead's argument

was again used in the 1960s when there were fears about school
geography: 'No subject can claim a place on the school curriculum
unless it has a clear structure, a precise theme and a worthwhile
purpose . . . if geography is to survive in school it, too, must
be a scholarly discipline with a clearly defined purpose and a
carefully organised structure.'[22] Nicholls began by conceding
that environmental studies were generally accepted as useful in
teaching 'young children' but then argued that: 'As the width
and depth of knowledge acquired increase so does the need to
specialise; subject divisions appear and the need for subject
disciplines arises. These codes of study are the framework or
basic principles which are necessary for specialised learning
and understanding.'[23]

The role of geography as a subject discipline ordering and
unifying the 'unrelated facts' of environmental studies was widely
promoted by geographers at this time. 'Geography because it
is an integrated discipline at the heart of environmental studies
is better placed than any of the other constituent nuclei to co-
ordinate and unify the larger body of studies of which it is the
core'.[24] The implicit hierarchy contained in this statement is
clarified by another geographer exploring the same relationship:
'To put it in terms of a model, geography may be likened to a
pyramid the base of which is environmental studies, but the
apex is the sharp intellectual discipline fashioned in the
university.'[25] A university professor confirmed this view, and
explained the implications for school geography: 'You need high
level theoretical development first of all . . . then you break it
down to digestible level in school.'[26]

The third strand of Nicholls' argument, undoubtedly the most
convincing aspect for the many teachers in the audience, dealt
with the 'practical realities' for 'practising teachers'. Crucial
to this argument was the recognition that:

> It is likely, but by no means certain, that if environmental
> studies or environmental education is considered as a subject
> in its own right, some, but not all, of the time previously
> devoted to constituent subjects will be made available to the
> new omnibus subject. With constant pressure on teaching time,
> headmasters are ever searching for new space into which
> additional prestige subjects can be fitted, and the total loss
> of teaching time to environmental subjects may be considerable.
> Nor, in my experience, have I found departments very eager
> to surrender precious teaching time, particularly with the
> more able classes, to make good other departments' losses.

Nicholls stressed a further practicality: 'If undifferentiated
environmental studies of an omnibus nature are to be introduced
into the school curriculum, which of the academic disciplines is
going to cater for suitably qualified men and women to take
charge of them?'[27]

A publication prepared by the Environmental Education Stand-

ing Committee of the Geographical Association, which included
Mr Nicholls, clarifies the nature of the fears over such 'wrang-
ling'. They assert that 'The concerns of environmental education
render the presence of a person with geographical training in
each team quite essential'; and similarly:' . . . that a team which
lacked a geographer would be handicapped; a team with one
would have a wider range of possible activities.'[28]

Nicholls explored this theme in considerable detail in his
address: 'Qualified men and women of academic stature have
selected their subjects because of their interest in them and the
importance they consider them to have. They also like to see
the inspiration of their teaching reflected in their pupils'
"advancement".' The relationship between subject expertise and
pupil advancement is later elucidated:

> A shallow approach to any subject inevitably becomes less
> satisfying, and finally utterly boring both to teacher and
> class. Not every question from a class calls for an immediate
> answer in depth, but when the teacher's ignorance of the
> subject becomes evident to the class the pupils lose confidence
> in their teacher, and more pitifully, the teacher loses confi-
> dence in himself, and confusion becomes chaos. The teacher
> must know his subject . . .[29]

The relationship between the status of a 'subject' and the
pupils which traditional subjects attract, is alluded to by
Nicholls in discussing a DES survey's findings with regard to
environmental studies: Four varieties were distinguished:
(a) one comprehensive school used environmental studies for all
first-year pupils and thereafter separate subjects were taught.
(b) two schools have environmental studies for slow learners
in years 1, 2 and 3 only; the average and able pupils did
ordinary subjects. (c) two schools gave environmental studies
in year 4 only for fourth-year leavers. These were non-
examination pupils. The rest did ordinary subjects. (d) one
school gave environmental studies for able fifth-year pupils for
'O' level as option against other subjects. From these findings
Nicholls concludes:

> First, average and above average pupils are considered to be
> able to cope with ordinary subjects, though it might be
> unsafe to assume they would rather not spread their abilities.
> Secondly, environmental studies are thought to be easier or
> can be made more attractive to less able scholars. Thirdly,
> separate subjects may be easier to teach successfully. Cynics
> might suggest that combined studies provide a more successful
> opiate to potentially rowdy classes. You as teachers, may
> reach other equally valid conclusions.[30]

The last sentence confirms that the message, despite its philosophical and logical shortcomings, aims to focus on the teachers'

perception of the practical realities of their work.

The final strand of Nicholls' argument concentrates on the need to keep geography as a unified discipline. An earlier President had touched on the socialising role of the university. Geography departments which 'have a duty to ensure that, at least at the first degree level, the core of our subject is neither forgotten nor neglected and that the synthesis of the specialist fields and their relevance to that core are clearly appreciated by our undergraduate students.'[31] The symbiotic relationship between the university geography and school geography is explored:

> There is now an intake from sixth forms, into our university departments of at least one thousand students each year to read geography. The recognition of our subject's status among university disciplines which this gives, together with the now costly provision made available for its study, could never have been achieved without this remarkable stimulus and demand injected from our schools.[32]

Nicholls argued from a similar position about what is required of geography as a subject:

> At sixth form level it must . . . provide a challenge to the young men and women who may have ambitions for the future and wish to carry their studies further and go to a university. They will become, in the best sense, students. Some of these will furnish the university schools of geography with young men and women who will expect to have some knowledge with sound and deep foundations so that understanding between them and their lecturers, readers and professors is mutual. We should be wise not to stray too far from the recognised routes – the frontiers of the subject are alluring, but not all are worth extending, at least in School. If we provide the universities with undergraduates who have a wide but shallow acquaintance with many subjects, will they prefer these students before those with a sound foundation in fewer relevant subjects?[33]

Nicholls' conclusion stressed the need for staying within 'the recognised routes':

> Ten years ago, almost to the day and from this platform, Professor Kirk said 'Modern geography was created by scholars, trained in other disciplines, asking themselves geographical questions and moving inwards in a community of problems; it could die by a reversal of the process whereby trained geographers moved outwards in a fragmentation of interests seeking solutions to non-geographical problems'. Might not this be prophetic for us today? Could it not all too soon prove disastrous if the trained teachers of geography

moved outwards as teachers of environmental studies seeking solutions to non-geographical problems?[34]

Nicholls' conclusion is as explicit a statement of the geographers' 'party line' as it is possible to make: in effect he is saying we must not allow the process which created geography to be repeated.

Negotiations for Environmental Studies as a Subject

Nicholls' only allusion to the Hertfordshire initiatives was obscure,[35] but support for environmental studies was actually voiced in the address which followed Nicholls'. Professor Wise, a university geographer schooled in regional geography and the fieldwork tradition, echoed the schism in the geographers' ranks noted earlier, when he said: 'we sometimes tend to assume that "geography" and "environmental studies" are synonymous. The theme of this paper is that, while they are not, geography has an essential contribution to make.'[36]

Following Nicholls' argument we can see why such an assertion was a dangerous heresy. The extent of this heresy was made clear later in the paper when he recommended the growing tendency to think in terms of replacing subject-oriented courses with the problem – or concept-oriented courses centred on aspects of the environment appropriate to inter-disciplinary attack. He added later that 'Clearly, the field is too wide to be the property of one or even a small number of academic disciplines.'[37]

Sean Carson, who concedes that Professor Wise 'has always been supportive' consulted a number of sympathetic geographers at about this time in the course of the negotiations for the London 'A' level. His reply to the geographers stressed a number of common assumptions in the arguments they deployed. Notably the tendency to argue that 'everything is geography' or that 'parts of geography can be expanded to comprise almost everything'. This he noted was in fact 'to say that geography is not in any way a specialism'.[38]

At an ATO DES course in March 1973, Carson offered a defence of his whole strategy:

If environmental education is to lead to the study of the problems I have outlined then a discipline of some recognisable sort must exist. For this reason I do not agree with those that suggest that existing subject definitions should suffice to cover these problems by an adjustment of their syllabuses. This is not in my view a practical proposition. A main subject in this area of curriculum is geography, but developments in geography are in another direction . . .[39]

Later he developed this last point:

I had thought . . . that in geography they have introduced
very much more the statistical approach and the idea of
patterns . . . Therefore they don't any more do geology, the
landscape and the rocks underneath. Well, this is good environmental stuff, understanding the landscape. So I said to the
geographers, 'you don't want to do that any more – our people
do! If you're worried about the technical barrier being drawn
between us, we'll do the landscape appreciation.'[40]

Though factually dubious, in that many geography teachers
continued to teach physical and regional geography, Carson's
strategy was a masterly way of exploiting the schism among
geographers, and serves to explain the passion with which his
initiatives were thereby greeted.

The answer provided by the Geographical Association to
Carson's strategy of defining a new discipline was to argue
against the feasibility of such a definition. A discussion paper
prepared by the Standing Committee on Environmental Education
in December 1974 argued that: 'There has been a growth of
environmental studies in schools which merely utilizes a wide
range of inter-disciplinary material as stimuli in the classroom.
This method lacks any real integration of the material, though
it does not create any new subject boundaries.'[41] In this way
the lines were drawn up for the negotiations inside Schools
Council, following a strategy of denying that geography and
environmental studies were sufficiently distinguishable for the
latter to be a separate discipline.[42]

Later, in 1975, a paper circulated to the Schools Council
Working Party on Environmental Studies noted that:

At present, students taking environmental studies at G.C.E.
'A' level are not allowed to combine this choice with geography.
Subject compatibility is frequently a source of discord but it
is important to prevent the perfectly legitimate misgivings of
academics about subject demarcations being turned into
obstacles unfairly placed in the path of students.[43]

In the event, the delaying tactics pursued by the geographers
have now produced a positive strategy along the traditional lines
of internal subject re-definition. Recently a number of syllabuses
entitled Environmental Geography have appeared and a new
'Handbook for Teachers' of this emerging synthesis produced.
The title Environmental Geography was used 'to emphasise our
aim of helping to restore the study of school geography to a
central role in the understanding of the human habitat . . . we
contend that geography, along with ecology, offers an important
way of comprehending environmental problems.'[44]

CONCLUSION

The historical background of the relationship between geography and integrated studies confirms the existence of a series of subgroups within the subject. In the early twentieth century those geographers arguing for an 'integrated subject', notably MacKinder, were opposed by those aspiring to an 'academic' subject. In the latter group Unstead characterised geography as 'an organised body of knowledge, the different parts of which naturally hang together' and the Geographical Association as 'a balanced subject with a unity of its own'. The process thereby initiated was later described by Marchant who noted that 'we geographers have built up our subject into a discipline which is at least treated with academic respect'.

Marchant was writing in 1967, but new schisms lay ahead. Most significant of these was the struggle between groups with allegiance to regional and field geography and those promoting new geography. Carson exploited this schism in promoting his version of 'environmental studies' and in doing so won a number of supporters within geography (e.g. Professor Bryan and Professor Wise). In the long run, however, new geography established a major place within the subject which could now claim to be a fully-fledged academic discipline. The role of university scholars in defining geography is noted in the phrase which portrays a subject whose 'apex is the sharp intellectual discipline fashioned in the university'.

The practical realities of academic status are clearly enunciated by Nicholls' speech. Hence 'average and above average pupils are considered to be able to cope with ordinary academic subjects' and these pupils at present are taught geography. Environmental studies 'are thought to be easier or can be made more attractive to less able scholars'. If, however, environmental studies were to be considered an 'academic subject in its own right', the 'total loss of teaching time to environmental subjects may be considerable'. Nicholls adds 'Nor, in my experience have I found departments very eager to surrender precious teaching time, particularly with the more able classes.' The threat of losing able students and departmental resources is thereby made real if academic parity is conceded to environmental studies. By placing the threat to resources and career at the centre of the debate about geography's future the implicit exhortation is to subjugate the claims of intellectual scholarship to those of subject self-interest.

BIOLOGY AND THE PROMOTION OF FIELD STUDIES

Biology and the emergence of Environmental Studies

In the fifties and sixties rural studies was viewed condescendingly by biologists - as courses of applied biology for the less able. The Report of the Study Group on Education and Field

Biology reflects the manner in which biologists kept rural studies at arm's length: 'In their present rather fluid state, rural studies are not at all easy to assess critically and realistically.'[145] Following the Keele Conference and later, the Hertfordshire Conference at Offley, some biologists began to consider the emerging 'environmental studies' more seriously. The 1960s and early 1970s were, as noted before, a time of rapid change and redefinition in the field of science education. Inevitably some of these reformist efforts overlapped into the domain of rural and environmental studies.

At this time a number of boards were reconsidering their science papers at 'O' level and 'A' level, particularly in subjects like 'rural biology'. This reconsideration coincided with efforts by rural studies advocates to redefine their subject and occasionally the two initiatives converged. For instance in June 1970 Carson reported to the Hertfordshire working party that Paul Topham: 'has been invited to be a member of the Biology Advisory Panel of the London University Examination Board. This panel are producing an "O" level syllabus which we expect will closely follow the Hertfordshire ideas (as does the Oxford Local Boards "O" level paper). The panel have raised the possibility of an "A" level and we have sent them our syllabus.'[146] The fraternisation of rural studies teachers and biologists was not all one way, however, for a number of prominent biologists became involved in new 'environmental' initiatives. A working party set up by the Joint Matriculation Board Examination Council to define an environmental studies/science 'A' level included several prominent biologists, notably Professor D.H. Jennings of the Hartley Botanical Laboratories. The working party was weighted with other 'science advocates', lecturers and teachers. Not surprisingly the group finally agreed to title the syllabus they drew up 'environmental science'.[147]

The manner in which biologists who became involved in new 'environmental' syllabuses still retained their affiliation to their parent discipline, is eloquently testified to by John Price. Price became Chief Examiner to the Associated Examining Boards new 'O' level in environmental studies. At a conference called by the Board to discuss the paper he had drawn up, he had this to say:

> The apparent biology weighting throughout was mentioned several times. I could justify this by claiming that Environmental Studies really is the ecology of man and to that extent is a biological subject but if you look at the syllabus you do in fact find that a lot of it could be described as biological. It may be the technology of agriculture or horticulture but it can still be called biology.[48]

The biologists who became involved with new environmental studies syllabi were mainly advocates of ecology and field studies. As we have noted the major developments in biology were at this time antagonistic to such approaches. W.H. Dowdeswell became involved with the Wiltshire working party on Rural and Environmental Studies, whilst Dr Perrot, the other major advocate of field biology, became involved in producing pamphlets for the National Association of Environmental Education. Yet the involvement with rural studies was always restrained and 'loyalty' to biology, even if in fundamental disagreement with the direction the subject was taking, was always paramount.

This paramount loyalty meant that rural studies teachers were left to dominate the emerging field of environmental studies, for developments in biology were clearly leading elsewhere. Dowdeswell saw this with remarkable clarity:

> Rural Studies, of course, was always the depressed area, they were always the underdogs, generally underqualified, they were always looked down upon by school staff . . . they always got the wrong end of the bone and all that. Through developing 'O' levels and 'A' levels in Environmental Studies they had a chance of finally achieving academic responsibility.

However rural studies and biology were viewed as very close in terms of content if not in terms of status: 'Rural Studies always looked to me like Biology . . . some of it is applied Biology in the sense that you get into the gardening and cultivation area. My students who go out to teach Rural Studies always end up teaching Biology.'[49]

The rapid expansion and final establishment of biology as a high-status school subject in the 1960s left the subject more or less unhindered by the challenge of rural and environmental studies. The only exception was in the combining specialist development of ecology and field biology. Hence the main challenge to biology was deflected from the mainstream hard science laboratory core of the subject towards the fieldwork elements which the subject was anyway concerned to play down. In the battle for control of 'field studies' the biology (and geography) fieldwork advocates were able to maintain a dominant influence over field studies, in spite of being only minority groups within their own subjects.[50]

Field Studies

The use of the rural environment as an educational resource, which had been traditionally advocated by rural studies teachers, was also promoted from 1946 onwards by the Field Studies Council (initially called the Council for the Promotion of Field Studies). The Council made very slow progress and in 1960 had only six centres in England and Wales (which existed alongside the rural studies centres run by three local education authorities). Even at this stage traditional disciplines seem to have dominated in the provision of courses in the centres. We are told they were: 'designed mostly for sixth-form pupils from grammar schools, and for student teachers and university undergraduates in biology, geography and geology.'[51]

In 1960 to overcome 'the shortage of data about the existing situation, results and trends within the education system and the consequent difficulties in directing field studies along lines likely to achieve desirable educational objectives',[52] the Nature Conservancy established the Study Group on Education and Field Biology. The Study Group's establishment marked the beginning of an effort to promote field studies work through close liaison with the traditional disciplines in the school curriculum, notably biology.

The Report of the Study Group in 1965, as the title 'Science out of doors' indicates, began to define ways in which the science teacher, particularly the biologist, could use field studies. Also at this time the Nuffield Foundation Science Teaching project were considering ways of utilising field study techniques.[53] The 1965 Education Conference sponsored by the 'Countryside in 1970 movement' confirmed that field studies and science were coming to be seen as closely related in school curricula. In his opening address to the Keele Conference, Lord Bowden assumed that studies of the countryside in schools would be the responsibility of the science teacher. After referring to the Nuffield initiatives, 'at this moment, as you probably know, the whole processes of organising and teaching science in schools are being completely transformed',[54] he went on to comment on the potential of this curriculum reform.

> To a certain extent physics is bound to be a formal subject, best taught in the lab. But this is not at all true of Biology, and I think it is extremely important that children should have opportunities of going out into the field and realising for themselves what the scientific method is.[55]

The synonymity of field studies of the natural environment and science is confirmed later: 'There is an immense merit for the whole of the future of science in the great development of a type of experimental work which children can do in the natural environment.'[56] In a similar vein Dr Pritchard of the Nature Conservancy, who acted as 'Scientific Secretary' to the Study Group on Education and Field Biology, argued that: 'Environmental Studies must be firmly anchored to Scientific disciplines because the problems created by the intermingling of natural and human forces can neither be understood nor interpreted without the use of science'.[57] Dr D.E. Perrot submitted a paper to Conference on 'Research on the Teaching of Field Biology' which reported a programme carried out at Keele University in 1964.[58] The programme indicated that field studies was

> a better stimulus to the recall of factual information than other types of work for pupils of 12-15 of all kinds of ability, but by mental age 16 pupils engaged in field problems showed the

greatest gains in recall . . . At that stage pupils engaged in field problems showed greater increases in problem-solving skills than those engaged in laboratory problem-solving and other types of work.[59]

Following the Keele Conference, geography teachers also became active, and the Geographical Association established a standing committee of field studies. In 1965 and 1966 the committee completed surveys of facilities for field studies and in 1969 a further survey was completed by the Geographical Association, covering local authority field centres and other sorts of centres for field study work. The interest of the Geographical Association was reflected in the growing use made by geography teachers of field studies to teach their subject.

The promotion of field studies was essentially linked to the traditional disciplines of biology and geography, and throughout left rural studies firmly outside the dialogue. From the beginning Carson had protested that field studies were being linked with only subjects recognised as academic disciplines. Speaking of the Study Group on Education and Field Biology he wrote: 'Because rural studies was not recognised as a discipline at any academic level, even at "O" level, the Group was prevented from giving it serious attention.'[60] And at the Keele Conference he twice protested at the apparent hegemony of the biologists: 'In spite of all that has been said about broadening the outlook, we still seem[ed] to be talking in the narrow context of biology.'[61] He asserted: 'The approach of biologists in schools, colleges and universities was too narrow and formally scientific and took insufficient account of agriculture and other land uses.'[62]

Carson wanted a more interdisciplinary conception of field studies of the environment. At Keele he said: 'We must break down the barriers between academic disciplines. In Secondary Modern Schools this [is] particularly important'.[63] His later writings confirm this vision: 'When it came down to terms it was unfortunate that the educationists present were so concerned to present their separate cases that there was no time for them to come together and agree.'[64] In another article, written under a pseudonym, Carson wrote that at Keele: 'A major weakness that still plagues efforts to establish Environmental Studies became evident. This was the inability of teachers representing school subjects to appreciate the interdisciplinary nature of environmental problems and to move from entrenched positions defending their own interests.'[65]

The degree to which biology and geography had come to dominate field study work can be seen in a survey carried out in 1965. Of the total number of centres doing field study work, 120 covered geography and biology as subjects, 53 'general environmental studies' and 40 agriculture, horticulture and forestry. (These figures and later figures partially confuse the issue by including rural studies under 'agriculture, horticulture and forestry', but also some rural studies teachers would have been involved in 'general environmental studies'.) In the Field Studies Council centres only 14 covered the two traditional disciplines, 6 general environmental studies and 3 agriculture, horticulture and forestry. By 1969 the number of centres having grown: 332 now covered geography and biology, 167 general environmental studies, and 123 agriculture, horticulture and forestry (including rural studies). In the Field Studies Council and school centres it was reported 'a distinct pattern of emphasis on rather more specialised subject treatment is available'. In the Field Studies Council centres 18 covered geography/biology, 5 general environmental studies and 5 agriculture, horticulture and forestry (including Rural Studies). In School Centres the corresponding figures were 32, 14 and 13.[66]

The figures from the 1965 and 1969 surveys show clearly that biology and geography were established as the main subjects using field studies of the natural environment. In this situation, claims that rural studies were uniquely concerned with the natural environment were rapidly losing credibility. Carson was clearly very worried and in January 1968 wrote to the General Secretary of the National Association, Richard Morgan, on the matter. Morgan replied that the Field Studies Association

cover a wider range of people than those interested in Rural Studies and we have no hope of carrying out the whole function they stand for. In this area, we have come to the conclusion that to fend them off our territory of study will only get us a poor name. . . . However, this does not prevent us existing – or being a strong voice in our own field. But I think that we shall be more effective in co-operation than in resisting and claiming that we already provide the service which they are trying to provide. Because this claim is not true; they are catering for a much wider range of environmental interest than we are.

Morgan's statement reflects the acceptance of the domination of field studies by groups largely drawn from biologists and geography. His comments provide an epitaph to the frustration of Carson's hopes for rural studies in this area by the existing field studies groups because 'they reach a wider membership than we can ever hope to reach they are bound to be stronger financially and in every other way than we are'.[67] In this manner rural studies was once again frustrated in colonising a viable area of curriculum activity.

CONCLUSION

In Chapter 4 we described how the competition in the 1960s within biology between the sub-groups representing field biology and ecology and those promoting a hard-science, laboratory-based version had ended with the subject dominated by the latter group. The field biologists for a time developed connections with environmental studies, rather in the manner of the geography sub-group that was on the defensive in the 1960s, the regional geographers. But in biology these connections were never very strong: the subject was rapidly expanding and about to achieve final establishment as a high-status school subject. Apart from this the field biologists secured a strong position inside the field studies movement and together with the geographers managed to control most of the field studies centres. In this position there was little reason to fraternise with rural studies.

Any challenge from the new environmental studies to the growing subject of biology was thereby deflected to and successfully managed by the 'field studies' group within the subject. For mainstream biology with its 'hard-science' image, and its rapidly growing number of departments (and associated laboratories) within schools and universities, the challenge of the new environmental subject was hardly worthy of consideration.

NOTES

1 Royal Geographical Society (1950).
2 C.B.G. Bull, I.D.E.: A Geography Teacher's Assessment, first printed in 'Geography 53' (1968), pp. 381-6, reprinted op. cit. Bale, Graves and Walford, p. 259.
3 E.O. Marchant, 'Some Responsibilities', p. 139.
4 A. Garnett, Teaching Geography: Some Reflections, 'Geography', Vol. 54, 4 November 1969, p. 396.
5 Geographical Association Notes of Meeting of Chairmen of Section/Standing Committee (28.9.70).
6 Ibid., p. 2.
7 S.W. Wooldridge and G.E. Hutchings 'London's Countryside', Geographical Field Work for Students and Teachers of Geography (London, Methuen, 1957), p. xi.
8 M.J. Wise Obituary: Prof. S.W. Wooldridge, 'Geography', Vol. XLVIII, Part 3, July 1963, p. 330.
9 C.A. Fisher, 'Whither Regional Geography?', 1970, p. 374.
10 Ibid., pp. 375-6.
11 R. Millward, Obituary: Patrick Walter Bryan, 'Geography' Vol. 54, Part 1, January 1969, p. 93.
12 P.R. Thomas, 'Education and the New Geography', pp. 274-5.
13 Interview, 14.12.76.
14 Offley transcript, p. 29.
15 Ibid., p. 27.
16 Department of Education and Science, Education Survey 19, 'School Geography in the Changing Curriculum' (London, HMSO, 1974).
17 Ibid., p. 6.
18 A.D. Nicholls, Environmental Studies in Schools, 'Geography',

Vol. 58, Part 3, July 1973, p. 197.
19   Interview, 14.12.76.
20   C. Ward and A. Fyson, 'Streetwork - The Exploding School',
     (London, Routledge and Kegan Paul, 1973), p. 106.
21   'Geographical Teacher', 1913.
22   N.V. Scarfe, Depth and Breadth in School Geography,
     'Journal of Geography', Vol. XXIV, No. 4, April 1965.
23   Nicholls, 'Environmental Studies', p. 200.
24   Ivor Thomas, Rural Studies and Environmental Studies,
     'See', Vol. 2, No. 1, Autumn 1969.
25   K.S. Wheeler Review of D.G. Watts' 'Environmental Studies',
     (London, Routledge and Kegan Paul, 1969), 'Journal of
     Curriculum Studies', Vol. 3, No. 1, May 1971, p. 87.
26   Interview, Leicester University, 14.12.76.
27   Nicholls, 'Environmental Studies', p. 200.
28   'Environmental Studies; A Discussion Paper for teachers
     and lecturers prepared by the Environmental Education
     Standing Committee of the Geographical Association',
     draft edition (January 1972).
29   Nicholls, 'Environmental Studies', pp. 200-1.
30   Ibid., pp. 204-5.
31   Garnett, 'Reflections', p. 389.
32   Ibid., p. 387.
33   Nicholls, 'Environmental Studies', p. 201.
34   Ibid., p. 206.
35   Ibid., p. 198.
36   M.J. Wise, Environmental Studies: Geographical Objectives,
     'Geography', Vol. 58, Part 4, November 1973, p. 293.
37   Ibid., p. 296.
38   S. Carson, review of 'Streetwork' in 'Environmental Edu-
     cation' (Summer 1974), pp. 56-7.
39   S. Carson, ATO/DES Course, Paper No. 2, 'Environmental
     Education: Design for the Future' (March 1973).
40   Carson interview.
41   'The Role of Geography in Environmental Education. A
     discussion paper presented by the Standing Committee for
     Environmental Education to the Geographical Association
     Executive' (December 1974), pp. 1-2.
42   Carson, memo to Broad (16.3.73).
43   University of London GCE 'A' level Environmental Studies,
     Paper presented to Schools Council Working Party on
     Environmental Education.
44   K. Wheeler and B. Waites (eds,), 'Environmental Geography:
     A Handbook for Teachers' (London, Hart-Davis Educational,
     1976), p. 9.
45   'Science Out of Doors', p. viii.
46   S. Carson at Hertfordshire Working Party, Hertfordshire
     File, 3.6.70.
47   'Joint Matriculation Board Proposals for the Introduction of
     a Syllabus in Environmental Science (Advanced)', (mimeo,
     n.d.).

48　'Associated Examining Board Environmental Studies: Report of a Conference' 23, October 1971, p. 46.
49　Dowdeswell interview 24.10.77.
50　Study Group on Education and Field Biology, 'Science Out of Doors' (London, 1963), pp. 94-5.
51　Ibid., p. 83.
52　A. Herbert, P.M. Oswald and C.A. Surkes, Centres for Field Studies in England and Wales, the Results of a Questionnaire Survey in 1969, 'Field Studies', Vol. 3, No. 4, 1972, p. 658.
53　Proceedings of the Conference on Education, 'The Countryside in 1970', Keele, 1965 (London, Nature Conservancy, 1965), p. 20.
54　Ibid., p. 7.
55　Ibid., p. 8.
56　Ibid.
57　Ibid., p. 11.
58　Ibid., p. 20.
59　Ibid.
60　Carson M. Ed., p. 61.
61　Op. cit. 'Proceedings of the Conference on Education', 1965.
62　Ibid., p. 16.
63　Ibid., p. 22.
64　S. Carson, 'N.R.S.A. Journal' 1964-5 p. 33.
65　W.P. Fenwick, Education and Environment, 'The Ecologist', August 1972, p. 8.
66　Herbert, Oswald and Surkes, 'Centres for Field Studies', p. 676.
67　Letter from R. Morgan to S. Carson, 19.1.68.

NEGOTIATIONS WITH THE EXAMINING BOARDS

In the period during which the Hertfordshire working party
were completing their final draft of the 'A' level, from late 1970
into the early months of 1971, only two examining boards were
actively involved. As has been noted, one board had been
scrutinising the various proposals ever since Topham's first
submission in 1967. A second board, London University, had
allowed an examinations officer to attend the working party
meetings, but it had stressed that she was attending only in 'a
private capacity'.[1]

In January 1971, Carson received two detailed replies from
the first board to his letter enclosing the working party's draft.
The first letter noted[2] that the secretary of the Board had
'shown the preliminary draft syllabus to a number of colleagues
and it has been generally well received'. The main objections
were to the fieldwork-oriented Section 2 of the syllabus. The
secretary stated that there was a 'need to know a lot more about
how to teach Section 2 in the schools', and added that this
would also 'resolve part of the examination problem. I doubt if
the large volume of fieldwork suggested is possible from the
examiner's point of view.' The uncertainties about Section 2
were amplified later in the letter; the secretary perceived two
main problems. The first was whether it could 'measure up to
the criteria for an "advanced level" study'. In other words 'can
it be made explicit that the studies undertaken will be equivalent
in intellectual demands made upon the pupils to studies undertaken as parts of other established courses leading to examination
certification at G.C.E. Advanced level?' In answer to this
question the secretary added 'my view is that it can, but that
more detail is required, perhaps in the form of notes for guidance, to make this clear'.

The second problem referred to assessment, and again the
secretary noted: 'I do not believe that this problem is as great
as the authors appear to fear': 'Any assessment method which
is proposed must be capable of producing reliable results: this
is essential for the sake of the pupils.' After listing 'a wide
range of organisations they must consult before embarking upon
this task' - for instance, the NFER, the secretary thought that
'the Schools Council might provide relevant information or be
prepared to help themselves'.

In a further letter, sent the following day,[3] the Board's

apparent optimism seems severely tempered:

> I have today received another commentary on your draft
> syllabus which is so detailed and obviously carefully thought
> out that I felt you would wish to see it even if it does arrive
> too late for your working party. The author indicates in a
> private letter to me that he is conscious of the blunt, destruc-
> tive nature of some of his comments but, as he is a man
> intimately concerned with environmental studies as such I
> feel sure you would welcome a verbatim transcription,
> especially at the preliminary draft stage of your syllabus.

His memorandum began with a series of detailed criticisms of the
sub-sections. In his more general comments which follow he
began by conceding 'that the time is right to regard environmental studies as a suitable medium to promote the intellectual
development expected of "A" level students.'
But in his reasons for his opposition to the Hertfordshire
proposals he elucidated points which had first surfaced at
Offley:

> My essential dissatisfaction with the proposals of Hertfordshire
> is that, like several other attempts at a syllabus for environ-
> mental studies, I cannot see it as a coherent discipline . . .
> The study must be a 'discipline' - a coherent body of fact and
> concept demanding an ordered mind for its appreciation and
> furtherance. It must be recognisable as such even by the
> student. The student must feel he is going somewhere, getting
> somewhere; and must feel he has accomplished something
> definable at the end of the course. The course must not be a
> collection of bits and pieces from other subjects - pursued by
> a hotch-potch of their disciplines. That is not sustaining food
> for a developing mind.

He then referred specifically to the Hertfordshire efforts to
define a discipline for 'A' level study.

> The Hertfordshire Conference was in part concerned to find
> some unifying theme which would serve as a backbone to the
> course. Hence the Energy Flow and Land Use ideas. But to
> my mind the only appropriate central theme to environmental
> studies is the organism that, in a sense, defines the environ-
> ment - man. The core of the proper study of man's environ-
> ment is man himself. Everything has a relevance and the
> whole has a coherence if man is consistently seen to be at the
> centre. This may seem to be a platitude, but it cannot have
> the unifying functions, cannot provide coherence and back-
> bone for a discipline, if it is taken for granted - as it is in
> the Hertfordshire syllabus.

Later in the memorandum he notes that most recent publications

derived from curriculum development work also devote considerable attention to the specification of teaching objectives. A clear
statement of the anticipated outcome of the proposed course in
environmental studies would ' . . . prevent many of the difficulties which might otherwise arise when the final version of
the syllabus is formally considered by examining boards and
the Schools Council.'

The latter prophecy was to prove, perhaps not surprisingly,
remarkably accurate. In fact as far back as June 1970, in reply
to a memo inquiring what the major problem was in getting the
'A' level accepted, Carson noted: 'It has proved very difficult
to get any information, but somewhere between the Board and
the Schools Council things are constantly stuck.'[4] The problem
continued throughout 1971. In March, in reply to Carson's
despatch of the final Hertfordshire draft, he was informed: 'In
recent weeks brief consultations have taken place but I have to
inform you that the general opinion is that your revised draft
does not meet the majority of the comments forwarded to you
from the Board in early January.'[5] In September, in a discussion
at the standing panel which Hertfordshire had set up to implement the 'A' level, it was minuted that the secretary of the
Board had 'turned down the proposals immediately on the argument that the method of examining was not suitable'.[6] In
December, S.T. Board wrote to Mr C. Mellowes at the Council
for Environmental Education, who was on the Board panel:

> I understand that Sean Carson has spoken to you about our
> 'A' level syllabus which had been turned down without its
> having reached your Education Committee, and I wonder if
> you could let me know what the position is. We are making
> some progress with other boards but a number of schools
> would still like to use the Board and to feel that the syllabus
> is receiving consideration by your Board also.[7]

Mellowes replied that he had 'already registered my opposition
to the ruling about the environmental studies "A" level proposals'.[8] In blocking the Hertfordshire proposals the Board
seemed to be in accord with the opinions of most of the examining
boards. Other boards had been sent the proposals and had
reacted with similar dissent. In December 1970 the senior
assistant secretary of another examining board approached by
Carson wrote,[9] somewhat increduously, about the first draft of
the syllabus prepared after Offley:

> The first reaction is that the syllabus is awesome in its
> demands. No proposals have been put forward in the confer-
> ence report or in the preliminary draft of the syllabus regard-
> ing the recording of examination results, but the allocation
> of time suggested under the heading Problems on the first
> page suggests that it is envisaged that the course is intended
> to be regarded as a single Advanced level subject.

He felt that:

> If this is the case then I fear that there is a serious danger
> that the approach to many of the topics included in the
> syllabus will inevitably be superficial. If the topics are to be
> dealt with in the depth implied by the draft, the syllabus is
> likely to be regarded as being far too overloaded and demand-
> ing.

Later in the letter this view was elucidated following a statement that the 'thematic approach of the syllabus is appreciated'.
'If an attempt were to be made to devise a syllabus without a
consistent, identified theme there would be a serious danger of
the subject matter being fragmented for both the teacher and
pupil.'

Some of the assistant secretary's fears appeared to be related
to notions about the 'new' clientele for 'A' levels which were
growing with the spread of comprehensivation. He argued that
some care would need to be taken to ensure that the 'A' level
proposals 'do not founder because they have been made with
too optimistic a view of what the sixth form pupil is capable of
achieving in one-part of his sixth form studies.' Again the
assistant secretary envisaged problems over the fieldwork:
'. . . the external assessment of such work is a difficult and
expensive operation and with the methods available the reliability
of such external assessments may be in doubt.'

By October 1971 with one board having turned the proposals
down and other boards plainly uneasy, Carson was beginning to
fear that no board would accept the Hertfordshire syllabus.
As a result new initiatives were taken and Carson attempted to
raise the matter with the secretaries of GCE examining bodies.
He received replies which made plain most boards' opposition to
the new syllabus.[10]

The opposition from the boards was reflected in the slow
progress with the London Board. Following the meeting of
GCE secretaries, the London Board had contacted Carson. The
original letter cannot be traced but Carson referred to it in
another letter written on 21 October to C.L. Mellowes: 'I have
received a letter from a secretary of London University
Examining Board saying he has become aware that it is being
suggested that his Board are going to service the "A" level
examination for everyone, but that this is not so. He seems
rather incensed by the suggestion.'[11] In spite of these fears
the London Board continued to follow the Hertfordshire developments closely and in December, after an invitation from Carson,[12]
sent a representative to a meeting of the Standing Panel of
Hertfordshire Schools set up to aid in the 'A' level's acceptance.
By January C.L. Mellowes was writing: 'I think there are
grounds for being hopeful about the response of the London
Board.'[13]

THE HERTFORDSHIRE STANDING PANEL

The Standing Panel was first mooted by Carson, after gaining the support of C.T. Broad, in July 1971. On 27 July the idea was put to Hertfordshire heads in a circular[14] saying there had been a number of suggestions that it might be appropriate for the schools intending to undertake the 'A' level environmental studies course to set up a Standing Panel so that mutual problems could be looked at as they arose. The Standing Panel representing the heads of schools and colleges was set up in order to keep an eye on the progress of the syllabus. It was hoped that official recognition by the Schools Council might be obtained by about March 1972 in time for schools to organise courses beginning in September 1972.[15]

The first meeting of the Standing Panel was on 27 September and the minutes[16] record that Mr Carson reminded members that all the work that had been done to have the syllabus accepted and all the publicity that had been received 'would count for nothing if in fact schools and teachers did not make arrangements to start the course and teachers did not take this opportunity'. At the second meeting of the panel on 15 December, attended by Miss Hopkins of the London Board, it was noted[17] that a meeting had been arranged for December 20. Miss Hopkins suggested 'that we did not push the board too quickly'. Carson reported to the heads on the London meeting:[18]

> The syllabus has been considered by four advisers of the London Board and their comments made no serious criticisms so the Board will be setting up a Subject Panel very shortly. It is hoped that this Panel will meet in January and that they will ask your representatives to meet them in February. As a result of this meeting a finally agreed syllabus will be put before the London University Council for approval on 2nd March. If they approve it will then be forwarded to the Schools Council for their May round of Committees and it is hoped that a result will be known in June 1972.

Carson then speculated on the implications for Hertfordshire schools:

> Although at this stage I cannot say anything definite I am very optimistic that we will have an examination available for students starting in September 1972 and I hope that you will feel confident enough to make your plans accordingly.

On 19 January a newly constituted 'ad hoc committee in environmental studies' of the London Board met in Gower Street, London, under the chairmanship of Professor Brown. The minutes noted that: 'The Hertfordshire Advanced level syllabus was dicussed and there was a general agreement that it should be considered as a London G.C.E. syllabus.' The syllabus was

considered in detail. Two main categories of revision were
suggested. Firstly, that in some sections 'syllabus content
could be considerably reduced, together with associated teaching
notes'. In some cases such reduction was suggested by subject
specialists on the panel: 'nothing is known about energy flow
in parasites - suggest this be removed from syllabus.' Secondly,
in Sections 2 and 3 particularly, there was a demand for more
consideration of the urban situation. In Section 2 the question
was posed: 'In this whole section, in the teaching notes, could
more guidance be given to the urban school?' In Section 3
'Urbanization should receive an earlier mention', 'notes should
include urbanization not being restricted to Britain'.[19]

On 4 February the ad hoc committee met the official representatives of the Hertfordshire Standing Panel: Mr Smith, Mr
Gwenlan and a biology teacher, Mr Lord. It was reported[20] that
the delegation agreed with the Board's committee that they
would recommend the syllabus to be put forward as a Mode II
'A' level syllabus in environmental studies which may be taken
by any school, either in Hertfordshire or outside on application.

At this stage Carson circularised[21] all those people who had
applied for information about the 'A' level. In the period after
the NFER publication many headmasters had written asking if
they could take the 'A' level.

> The syllabus is now ready to go forward as a Mode II syllabus,
> that is to say it will be limited to schools who have applied to
> take it rather than be available in the general circular. I have
> agreed with the London Board Environmental Studies 'A' level
> committee that membership of the Standing Panel of Heads
> concerned with environmental studies at 'A' level, which has
> been the negotiating body so far, may now be widened to
> include Heads from schools anywhere in the United Kingdom
> and that this would be the appropriate channel for application
> to take the examination.
> I am, therefore, inviting Headteachers to join the Standing
> Panel. Obviously it will not be necessary for their Heads to
> attend meetings although they would be welcome to do so,
> either personally or by sending a representative from the
> school. All the information will be centralised through this
> arrangement.

In advising the Hertfordshire schools to complete plans to
begin the 'A' level and the following year and in encouraging
schools from all parts of England to join the Standing Panel,
Carson was clearly anticipated a successful outcome at Schools
Council. In fact the negotiations with the university dragged on
until late May. On 10 May the Schools Council Geography Subject
Committee saw the syllabus and on 22 May the Science Committee.
On 7 June Carson circulated[22] members of Standing Panel:

> The representations to the Schools Council by the London

Board, on behalf of our 'A' level submissions, have not so far
proved successful and it is now likely that there will be further
discussions in the Autumn.
I regret to advise you that in the circumstances it seems most
unlikely that an examination will be available before June
1975, in other words students beginning the course in
September 1973.
This is a major setback but there appears to be no way round
it at the moment.

Carson reported the implication of the setback:[23]

We have suffered a setback from the Schools Council and it
does not appear possible for schools to take this examination
in 1974. That means that schools setting up courses this
September will have to aim them at alternative and less demanding examinations. At the meeting of the Standing Panel yester-
day, some agreed that they would do this and others thought
they might follow the 'A' level syllabus even if they had only
their own certificate to award at the end.
I hope we can still make grants this year to those schools
beginning sixth form courses in spite of this setback . . .

NEGOTIATIONS WITH SCHOOLS COUNCIL

The Standing Panel received detailed reports of the abortive
Schools Council negotiations on 21 June:[24]

On 10th May, Mr. Topham had attended the Geography Subject
Committee of the Schools Council. The syllabus was discussed
in detail, questions were particularly asked about the Section
on 'entrophy'.
On 27th May he had attended the Science Committee. This
committee had consisted of eight members only out of twenty-
four, of whom most seemed to be physicists and only one a
serving teacher. They had studied the first section of the
syllabus only and asked no questions about any other area.

The minutes add that Sean Carson reported that on 24 May 'we
were informed by 'phone from London University that the
syllabus had not been approved by either committee'. The
opinions of the geography and science sub-committees were later
detailed in a letter from Schools Council to the London Board:[25]
'It was felt that the syllabus was too extensive, not only because
it would lead to the superficial treatment of many topics, but
also because a number of sections appeared irrelevant to the
central concern of environmental studies.'
    The letter gives as an example of superficiality the case of
entropy: 'Members felt that this was a difficult concept and that
it should not be studied in isolation. It would be necessary to

know the difference between enthalpy and free energy before entropy could be understood.' The judgement as to the superficiality of topic coverage was quite clearly based on the specialists' knowledge of their own subject. The letter notes that a significant criticism was that: 'The depth of treatment of the science in the syllabus was not comparable with that of similar topics in an "A" level physics or chemistry syllabus.' If an interdisciplinary syllabus is judged for superficiality only from 'single subject' perspectives, the judgement is virtually self-fulfilling. Similarly with the criticisms as to the irrelevance of certain topics:

> The parts of the syllabus that seem to be quite removed from the core interests of the subject include (a) most of the work on geology, e.g. theories of the origin of land masses, plate tectonics, isostasy, (b) man as a heterotrophic organism, and (c) the historical evolution of man.

Following these judgements the letter proclaims in paragraph V (see later note 32).

> If such irrelevant topics were envisaged as removed, the effect would be to reveal how close the resulting syllabus would be to existing syllabuses in geography. Concern was expressed at the heavy overlap between this syllabus and syllabuses in both geography and biology. For example it was thought that a candidate prepared for geography would have little difficulty in answering many of the questions. The suggestion was therefore made that there should be some restriction on the subjects that could be offered at 'A' level along with environmental studies.

Two other criticisms were noted: firstly, that there was a clear feeling that by 'trying to make an umbrella for everything that might excite sixth-formers they were trying to do the impossible'. To some extent linked to this was concern 'at the view put forward during discussion in support of the syllabus that the syllabus was designed for the new sixth form, and not necessarily aimed at the pupil requiring an academic "A" level with a view to going on to university.'
A participant recalled the meetings with the two sub-committees representing geography and science. 'It was a territorial response . . . fair enough – it's a natural response. I think it was taken to extremes.'
He commented on the general 'climate of opinion' at the time of the meetings: 'What worried me is that the Schools Council at the point in time our syllabus was going up, was calling out for integrated approaches and types of syllabuses. This was the first one that came up and they didn't know how to manage it.'
He described how he considered Schools Council had reacted to the Hertfordshire initiative:

They brought together a bunch of geographers and scientists,
who were orientated to their own subjects and couldn't see
outside. That's the way they'd been educated and it's the way
they see their disciplines . . . and it's not their fault . . .
Those aren't the right people to get to comment on it.

Carson was particularly incensed by the science sub-
committee's position on entropy:

The Chairman said 'you can't mention Entropy unless you quote
the two laws of thermodynamics and then you must do the
supporting experiments.' Well, this would have taken two terms
and would have been so much physics it would have unbalanced
the whole thing. We had great arguments about this, went
back to the university – the university science people said
'how ridiculous'.[26]

Ivor Goodson: How do you explain the scientists' reaction to
that?
Sean Carson: In my opinion the scientists' view was 'we're not
having these people teaching that.' They're not doing it
properly . . . in science you don't make a statement, you arrive
at a conclusion based on experimental data – they would say.
I would say, they make experiments to fit the answer they want
. . . 'This is the scientific method . . . if you're not using that
method we don't want you making these statements.'
The point we were making is that you're not teaching physics,
you're using certain scientific information. You cannot go
through the process of building up each time you want to use
scientific or biological information.
Ivor Goodson: In which case you don't need a scientist to teach.
Sean Carson: No . . . we'd already said 'you don't need a
physical scientist'. A confident broadminded geographer or
biologist could teach it. We're already teaching combined
sciences in schools . . .
With the geography sub-committee Carson felt 'they were
anti the whole thing – more so than the scientists':

People would say 'there is nothing in this that couldn't be
taught in an "A" level geography syllabus.' We'd say 'no, it
isn't' and itemise how it was quite different . . . Some would
say silly things, for example, 'you won't get geographers
to teach this, so you won't be able to manage it' . . . I said
'we have geographers to teach it now' . . . They didn't want
to know that. They continually said we wouldn't get it
accepted by universities. So I said, 'Until I've got it finally
prepared I can't submit it to find out what universities would
accept it, but in fact here is the conference, here are these
people, some geographers, who have said they will accept
it' . . .

A Hertfordshire teacher commented on the immediate response to the Schools Council rejection: 'We were furious about it . . . Sean started a press campaign . . . the university were absolutely livid . . . So was Broad.' Carson recalled his reaction: 'At first I was lost . . . But I'm very stubborn, I became determined to get it through Schools Council . . . even at the expense of my health.' In a letter to Standing Panel members Carson commented on the letter received from Schools Council. Referring to the geography sub-committee's exhortation to remove 'irrelevant topics', he noted: 'Obviously if everything else is removed there would be nothing left but geography. Their suggestion shows clearly that they do not understand what we are after.'[27]

The first protests to the Schools Council came from the London Board. An assistant secretary informed Carson:[28] 'I am very disturbed at the slow progress of this business and have been in frequent communication with Schools Council to try to hasten the process.' A detailed letter from Hertfordshire to Schools Council expressing the dismay at the rejection:

Of our twenty-four schools, twelve have planned to start courses in September 1972 for examination in June 1974 and the authority has been generous in allocating funds for this development. I believe that it now appears unlikely that the one hundred and twenty students concerned will be able to begin the course after all. Already after a series of curriculum development workshops at teachers' centres, environmental studies courses at C.S.E. and 'O' level are running in many of our secondary schools and we have a pilot environmental studies scheme for examination at C.E.E. level. Both the regional C.S.E. Board and the London University Schools Examinations Department have established environmental studies panels composed of people practising in the field of environmental education to reflect the needs of our schools.[29]

The letter ended with an offer of help which indicated his desire for a speedy response and saying that he understood 'that you may be setting up an environmental studies panel, and if this is the case we would be glad to offer the services of some of our experienced environmentalists . . .' A week after this letter the Standing Panel met to consider their response. They 'unanimously agreed to ask the Chairman to prepare a letter to the Schools Council'[30]

asking them in what ways was the syllabus unsatisfactory; to set up an interdisciplinary committee; reminding them of their recent publication, 'Growth and Response' on sixth-form work which very much supported our approach, and pointing out the urgency necessary if agreement is to be reached this Autumn and another year is not to be lost.

The response of the University Examination Board was similar to the reaction in Hertfordshire, as a Hertfordshire adviser recalled: 'The University were absolutely livid that it had come back . . . especially those who had steered the whole thing through.' The university's letter to Schools Council followed closely the conclusion of the Standing Panel at a meeting on 12 September. Carson summarised their conclusions in a letter to Barbara Hopkins. He began by listing changes in the syllabus. Besides some changes in title the panel were willing[31] 'to accept the criticisms about Entropy and omit it, and also to omit much of the geographical material . . . we have also included some detail on the statistics required.' (The Schools Council letter of 13 July had stated 'In statistics it was felt more guidance should be given.') Carson then noted, 'I must report that they objected to Paragraph V[32] of the Schools Council's letter to Mr Stephenson and we have not made any major change in principle in the coverage of the syllabus.' Following several meetings between the university's advisers and Carson and Topham, Barbara Hopkins wrote to Schools Council.[33] The letter reiterates the changes listed by Carson and also notes:

> The comments in V caused some surprise. It would seem that the objectives of the syllabus have been misunderstood by the subject committees. The syllabus is considered to be a demanding one for any sixth former to study. It is felt that the views recorded in the last sentence of V did not accord with the tenor of the Schools Council Working Paper 45, 16-19 'Growth and Response' 1. 'Curricular Bases'.

A further section requested 'that the modified syllabus may be discussed with a single Schools Council representative body which includes experts with a professional concern for environmental studies'. One concession that the university had agreed with Carson and Topham was noted:

> The possible overlap with other London examination syllabuses[34] was discussed in some detail. The University advisors finally decided, with some reluctance, to recommend that candidates taking the syllabus should not be allowed to sit geography at the same examination.

The university representatives met the Schools Council committee on 17 January 1973. They were Professor E.M. Brown, Department of Geography, University College, London, and Moderator in Environmental Studies; Professor G.W. Dimbleby, Professor of Human Environment, Institute of Archaeology; Sean Carson and Paul Topham. Carson reported the results of the meeting in a memo:

> The Panel was a more representative one and included people prominent in the environmental studies field, as well as

representatives of all the G.C.E. Examining Boards and the Chairman of the Science and Geography Committee. The Panel was chaired by Mr. Sibson, Secretary of the Schools Council. We had an hour and a half's interrogation and then had to leave. I understand from my sources that the Panel then agreed to recommend the syllabus almost unanimously. It has to go to the Geography and Science Panels for their final approval which it will do in the next few weeks, but I am assured, privately, that this time there will be no trouble. As soon as we get official confirmation of its acceptance, schools will be able to begin to organise courses for September 1973, to be examined in June 1975. There are likely to be two restrictions on the syllabus - (1) it may not be taken with geography at the same examination, and (2) it will be limited to schools in the Standing Panel although how flexible this will be remains to be seen.
Everything seems to be over now, bar the shouting, and the next job will be to encourage schools to develop their courses.

The acceptance by the Schools Council's ad hoc committee on environmental studies was confirmed by letter on 21 February 1973.[35] The syllabus was to be offered 'on an experimental basis for a period of five years'. The general tenor of the remarks is markedly different from those received from the science and geography sub-committees the year before. For instance: 'Commenting on the way in which assessment and moderation were to be carried out the plea was made that in the initial stages these operations should be as complex as time and money would allow.' In several cases previous exhortations were reversed: 'The suggestion was made that less emphasis should be put on the mathematical treatment of statistics. Instead students should be encouraged to use the laboratory approach in the recording of data.'
The schools taking the examination were now organised by the University Examinations Board into a 'consortium'. In the final list of schools submitted to Schools Council on 5 July 1973 there were 24 schools and colleges from Hertfordshire and 16 from other parts of the country.[36] These schools began the course in September 1973.
Fittingly, the last word in the negotiations with Schools Council came from the science and geography sub-committees. The assistant secretary had written on 18 February and 11 April to ask about the general availability of the syllabus. In reply, on 23 April, the Sixth Form Curriculum and Examinations Officer stated:[37]

I put the question of general availability of this syllabus to our Science and Geography 'A' level committees and as you know they were most unhappy about its being generally available and wished me to say just this.
In order to be as helpful as possible, I did, however, circulate

the syllabus in its revised form to members of the ad hoc
group and asked that they assess the syllabus pointing out
where they felt it unsuitable.
In the light of the comments received, the Chairman of the
Geography 'A' level sub-committee has now been through the
revised syllabus and made the comments which are attached . . .

In many ways the Chairman's comments resemble unrepentant
reiterations of the sub-committee's earlier position. This is
made clear in the first comment: 'It was noted with approval that
candidates could not take this examination together with
Geography'. The major concerns were again

about the breadth of coverage that may lead to a consequent
superficiality of treatment. There was concern also about the
continued inclusion of aspects that seem to have no direct
relevance to the main objective of the syllabus and it was felt
that certain parts of it could be reduced or omitted thereby
achieving greater focus on the main aims of the syllabus.

The final point was again familiar:

There is as yet no indication that universities would be prepared to accept a pass in this subject as an entry qualification
for degree courses and in order to gain acceptance by the
Council it may be necessary for a statement to this effect to be
a preface to the syllabus.

Sean Carson's recollection of the negotiations with Schools
Council is inevitably somewhat bitter. Of the detail of the
negotiations, he remembers disconcerting factors related to the
'architecture' of committee meetings, which he found intimidating:

A big room . . . right round the chairman. You're under fire
in a sort of desk situation. They will have considered it
already . . . and will put their points to you and you can
reply. The other people will support them. The whole thing
lasts less than . . . maybe an hour . . . They're polite but
hostile.

He felt that

The Schools Council finally cracked through too much pressure
. . . What can you say? This was a school-based piece of
work. This is what schools and teachers wanted - not what
the hell the Council wanted . . . This is the fundamental
point about it that really got under my skin . . . Curriculum
development should not be done by Schools Council, then be
imposed on schools. I'm not decrying them but it should be
the other way round. This is the first piece of curriculum
development from schools and teachers in the history of

English education to reach Advanced Level. If the needs are
there what right have Schools Council . . . All right, tell us
about standards, advise us about content and where we might
be falling short on skills and abilities. All right . . . but
they're not right to put down the syllabus . . .

In a letter to a leading advocate of environmental education.
Carson confirmed these opinions:

> The problems are enormous, but although there has been
> considerable support from the universities the group [Hertford-
> shire Working Party] are not happy about the reaction of
> Schools Council, who have the final say in allowing schools to
> take the syllabus. In their opinion the fact that the Schools
> Council is organised in subject committees means that these
> committees jealously guard the preserves of their subject.
> There is no environmental studies committee, but after con-
> siderable pressure the Schools Council set up an Ad Hoc
> Environmental Studies Committee to vet the syllabus. Unfortu-
> nately this consists of the chairman or representatives of
> other subject committees, who are more concerned to obstruct
> rather than to encourage the development of a cross-
> disciplinary subject such as this is (it is true there is one
> environmentalist co-opted to the committee). By their con-
> stitution, the Schools Council's committees should have a
> majority of serving teachers . . . This committee, however,
> has to the best of my knowledge no serving teachers at all
> and certainly none representing environmental studies as
> such although we have asked for this a number of times.[38]

CONCLUSION

The negotiations for the Hertfordshire 'A' level show clearly
how the process was dominated at key points by the academic
subject tradition. The comments made by the representative
from the examining board strongly reiterate points raised at
Offley. He wrote: 'The study must be a discipline   a coherent
body of facts and concepts demanding an ordered mind for its
appreciation.' The thorough renunciation of the pedagogic
tradition was implicit in the statement that the syllabus should
be a discipline and must be recognisable as such, 'even by the
student'.

The dominance of the academic subject tradition was confirmed
not only by ideology but by the organisational structure through
which the Hertfordshire 'A' level had to pass before recommendation. The 'A' level, an avowedly interdisciplinary scheme,
was perused at Schools Council by traditional subject committees
who made comments which reflected a profound misunderstanding,
or wilful disregard of the 'A' level's interdisciplinary intentions.

Thus the science sub-committee found to its apparent amazement that 'the depth of treatment of the science in the syllabus was not comparable with that of similar topics in an "A" level physics or chemistry syllabus.' When an interdisciplinary syllabus combining academic, utilitarian and pedagogic intentions is appraised by such committees only in terms of the academic content of existing disciplines the judgement is merely self-fulfilling and serves to duplicate the traditional academic content of existing disciplines within the new subjects. This renders the subject committee's second line of defence similarly inevitable. Since 'irrelevant topics' have to be removed so that the main (academic) topics can be covered in single subject 'depth', it follows that the effect is 'to reveal how close the resulting syllabus would be to existing syllabuses'.

The intransigence of the subject sub-committees seems to have caused embarrassment inside the Schools Council and fury among those involved at the London Examining Board. The Schools Council responded by forming a new panel to sidetrack the subject committees, the Examination Board reacted by sending two well-known professors to argue the syllabus's case. Even then the subject committees responded with evident resistance, still being 'unhappy' at the syllabus being 'generally available'. As a result the syllabus was limited to a five-year experiment within schools in the Standing Panel and was not to be offered with geography. These conditions, which express the continuing power of the traditional academic subject committees, were enough to ensure the syllabus would not gain many recruits. Carsons's judgement of the Subject Committees reflected his disappointment. In 1974 he wrote: 'The fact that the Schools Council is organised in subject committees means that these committees jealously guard the preserves of their subject.' These committees he thought come from 'the descendants of the old Schools Council, which was called the Examination Council'. He saw them as 'the status quo, what they call "standards" and all that', and felt they were made up of the 'most conservative academics' in universities and the 'uncommitted and conservative elements among teachers'.

Certainly the judgement that the subject committees 'jealously guard the preserves of their subject' seems to be substantiated by the record of events, although this was true for the 'middle of the road' subject specialists as well as the conservative elements which Carson, probably unduly, draws attention to. The range of limitations put on the new 'A' level and especially the one-year delay must have substantially affects its progress. The 'A' level has in fact been adopted in only the small minority of schools associated with the Standing Panel, and they base the 'A' level within their old rural studies departments. In 1972 there were 28 schools preparing for the examination, 19 of them in Hertfordshire. By 1975 this had increased to 35 schools, 20 in Hertfordshire. Only in Hertfordshire has there been encouragement at county level to provide graded posts for heads of environmental studies departments.

Since 1975 the pattern of financial retrenchment has adversely affected the prospects even for those dedicated schools taking the 'A' level. This will have an influence on the Hertfordshire 'stronghold' as Carson recently noted: 'The economic cuts will no doubt effect the spread of the "A" level, as will the present attention given to a core curriculum. Already several schools and F.E. colleges have packed up because they could not get enough candidates . . . and I hear that more plan to drop out.'[39] The recent examination board figures for June 1979 record that in secondary schools 168 candidates took the examination.[40] As a final footnote, in 1979 Sean Carson retired. Without its leading advocate in Hertfordshire and the NAEE the 'A' level plainly faces a very difficult future. The prolonged 'filibuster' engaged in at examination board and School Council level together with the restrictions initially placed on who could take the 'A' level may have ultimately blocked the aspirations of environmental studies not only to broad-based acceptance but to actual survival at 'A' level.

NOTES

1   Hopkins to Carson, 4.1.71.
2   Letter to S. Carson, 7.1.71.
3   Letter to S. Carson, 9.1.71.
4   Memo 5048 SMC.BC/RS/01/2, S. Carson to S.T. Broad, 17.12.70.
5   Letter to S. Carson, 26.3.71.
6   Minutes of the meeting of the Standing Panel held at Offley Place on Monday 27 September, Hertfordshire File 07/2.7.
7   S.T. Broad to C.L. Mellowes, 13.12.71.
8   C.L. Mellowes to S.T. Broad, 4.1.72.
9   Letter to S.T. Broad, 14.12.70.
10 W.G. Bott to S. Carson, 15.11.71.
11 S. Carson to C.L. Mellowes, 21.10.71.
12 S. Carson to Miss B. Hopkins, 25.11.71.
13 C.L. Mellowes to C.T. Broad, 4.1.72.
14 S. Carson to all Heads, 27.7.71, Hertfordshire File SMC. BC/RW/01/2.
15 S. Carson to Heads, undated, Hertfordshire File SMC. BC/RW/07/2.7.
16 Minutes of Standing Panel, Hertfordshire File 07.27, 27.8.71.
17 Minutes of Standing Panel, Hertfordshire File 07.2.7, 13.12.71.
18 S. Carson to all Heads, 3.1.72, Hertfordshire File SMC. BC/RW/07.2.7.
19 University of London School Examinations Department Ad Hoc Committee in Environmental Studies. Notes from first meeting on 19 January 1972.

20   Report to Standing Panel, Hertfordshire File, 8.2.72.
21   S. Carson to past applicants, undated, Hertfordshire File
      SMC.BC/RW/07.2.7.
22   S. Carson to Standing Panel, 7.6.72, Hertfordshire File,
      SMC. BC/CCR.
23   S. Carson to S.T. Broad (and Mr Carter and Mr Barr),
      20.6.72, Hertfordshire File SMC.BC/MMD/07.2.7.
24   Members of Standing Panel, 21.6.72, Hertfordshire File,
      SMC.BC/MMD/07.2.7.
25   Letter, 13.7.72, Schools Council, Sr/L/G/191.
26   Interview, 30.10.75.
27   S. Carson to members of Standing Panel, 21.7.72, Hertford-
      shire File, SMC.BC/DP/07/27.
28   E.B. Champkin to S. Carson, 10.7.72.
29   S.T. Broad to R. Sibson, 14.6.72, Hertfordshire File,
      B/SMC.BC/CCK/07.2.2.
30   Minutes of Standing Panel, 19.6.72, Hertfordshire File,
      SMC.BC/MMD/07.2.7.
31   S. Carson to B. Hopkins, undated, Hertfordshire File,
      SMC.BC/CAS/07.2.
32   Schools Council letter, 13.7.72.
33   B. Hopkins to F.T. Naylor, University of London Examin-
      ations Department, 2.11.72, 21.2.73, GC/BMA/PC.
34   Letter Schools Council, 21.2.73, SS/L/G/191.
35   Letter Schools Council, 21.2.73, SS/L/G/191.
36   Appendix 2, List of Consortia submitted to Schools Council
      by London University 5 July 1973.
37   Schools Council, 23.4.74, SC/72)225(322/0/SS/1/G/191.
38   Letter, 2.7.74, Hertfordshire file SMC.BC/DS/07.2.
39   Letter from S. Carson, 5.11.76.
40   University of London, General Certificate of Education
      Examination Statistics (University of London, 1970).

CONCLUSIONS

In summarising the research reported in this book it is perhaps appropriate to begin by re-examining our original hypotheses. Firstly, the book provides support for the initial hypothesis that subjects, far from being monolithic entities, are comprised of shifting sets of sub-groups, 'delicately held together under a common name at particular periods in history'.

Obviously this pattern would appear most strongly in subjects representing 'fields' rather than 'forms' of knowledge. The history of geography, for instance, shows that in the early stages the subject was made up of a variety of idiosyncratic local versions devised or taught by specialists from other disciplines. During the period in curriculum history that is the concern of this book, the battle over environmental education in the late sixties and early seventies, the sub-groups within geography can be seen 'pursuing different objectives in different manners'. So much so that in 1970 Professor Fisher wrote that 'The light-hearted prophecy I made in 1959 that we might soon expect to see the full 57 varieties of geography has been almost literally fulfilled, and my personal collection of different categories of geography that have seriously been put forward in professional literature now stands at well over half that number.' At about the same time, the President of the Geographical Association was warning that new geography created a problem because 'it leads towards subject fragmentation', so that ultimately 'the question must arise as to how much longer the subject can effectively be held together.' The potential danger of new versions of geography was touched on by Walford who argued that 'unity within the subject' was 'a basic requirement for the continued existence of the subject'.

The tendency to fragmentation in geography through the proliferation of sub-groups and sub-versions is a recurrent feature of the subject's history (see Chapters 5 and 10), and was echoed by the Norwood Report's fear about the 'expansiveness of geography'. At this earlier stage, 1943, they saw geography as 'The study of man and his environment from selected points of view' - a definition at that time leading to fears that through its expansiveness geography was becoming 'a "world citizenship" subject, with the citizens detached from their physical environment'. As a result at this time 'geography had become grievously out of balance; the geographical synthesis

had been abandoned'. The problem was rapidly addressed and
a decade later Garnett claimed that most school departments were
headed by specialists so that 'The initial marked differences
and contrasts in subject personality had been blurred or
obliterated.'

The means by which the fragmentary sub-groups were
monitored, controlled and periodically unified will be dealt with
later. However, in the period of the battle over 'environmental
education', two, or more accurately three, major sub-groups
within the subject were actively concerned: the regional geographers, the field geographers and, the fastest-growing sub-group,
the new geographers. The first two groups representing strong
traditions within the subject had large support among school
geography teachers. The latter group was largely derived from
new developments in the subject within the universities. As
related in Chapter 10 the first two sub-groups were considerably
more sympathetic to environmental initiatives than the new
geographers. This was because the environmental lobby offered
aid and sustenance to the field and regional geographers. Hence
we find eminent regional geographers like Professor Bryan
promoting conferences in environmental studies because this
expressed more clearly than new geography 'his own life's work
and ambitions as a geographer'. P.R. Thomas explained the
affection for environmental approaches entirely in terms of the
struggle for survival of the regional sub-group and a college
lecturer in geography judged that the new crisis among
geography sub-groups 'caused traditional (i.e. regional and
field) geographers to flee into environmental studies' for a time.
This flirtation proved a short-run phenomenon because of the
overwhelming desire for fully-fledged academic status among
all geographers; because new geography carried within it the
seeds of this final acceptance; and because the activities of the
Geographical Association and the university schools of geography
together directed and managed the change towards a new
'geographical synthesis' where once again the sub-groups were
'delicately held together'.

The pattern discerned among geography sub-groups in the
period of environmental education's emergence is partly echoed
when considering biology. Again the subject began with a variety
of idiosyncratic versions and groupings devised and taught by
specialists from other disciplines, in botany and zoology. By
the 1960s biology had also developed a major sub-group whose
concern with ecology and field biology bordered on the new
environmental approaches. For a time this sub-group gained
considerable momentum from initiatives like the Keele Conference
which saw this version of biology as promoting environmental
awareness.

Alongside field biology a sub-group promoting biology as a
'hard science' based in laboratories gained increasing adherents.
The rise of molecular biology with the work of Crick and Watson
in the 1950s gave a changed impetus to the work of this group.

In the new universities opening up in the 1960s and in schools
following the Nuffield project, this group managed to dominate
the versions of biology that were accepted. Hence the 'hard
science' version was embodied in the new laboratories that were
then being built and in the departments that were set up.

So dominant did the 'hard science' group become in biology,
that for a time the ecology and field biology sub-group developed
defensive connections with environmental studies. As with
geography a number of professors associated with the sub-
group appeared at events or in publications sponsored by the
National Association for Environmental Education. However,
although only a sub-group on the defensive within biology, the
field biologists secured a dominant position (along with the field
geographers) in the field studies movement which grew rapidly
as the 'environmental lobby' gained momentum. The field biology
sub-group was thereby able to develop important new 'territory'
inside the growth area of field studies which partly compensated
for losing the battle for mainstream biology to the hard-science
sub-group. By securing this leading role in field studies any
permanent collusion with the rural studies groups promoting
environmental studies was rendered both unnecessary and un-
desirable.

In both geography and biology the sub-groups allied to distinctive versions of the subject often gathered very different
degrees of support according to whether school or university
groups were being considered. Sometimes this reflected a time-
lag effect as the new versions of the subject only slowly worked
their way into the schools with new graduates taking up teaching posts in them. This was for instance the case in the battle
between the regional geography and new geography groups: a
long time after new geography was well established in universities, regional geography retained the allegiance of the majority
of school teachers.

In rural studies the varying support according to whether
one concentrates attention on school or university groups, was
never an issue as the subject was not taught in universities.
The sub-groups within rural studies therefore concentrated on
particular versions of the subject within schools. In the period
when environmental studies was launched, the two main groups
were those who wanted to quickly attach rural studies to a new
examination subject with some connections in the tertiary sector
and those who wanted to retain traditional rural studies as a
subject of outstanding appeal to the more 'practical' pupil. The
battle over the name of the subject association and the new
subject recorded in Chapter 8 was essentially a battle between
these two sub-groups and ended in resounding victory for the
first group.

The second hypothesis examined within the book relates to
three major traditions discerned in school subjects: the academic,
the utilitarian and the pedagogic. It was thought that an
evolutionary profile of the school subjects under study would

show a progressive movement away from stressing utilitarian and pedagogic versions of the subjects towards increasing promotion of more academic versions. We have already seen when discussing the nature of school subjects that sub-groups representing new geography, 'hard science' biology and examinable environmental studies, had come to be leading promoters of their subjects by the early 1970s. The process and rationale behind this outcome require fairly detailed understanding, representing as they do the culmination of a contest between a range of well-supported alternative definitions within each of the subjects.

The model of subject establishment towards a culminating 'academic' discipline was found to be closely applicable to both geography and biology. Once successfully promoted as an academic discipline the selection of the subject content is clearly considerably influenced 'by the judgement and practices of the specialist scholars in the field'. Subjects defined in this way, require a base of 'specialist scholars' working in universities to continue the definition and legitimation of disciplinary content.

The strategy for achieving this third stage received early recognition in geography. MacKinder's 1903 four-point plan provides an explicit statement of a subject aspiring to academic acceptance. The key to the strategy was the first point, the establishment of 'university Schools of Geographers where Geographers can be made'. To complete the control of the subject's identity, geography teaching and examination construction was to be placed in the hands only of teachers 'made' in the universities. The mediation between university and school was in geography, placed in the hands of the Geographical Association. The Association, founded in 1893, played a central role in the promotion of geography, since in its early days the subject was confined to idiosyncratic schools-based versions and had obtained a tentative place in only a few universities.

The close linkage between the growth in schools and the establishment of the subject elicits regular comment in the pages of 'Geography'. The President of the Geographical Association paid homage to 'fruits of inspired teaching' which have led to the 'intense and remarkable upsurge in the demand to read our subject in the universities'. The result has been 'the recognition of our subject's status among university disciplines . . . together with the costly provision made available for its study'. The latter point shows the direct link between academic status and resources in our educational system: the triumph of the 'academic' tradition over the utilitarian and pedagogic traditions which played such a prominent party in geography's early days is to be partly understood in these terms.

The establishment of 'discipline' status inside the universities which had been so systematically pursued since MacKinder's 1903 proclamation provided a range of material improvements in the subject's place within schools. In 1954 Honeybone could claim that 'at long last, geography is forcing its complete acceptance as a major discipline in universities, and that geographers are welcomed in to commerce, industry and the professions, because they are well educated men and women.' Acceptance as a major vocational qualification finally meant that geography could claim its place in educating the most able children, and thereby become established as a well-funded department inside schools staffed with trained specialists on graded posts. By 1967 Marchant noted that geography was 'at last attaining to intellectual respectability in the academic streams of our secondary schools'. But he noted that the battle was not quite over and gave the instances where the subject was still undesirably taught as a 'less able' option. With the launching of new geography the subject finally attained total acceptance as an academic discipline in universities and as a fully-fledged 'A' level subject in all schools, with the resources and 'costly provisions' which such status attracts.

In biology the evolution of the subject is distinguishable from geography because from the beginning there was an associated and well-established university base in the form of botany and zoology. For this reason and also because from the outset the subject benefited from the side-effects of the influential science lobby the task of subject promotion never totally resembled geography's 'beginning from scratch'. Biology's task was more to present a case for inclusion within the, by then well-established (and consequently well-resourced) science area of the curriculum. This task was often pursued within the overall arena of the Science Masters Association, who from the 1930s onwards played an active role in promoting biology. In 1936 an influential biology sub-committee was formed to promote biology syllabuses, and many articles in the Association's 'School Science Review' argued the case for biology's recognition as an examination subject for the able student. The problem was best voiced by the Ministry of Education in 1960: 'The place which is occupied by advanced biological studies in schools . . . is unfortunately that of vocational training rather than of an instrument of education.' The need to be seen as an 'instrument of education' meant that the promoters of the subject needed to move away from the utilitarian towards more academic versions - only then could an 'A' level subject command sufficient pupil numbers to warrant 'departmental' status and resources in schools. Hence we find the common theme being advocated: biology must be treated 'as a comprehensive discipline in its own right'.

In the final stages in the promotion of biology as an 'academic discipline', the two main initiatives stressed the subject as a hard science needing 'laboratories and equipment'. In the rapidly expanding universities it was this version of the subject which was widely introduced, thereby establishing the academic discipline base; likewise the Nuffield Biology Project for Schools centred on 'a crusade in terms of equipment and laboratory staff'. With the new generation of biology graduates trained in

this hard science at universities, the establishment of the subject
as a fully fledged academic 'O' and 'A' level subject was finally
assured.

Unlike biology and geography, rural studies remained for
generations a low-status enclave, stressing highly utilitarian or
pedagogic values. Confirming Ben-David and Collins' contention,
the move to a change in intellectual and occupational identity
came at the time when the subject was faced with survival
problems in a reorganising educational system stressing the
academic tradition. The pervasive influence of this tradition
can clearly be seen in the following quote: 'The lack of a clear
definition of an area of study as a discipline has often been a
difficulty for local authorities in deciding what facilities to
provide . . . It has been one of the reasons for the fact that
no "A" level course in rural studies exists at present.' The
Schools Council working party in 1968 confirmed this with the
broad hint that there was the 'need for a scholarly discipline'.

With no tertiary base and hence no specialist scholars involved,
except random specialists from other disciplines, the Hertfordshire strategy was to develop an 'A' level syllabus from groups
working in the secondary schools. This offered the promise of
tailoring 'a course to the needs of the kids' and not to 'have
to meet the requirements of other people's courses'. But the
crucial reason in terms of the subject teachers' material self
interest was often frankly admitted: 'I think we had got to
prove that environmental studies was something that the most
able of students could achieve and do something with . . . if
you started off there all the expertise and finance that you put
into it will benefit the rest – your teaching ratio goes up etc.
and everyone else benefits.' Likewise, another leading advocate
admitted that they had seen that 'the only way to make progress
was to get in on the examination racket . . . the exam. was
essential, otherwise you couldn't be equal with any other subject.
Another thing was that comprehensive education was coming in.
Once that came in, no teacher who didn't teach in the fifth or
sixth form was going to count for twopence. So you had to have
an "A" level for teachers to aim at'. The survival rationale
was always a strong factor: 'I just thought if you're outside this
you've had it in schools: it was already happening in some
schools where a [rural studies] teacher was leaving, they didn't
fill the place, because they gave it to someone in the examination
set up.' And beyond survival the reasons for an academic 'A'
level were simply 'because if you didn't you wouldn't get any
money, any status, any intelligent kids'.

The 'A' level in environmental studies is a recognition of
the factors defining the aspirations and efforts of these rural
studies teachers. What was subsequently been denied is not that
environmental studies represents a valid area of curriculum,
but that it can thereby claim to be an academic discipline. Such
claims it would appear are best validated through university
scholarship and without a university base status passage to

acceptance as an academic subject has been denied. As Carson
noted at Offley, new contenders for academic status are often
placed in an impossible situation since they are asked 'What
evidence have you that universities would accept this sort of
"A" level?' On making enquiries to universities, the reply was
'show us the successful candidates and we will tell you'. A
chicken and egg situation!

The third hypothesis in the book follows on from consideration
of the patterns of internal evolution in school subjects to investigate the role that the pursuit of academic status plays in the
relationship between subjects. In continuity with the second
hypothesis we would expect established subjects to defend their
own academic status at the same time as denying such status to
any new subject contenders, particularly in the battle over new
'A' level examinations.

In the struggle to launch environmental studies as an 'A' level
subject, the geographers' reaction strongly, and the biologists'
much more mildly, followed the lines of the hypothesis.
MacKinder, the founding father of geography's road to academic
establishment, would have understood this. In explaining the
geologists' opposition to geography he saw their fear of the new
subject making 'inroads in their classes' as the reason for their
response and noted that 'even scientific folk are human, and
such ideas must be taken into account'. In continuity with this
the geographers strongly opposed social studies, an integrated
package that predated environmental studies by several decades.
The geographers, it was claimed, 'saw the new proposals as a
threat to the integrity and status of their own subject'.

The growth of environmental studies was treated in similar
manner by the geographers. The discussion of the Executive
Committee of the Geographical Association show precious little
concern with the intellectual or epistemological arguments for
environmental studies. The discussion focused on 'the threat to
geography involved in the growth of environmental studies'.
Indeed, when the possibility of a dialogue with environmental
studies teachers was suggested 'some members felt that to do so
would be tantamount to admitting the validity of environmental
studies'. Carson's reminiscences of his talk to the Geographers'
Conference tends to confirm the spirit in which new contenders
for academic status were viewed if they were at all adjacent to
geography's broad and shifting frontiers. The response was
patently directed towards territorial defence – not academic
dialogue. The most overt plea for defence rather than dialogue
came in the Presidential Address to the Geographical Association
in 1973. Mr A.D. Nicholls laid great emphasis on the 'practical
realities' for 'practising teachers'. 'With constant pressure on
teaching time, headmasters are ever searching for new space
into which additional prestige subjects can be fitted, and the
total loss of teaching time to environmental subjects may be considerable.' Beyond these practical fears about the material
interests of geography teachers, environmental studies evoked

a particularly emotional response among geographers because of
its proximity to geography's continuing identity crisis. Nicholls
provides an unusually frank admission of the need for territorial
defence being placed above any intellectual imperatives:

> Ten years ago almost to the day and from this platform,
> Professor Kirk said 'modern geography was created by scholars,
> trained in other disciplines, asking themselves geographical
> questions and moving inwards in a community of problems; it
> could die by a reversal of the process whereby trained geogra-
> phers moved outwards in a fragmentation of interests seeking
> solutions to non-geographical problems.' Might not this be
> prophetic for us today? Could it not all too soon prove dis-
> astrous if the trained teachers of geography moved outwards
> as teachers of environmental studies seeking solutions to non-
> geographical problems?

The fears which geographers expressed so strongly and
emotionally about the emergence of environmental studies were
not shared to the same degree by biologists. As we have seen
only the field biology sub-group was threatened and they
managed to expand into the growing territory of field studies.
However in the negotiations at Schools Council the science sub-
committee, which included a number of biologists, joined forces
with the geographers in their opposition to the environmental
studies 'A' level. In both sub-committees 'concern was expressed
at the heavy overlap between this syllabus and syllabuses in
both geography and biology.' The alleged overlap was coupled
with exhortations to remove those 'irrelevant topics' not related
to geography and biology. The result was the self-fulfilling
indictment 'if irrelevant topics were envisaged as removed, the
effect would be to reveal how close the resulting syllabus would
be to existing syllabuses in geography'.
The judgement quoted by Carson that the Schools Council
sub-committees 'jealously guarded the preserves of their subject'
was confirmed by the comments from the geography sub-
committee when the decision on the 'A' level was finally
announced. They were plainly fairly satisfied with their territorial defense and 'noted with approval that candidates could
not take this examination together with geography'. A final
point was added that there was 'as yet no indication that
universities would be prepared to accept a pass in this subject
as an entry qualification for degree courses'. The restriction on
environmental studies being offered with geography, together
with the initial restriction to a five-year period and to only the
Standing Panel schools, placed enormous practical obstacles in
the way of any widespread adoption of the subject. By ensuring
these obstacles faced the new subject in the early years when
the momentum for change was strong, the opponents to the new
subject effectively extinguished the chances of its establishment
in the school curriculum.

The book provides evidence of three subject communities in evolution and in conflict. It shows a range of conflicting sub-groups within the subjects and that these often concentrated around the three major 'traditions' discerned. The pursuit of material self-interest ultimately ensured that the sub-groups attached to the academic tradition came to dominate the subjects. This was because the flow of resources, finance and recognition of 'departmental' territory and needs has been linked especially to 'scholarly disciplines' that can be taught to 'able' students. We have seen how the promotion of a subject as a scholarly discipline was systematically co-ordinated by subject associations and by groups of university scholars. Once the academic base of the scholarly discipline was established within the universities the dominance of the academic tradition within the subject was firmly wedded to the vested interests of the university scholars. The university departments then played a major role in defining the subject (though often with significant time-lags) through their control of the training of the school teachers of the sub-jects; through their role in the major influential committees, such as the Schools Council Subject Sub-Committees, and within exam-ination boards; and through their role in decisions about which 'A' levels are acceptable qualifications for their degree courses. The subject communities and associations representing the school teachers accepted, indeed at points conspired to produce, this dominant university role because the teacher's career was so crucially dependent on the flow of resources linked to the sub-ject's continuing status as a scholarly discipline for 'O' and 'A' level students.

In the battle to promote environmental studies we have seen how the rural studies advocates were barred from following the route to academic establishment. With no prospects of a scholarly discipline of environmental studies coming from the universities, the Hertfordshire advocates were forced into attempting to define 'a discipline' from the school level. This allowed opponents of the new subject, whilst broadly conceding its value to young and less able students, consistently to deny that it could be viewed as in any sense 'a scholarly discipline'. With a few exceptions school subject groups and university scholars of geography and, to a much lesser extent, biology, stuck firmly to the defence of subject integrity epitomised in Nicholls' speech to the Geographical Association. Considerations of an intellectual sort were thereby subordinated to the defence of subject territory which ensured that scholars and teachers of the subject would continue to benefit in terms of resources and career prospects.

COMPLEXITIES

In summarising the studies undertaken in this book it is import-ant to examine whether the patterns of control discerned add up to 'domination' by powerful high-status groups as has been contended by M.F.D. Young et al in 'Knowledge and Control'[1] The role of dominant groups shows perhaps most clearly in the victory of the academic tradition in the early years of the twentieth century. This victory was embodied in the influential 1904 Regulations and most significantly, the 1917 School Certificate. Once established, however, these curricula patterns (and their associated financial and resource implications) were retained and defended in a much more complex way and by a wider range of agencies. It is therefore correct to assume that initially the rules for high-status knowledge reflected the values of dominant interest groups at that time. But it is quite another issue to assume that this is inevitably still the case or that is is dominant interest groups themselves who actively defend high-status curricula. It is perhaps useful to distinguish between domination and structure and mechanism and mediation.

By focusing on subjects in evolution and the conflict over 'A' level examinable knowledge the studies in this book clearly indicate the central role played by school subject groups. The most powerful of these agencies are these school subject groups promoting the academic tradition. Successfully in geography and biology, but unsuccessfully in environmental studies, these groups demanded the creation of an academic discipline based in the universities. The 'academic tradition' sub-groups act in this way because of the legacy of curricula, financial and resource structures inherited from the early twentieth century (when dominant interests were actively defended). Because of this legacy able pupils and academic examinations are linked and consequently resources, graded posts and career prospects are maximised for those who can claim academic status for their subject.

The evidence indicates not so much domination by dominant forces as solicitous surrender by subordinate groups. Far from teacher socialisation in dominant institutions being the major factor creating the patterns discerned it was much more considerations of teachers' material self-interest in their working lives. Since the misconception is purveyed by sociologists who exhort us 'to understand the teacher's real world', they should really know better. High-status knowledge gains its school subject adherents and aspirants less through the control of the curricula which socialise than through well-established connection with patterns of resource allocation and the associated work and career prospects these ensure. The studies in this book argue that we must replace crude notions of domination with patterns of control in which subordinate groups can be seen actively at work.

But if domination by the universities fails to characterise a complex process correctly, the activites of 'academic' subgroups in school subjects clearly do conspire to increase the control over the definition and direction of subjects by university scholars. The conflict then focuses on the alliance between the universities and the academic school subject groups and those other subject traditions, notably the pedagogic and utilitarian, which often express internal school needs. In this continuing contest the academic tradition holds all the cards. Reid contended that within schools a

> major area of conflict is . . . between the external constraints arising from university requirements and the internal pressures which have their origin in the school. Schools are, however, poorly equipped to resist university pressures. To a large extent they allow the legitimacy of university demands, and have evolved an authority structure which is linked to them . . . They are, by contrast much better placed to deal with internal demands, and have a variety of means at their disposal for clamping down pressures which conflict with the responses stimulated by university influence.[2]

The existence of academic, pedagogic and utilitarian traditions in school curricula has its origins in the separate sectors of the educational system which preceded the comprehensive era. The continuance of these traditions and the continuing dominance of the academic tradition bear testimony that the fundamental structures of curriculum have withstood comprehensive reorganisation. As in the tripartite system so in the comprehensive system, academic subjects for able pupils are accorded the highest status and resources. The triple alliance between academic subjects, academic examinations and able pupils ensures that comprehensive schools provide similar patterns of curriculum differentiation to previous school systems. For the teachers who have to cater for all kinds of pupils this concentration on a particular kind of pupil and a particular kind of educational success poses the same dilemma voiced by the rural studies teacher in response to the promotion of academic examinations in his subject: 'Once again we can see the unwanted children of lower intelligence being made servants of the juggernaut of documented evidence, the inflated examination.' This conclusion summarises the continuing choice:

> True education is not for every man the scrap of paper he leaves school with. Dare we as teachers admit this? Dare we risk our existence by forcibly expressing our views on this? While we pause after the first phase of our acceptance are we to rely on exams for all to prove ourselves worthy of the kindly eye of the state?[3]

The deep structures of curriculum differentiation are historically linked to different educational sectors, to different social class clienteles and occupational destinations, to different status hierarchies. Differentiated curricula and the social structure are matched on very firm foundations: by building on these foundations comprehensive reorganisation has had to accept the antecedent structures which contradict its stated ideal.

CONJECTURES AND CURRENT DEBATES

Beyond the specific conclusions and complexities noted there seems some evidence for suggesting that the embryonic theoretical framework of this study provides a useful starting point for other studies. Such studies, by extending the focus and the analysis, will test the generalisability of some of the broader conjectures contained herein.

In considering future studies it is perhaps worth re-examining the limitations of the current study. Firstly the research focused on the promotion of only three school subjects and the detailed negotiation of just one examination syllabus. Clearly then studies are needed to elucidate further the detailed connection between promotional strategies and 'rhetorics' and the 'reality' of the curriculum content and classroom practice. There are a number of levels within the educational system each with varying degrees of autonomy. Hence whilst we have seen that the academic tradition is most commonly used to promote school subjects far more detailed study is required of how far this promotional activity effects the 'small print' of curriculum content, both within the range of examination syllabuses, in the associated but by no means directly related examination question papers and within school classrooms. Above all, in following up the studies in this book, such detailed investigation of the relationships between these complex arenas and levels of curriculum negotiation must be undertaken. With rural studies we know that promotional rhetoric substantially affected the curriculum 'reality' of a new 'A' level syllabus in environmental studies. We also know that this process of translation from rhetoric to notional reality was deeply contested by groups inside and outside the subject community.

Secondly the study was specific to a particular period of time in the evolution of three school subjects. The concern was with subjects during the period when academic establishment was the primary pursuit. For geography and biology we have not investigated whether the patterns were modified after broad-based acceptance and for rural and environmental studies this remains a hypothetical issue. Certainly there seem grounds for believing that the periods when subjects pursue and achieve academic establishment (with the associated status and resources) may be times of particular concern with, and acceptance of, unity within the subject. Nonetheless comparison between the subjects studied illuminates a number of important and suggestive differences. The description of the evolution of geography, for instance, shows that here was a subject with a profound and continuing identity problem. In such a situation a firm alliance was moulded between academic geographers and the school teachers who were organised in the Geographical Association. The case of biology, however, shows that other subjects do not necessarily share to the same degree either the geographers' paranoia nor their strong sense of alliance in the face of new contenders for academic status. It is therefore possible that subjects with higher academic self-confidence would not act in the starkly territorial manner discerned in this book.

In considering other subjects, classics would seem to offer an interesting study of an 'academic' subject representing powerful interest groups which has nonetheless declined. Perhaps this indicates a paradox: that although subjects must grow out of their utilitarian origins to become 'academic' they need to continue to be generally accepted as 'vocational' qualifications in order to survive. Likewise once accepted as 'academic' subjects, they must continue to appeal at a pedagogic level to learners. Hence in the era following academic acceptance such issues sometimes receive considerable attention as was the case with the Nuffield projects in science subjects.

Some subjects have successfully followed the route to academic acceptance so hopefully pursued by environmental studies advocates but still encountered barriers to total entry into the secondary school curriculum. For instance politics, economics and psychology have developed as disciplines in universities and been broadly accepted at 'A' level yet are still rarely found in the general curriculum of secondary schools. This could again illustrate the negative territorial power of school subject groups.

Whilst certain aspects of curriculum control and 'territorial' response therefore seem complex and difficult to generalise about, other issues are less so. The general nature of subject communities and the pervasive direction of subject definition and promotion can be clearly discerned. Subject sub-groups (and versions of the subject) may focus on issues such as pedagogy and utility as well as intellectual worth. In the long run, however, the sub-group and the version of the subject which is likely to be successfully promoted is that most in harmony with the material interests of the subject's scholars and teachers. Given the link between knowledge status and resources, subjects can best promote themselves through the academic tradition.

The legacy of differentiated status for the academic, utilitarian and pedagogic traditions draw on tripartite patterns of educational organisation. In considering curriculum change it is vital to understand that this tripartite hierarchy of status has been reproduced not only in the respective parity of esteem between different categories of subject but also to kinds of knowledge within subjects. At the latter level, scrutiny of 'what counts as education' is necessary. For instance, much of the debate about teaching craft and technology as a way of reinstating practical curricula has missed this point. Given the status patterns discerned one might expect that even if technology were to achieve high status and acceptance the

version which would 'count as education' would be academic
and theoretical and therefore stand in contradiction to more
practical objectives. The differentiated status of academic,
utilitarian and pedagogic traditions pervades both the type of
subject and the internal form of each subject. Curriculum reform
needs to address both of these levels of differentiation.

The differentiated status of the three curriculum traditions
discerned and their link with the way finance and resources are
allocated and pursued is confirmed by a number of studies
already undertaken.

Banks' study of parity and prestige in the English secondary
system ends by stressing 'the persistence of the academic
tradition' throughout that period of the system's existence.[4]
Hanson's study of art education and Dodd's work on technology
offer similar evidence.[5] The latter speaking of the Crowther
Report noted that they had shown how 'an alternative route to
knowledge' lay through practical subjects which did not destroy
the intellectual curiosity of the pupil in the way associated with
the 'academic' ones. Dodd notes that 'the problems lay in the
status of practical subjects by tradition second class . . . Discussion on its own is insufficient and it requires legitimization
by those institutions who hold this facility (universities,
examination boards, employers and society at large).[6]

As we have seen, the legitimising institutions together with
established and indeed aspiring subject groups share the vested
interest in the belief that 'a scholarly discipline' is needed if a
school subject is to be granted high status. The stranglehold
of the academic tradition has seldom been seriously threatened
by its overwhelming need to shun 'practical utility'. The theme
which Dodd points to was just as common when the 1904 regulations were established. A contemporary noted that the school
curriculum was 'subordinated to that literary instruction which
makes for academic culture, but is of no practical utility, to
the classes for whom the local authorities should principally
cater.'[7]

The dominance of the academic tradition is patently supported
by the major vested interest groups within education and the
broader society. Yet the very need for academic subjects to
escape from the allegations of 'practical utility' may yet lead
to irresistible pressure for change in the period of economic
malaise which we currently confront.

The studies in this book show clearly that school subject
groups tend to move progressively away from concerns with
'utilitarian' or 'relevant' knowledge. High status in the secondary school curriculum is reserved for abstract theoretical
knowledge divorced from the working world of industry and the
everyday world of the learner. As we have seen this is not
coincidental. The very price of success in achieving high status
in an academic discipline is to renounce practical connections
and relevance to the personal and to the industrial and commercial world. To these high-status academic subjects go the main

resources in our educational system: the better qualified
teachers, the favourable sixth form ratios and the pupils that
are deemed most able. Hence the main flow of financial support
in our school curriculum is invested in those subjects which
have promoted themselves as academic disciplines. In short the
politics of curriculum, the process of becoming a high-status
subject and discipline, ensures that most money in education is
invested in subjects which stress their divorce from practical
relevance and the industrial and commercial world. As a formula
for economic decline such a pattern of curriculum negotiation
and investment could hardly be perfected.

Economic disfuctionality is, however, not the only indictment.
As a formula for the education of a mass clientele the system is
similarly diametrical in its misdirection. We have noted that
Layton sees the academic tradition as the prelude to disenchantment for most pupils. Hemmings has likewise inveighed against
the 'academic illusion', which he says 'bristles with anti-
educational consequences'.[8] There is indeed a good deal of
evidence that the academic subject is profoundly unsuitable
for many pupils, specifically those from working-class backgrounds. For instance Witkin has shown how working-class
pupils actively prefer and choose lessons they can relate to the
everyday world.[9] The teachers of such pupils constantly confirm
this view; their mode 3 CSE syllabuses devised for these pupils
provide documentary proof that they judge practical relevance
to be the best motivational material for 'average' and 'below
average' pupils. Unfortunately school teachers have career
interests as well as classroom interests. As we have seen the
former may subjugate the latter: the pursuit of academic status
whilst providing the gateway to career success for the teacher
simultaneously inaugurates the prelude to disenchantment for
his pupils.

In summary the politics of the school curriculum and the
predominance of the academic tradition present the dominant
interests in our society with a classic contradiction. The
academic subject curriculum undoubtedly works smoothly to
educate a meritocratic minority although meanwhile disenchanting
the majority. The social class status quo is thereby preserved
along with the requisite ratio of managers and workers. But the
price to be paid is high for managers as well as workers. The
academic curriculum renounces practical relevance and industrial
and technical skills. To succeed in the educational system our
future managers must share this renunciation. Not surprisingly
our educational priorities are reflected in our management teams:
most are high-status academic specialists, few have technical
or engineering skills. A recent report, after noting the large
numbers of engineers among West German and French managers,
commented that in England 'too few of our graduates go into
industry and those that do tend to have an irrelevant educational
discipline.'[10]

Given the academic curriculum to which managers owe their

success this industrial illiteracy is an inevitable corollary. The academic curriculum produces industrial illiteracy for its successful minority, pervasive disenchantment for the majority. How much longer such an educational recipe will be deemed suitable in a country on the verge of economic crisis and social conflict remains to be seen.

NOTES

1   M.F.D. Young (ed.), 'Knowledge and Control' (Collier Macmillan, 1971).
2   W.A. Reid, 'Sixth Form', p. 106.
3   P.L. Quant, See Chapter 6, p. 163.
4   See Banks, 'Parity and Prestige'.
5   See Chapter 1, footnotes 12 and 13.
6   Dodd, 'Design and Technology'.
7   Quoted in Banks, 'Parity and Prestige', p. 41.
8   J. Hemmings 'The Betrayal of Youth' (London, Marion Boyars, 1980).
9   B.W. Witkin, Social Class Influence on the Amount and Type of Positive Evaluation of School Lessons, 'Sociology', Vol. 5, No. 2, 1971.
10 'The Times', 14 February 1978.

UNIVERSITY OF LONDON SCHOOLS EXAMINATION
DEPARTMENT HERTFORDSHIRE MODE TWO SYLLABUS IN
ENVIRONMENTAL STUDIES AT THE ADVANCED LEVEL

The aims and objectives of the two-year course are that the
student should be better able:

(a) to identify and appreciate the inter-relationships of the
physical and biological factors that make up the environment;
(b) to analyse and synthesise the ways in which man may
control his environmental impact and to recognise the
values by which such control may be guided;
(c) to evaluate and establish a set of personal values towards
the place of man in the environment, and the impact of
human society on its biophysical surroundings.

The working party felt that these objectives would be better
advanced by placing the student in a situation of personal
involvement, and contributing to his own studies as far as
possible through extensive activities in the field and laboratory
rather than by too much authoritative teaching.

The examination will consist of two theory papers and the
teacher's assessment of project and field work which will be
weighted as follows:

Paper 1 (3 hours) 30% } 70%
Paper 2 (3 hours) 40% }
Teacher assessment of field work of Section 2   10% } 30%
Teacher assessment of field study of Section 4   20% }

Both theory papers will be externally set and examined.

Paper 1 will normally consist of approximately 10-12 compulsory questions of a structured format with the answers to be
written or drawn in spaces provided in the question booklets.
The questions will cover Sections 1, 2 and 3 of the syllabus
and will be of approximately equal weighting and the mark
allocation will be indicated on the paper. The questions will be
designed to test the candidate's familiarity with the contents of
Section 1, 2 and 3, his ability to interpret and apply relevant
data, draw conclusions, state them effectively, recognise the
limitations of data and draw accurate inferences. Candidates
should be able to present their answers in diagrammatic and
graphical form where appropriate.

Paper 2 will consist of approximately ten questions. Candidates
may answer question one and any other three questions. The

mark allocation will be higher for question one than each of the other three questions and will be indicated on the question paper. Candidates will be allowed to bring in their field notes for reference purposes. Paper 2 is designed to test the candidate's ability:

(a) to apply knowledge of basic principles gained in syllabus Sections 1, 2 and 3;
(b) to use skills developed in the field study in Section 4;
(c) to integrate the above in the analysis of new situations.

The field work of Section 2 and the field study of Section 4 will be assessed by the teacher (an outline scheme for marking the field study is included at the end of the syllabus) and externally moderated. Further information on the moderation of the field study is given in the appendices to the syllabus. Candidates must satisfy the examiners in both the field and theory work.

The syllabus is designed and teaching notes have been drawn up to fit a situation where the course is taken by a single teacher (eight periods a week) or by two teachers (four periods a week each). Training courses for sixth-form teachers of environmental studies in Hertfordshire have been held and further courses for teachers, to cover the background of different parts of the syllabus, are planned.

SYNOPSIS OF SYLLABUS HEADINGS

Section One: Processes and Systems of the Natural Environment and the Limits of the Resource Base

1.1   *The Source of Energy: The Solar System*
        1.1.1   Sun as a source of energy

1.2   *The Transport of Energy: Radiation*
        1.2.1   Atmospheric layers and filtering effects
        1.2.2   Insolation
        1.2.3   Weather systems, air masses and climate
        1.2.4   Water cycle

1.3   *The Lithosphere*
        1.3.1   Energy and mineral resources in the lithosphere
        1.3.2   The soil

1.4   *Transference of Energy in the Biosphere*
        1.4.1   Conception of the circulation of elements
        1.4.2   Methods of obtaining energy

Section Two: The Ecosystem

2.1   *Climatic and Edaphic Factors*

2.2   *Pyramids of Numbers and Energy*